Postwar Journeys

POSTWAR

JOURNEYS

American and

Vietnamese

Transnational

Peace Efforts

since 1975

Hang Thi Thu Le-Tormala

University Press of Kansas

Published by the University Press of
Kansas (Lawrence, Kansas 66045), which
was organized by the Kansas Board of
Regents and is operated and funded by
Emporia State University, Fort Hays
State University, Kansas State University,
Pittsburg State University, the University
of Kansas, and Wichita State University.

Library of Congress Cataloging-in-
Publication Data

Names: Le-Tormala, Hang Thi Thu, author.
Title: Postwar journeys : American and
Vietnamese transnational peace efforts
since 1975 / Hang Thi Thu Le-Tormala.
Other titles: American and Vietnamese
transnational peace efforts since 1975
Description: Lawrence : University Press
of Kansas, 2021 | Includes bibliographical
references and index.
Identifiers: LCCN 2020040398
ISBN 9780700631902 (cloth)
ISBN 9780700631919 (epub)
Subjects: LCSH: United States—Relations—
Vietnam. | Vietnam—Relations—United
States. | Vietnam—History—1975– |
Vietnam—Social conditions—1975–
Vietnam War, 1961–1975—Peace. |
Peace-building, American—Vietnam. |
Humanitarian assistance, American—
Vietnam. | Transnationalism—Social
aspects—Vietnam.
Classification: LCC E183.8.V5 L417 2021 |
DDC 327.730597—dc23
LC record available at https://lccn.loc
.gov/2020040398.

British Library Cataloguing-in-Publication
Data is available.

Printed in the United States of America

10 9 8 7 6 5 4 3 2 1

CONTENTS

A photo gallery follows page 114.

ACKNOWLEDGMENTS

It was an unforgettable moment when I bid farewell to Dr. Norman Yetman, chair of the Department of American Studies at the University of Kansas (KU) in May 2004, before I returned to Vietnam upon completing my master's program. He said, "Look at me in the eye, and tell me if you plan to further your studies." In all honesty, I had not seriously thought about a PhD, but his firm handshake and the great encouragement in his eyes gave me no other options.

I replied, "Yes, I will go back to graduate school. I just don't know when yet because I have family obligations awaiting me in Vietnam."

He smiled happily. "Of course you don't have to do it right now. I just want to hear you confirm that you will, and I would be very disappointed if you don't want to further your academic career." Thus I left KU with a promise, which was also a great debt for me, and at the time, I could not imagine how I was going to live up to my promise. To make a long story short, Dr. Yetman's encouragement was a great source of academic aspiration. He has my deepest gratitude.

This book was developed from my dissertation at KU. I had the great fortune to receive the guidance and support of extraordinary historians who comprised my dissertation committee. The wisdom and insight of my advisor, Dr. Theodore A. Wilson, has significantly contributed to my academic progress, especially the completion of this challenging project. His expertise in both diplomatic history and military history has been extremely helpful to my topic. I am deeply indebted to him for his timely advice, generous support, and great patience. I owe my interest in history to Dr. William Tuttle, whose knowledge, inspiration, and dedication reshaped my academic path more than a decade ago. Since then, he has been endlessly nurturing and has generously devoted his time to the details of my project. To him, I am forever thankful. Throughout the completion of my research, I have received invaluable suggestions and encouragement from Dr. Sherrie Tucker. She graciously listened to my ideas and challenged me to deepen my thoughts. Her cheerful spirit was also helpful during stressful moments of graduate school. I deeply appreciate her presence and dedication. I owe Dr. Sheyda Jahanbani for the conceptualization of my historical approach for this study. Thanks to her wonderful classes and apt reading selections, I "discovered" historian Akira Iriye's "cultural transnationalism." Dr. Jahanbani's passion for transnational history has served as great guidance for my research. Since the first days of my PhD program, I have also received great assistance from Dr. Jeffrey Moran. He patiently listened to my inchoate ideas for an ambitious project and, again patiently, endured the twists and turns in my academic interests. It is with profound gratitude that I acknowledge Dr. Moran's generous support. I was fortunate to also have Dr. James Willbanks on my committee. As an expert in US-Vietnam relations and American veterans, he has been of vital help. I am very grateful for his speedy and insightful feedback.

To complete this research, I relied largely on the Vietnam Center and Archive at Texas Tech University in Lubbock, Texas, for its invaluable collections of materials and helpful staff. I am especially thankful to archivist Sheon Montgomery for her hard work. Her resourcefulness and enthusiasm made my time at the archive much easier and more productive. In similar manner, the library staff at KU quietly but greatly contributed to my studies. I also deeply appreciate the staff and residents of the Vietnam Friendship Village (Project USA) in Van Canh, Hanoi, especially the director Dinh Van Tuyen and the manager Nguyen Ngoc Ha, for their helpfulness and hospitality. My heartfelt thanks also go to Nguyen Thanh Phu, the manager of Project RENEW's Mine Action Visitor Center in Quang Tri, Vietnam. Visits to the Friendship Village and the Mine Action Visitor Center were very insightful and inspiring. My deepest thanks go to the interviewees for their crucial contributions to the research. During my stay in Hanoi for my research, I also received great assistance from my friends Nguyen Hien Thi and Tran Thanh Binh. Thi loaned me her scooter and Binh provided me with motherly care in her home. They made my intense trip enjoyable and unforgettable. I am grateful for their friendship and generosity.

I owe a great deal to KU for its generous University Graduate Fellowship and the Doctoral Student Research Fund, without which this project simply could not exist and my dream of becoming a historian may have never come true. I would like to extend my sincere thankfulness to the following professors for broadening my historical knowledge through their wonderful courses: Dr. Paul Kelton, Dr. Kim Warren, Dr. Jennifer Weber, Dr. Jonathan Earle, Dr. Adrian Lewis, Dr. Ann Schofield, and Dr. Benjamin Chappell. They made my academic experiences at KU extraordinary.

In the process of transforming my dissertation into a book, I am deeply grateful to the reviewers chosen by the University Press of Kansas (UPK). Their insightful comments broadened my views and helped improve the manuscript significantly. I thank UPK Editor in Chief Joyce Harrison for her enthusiasm and encouragement throughout the process. Special thanks to Production Editor Colin Tripp for his great assistance and patience. His quick responses were comforting as I was racing to meet deadlines. I also owe a great deal to my copyeditor Jenn Bennett-Genthner, whose diligence and attention to details are invaluable. I benefited greatly from her keen queries. To other staff members of the UPK, I thank you for your hard work during this difficult time as the COVID-19 epidemic is raging through our country.

I have never adequately acknowledged my family for their endless support. My mother, mother-in-law, and siblings on both sides have been the greatest "cheerleaders" for my academic pursuits. They are also a source of humor that kept me sane during stressful times. The greatest supporter, and probably the one having to put up with me the most, however, is my husband, Peter Tormala. He endured my insane schedule, shouldered much of the housework, and listened to my frustrations. He also accompanied me to the Vietnam Center and Archive at Texas Tech University as well as conferences, and he diligently proofread every page of this book. His love and support are beyond expectation. To my husband, I dedicate this research.

Postwar Journeys

Introduction

In early 1992, I was visiting my best friend's farm in a remote area in Tay Ninh, Vietnam, and found myself in conversation with her father. Having learned that her family had applied to immigrate to the United States under the Orderly Departure Program, which was created in 1979 under the auspices of the United Nations High Commissioner for Refugees to allow certain Vietnamese people to resettle in the United States or other Western countries, I asked her father if he knew when his family would obtain immigrant visas. He said, "We don't know yet. If Bill Clinton wins the presidential election, we will have the visas sooner. Otherwise, it could be a long wait." His answer was impressive to me, an ignorant college student. I was curious how this middle-aged farmer living in such an isolated place where newspapers and the mailing system were not available knew what was going on in the United States. More astoundingly, how did he know a "somebody" in the United States would have direct effects on the future of his family? Later, I learned that he had been secretly listening to the Voice of America's and British Broadcasting Corporation's Vietnamese programs, which was an illegal activity in Vietnam at the time.

In retrospect, this anecdote is a perfect example of transnationalism, and the farmer was a historical actor who transcended boundaries at great risk. While geographically and physically isolated, the farmer was mentally transnationalist. He understood the interconnectedness in world politics and was able to make connections between high politics and individuals' daily lives. He connected the dots of national interests and citizens' interests across borderlands. He might have faced imprisonment if he got caught listening to those radio programs, especially because he had been a South Vietnamese officer and had an "unclean" record as a re-education camp detainee. Ironically, his determination to retain his freedom to access information could have cost him his freedom. Despite his circumstances, the poor farmer was a transnational historical actor who refused to allow national and political boundaries to dictate his options.

This study seeks to understand the transnational peace efforts of American and Vietnamese people since the Vietnam War ended in 1975. Within the framework of this research, peace efforts are defined in their broadest sense, ranging from individuals' search for peace of mind to reconciliation and peaceful relations among former antagonists. Examples include, but are not limited to, searching for family members or friends who are missing because of war, helping people overcome the ordeals resulting from the war, and meeting or working with former opponents for the betterment of their societies. The withdrawal of US troops from Southeast Asia in 1973 and the end of the war in Vietnam in 1975 did not necessarily mean peace to all US and Vietnamese people. For many, those historical milestones were only the beginning of another struggle—another journey in search of a missing piece of their lives.

This research unfolds the painstaking journeys of individuals from varied political, cultural, and social backgrounds, who nevertheless shared unpleasant memories of a brutal war and a strong desire for peace. Their "journeys" could literally involve trips from one place to another or figuratively mean their undertaking in the aftermath of war. How did these people overcome their personal pain and help one another confront and/or reconcile their pasts? How did they improve relationships with their former foes? How did they bring peace to others and find inner peace for themselves? How did their governments help or hinder their peace efforts? How did these individual acts help reshape the relations between the two countries? What were the personal and social effects of transnational interactions? In an attempt to answer these questions, the research brings forth hidden historical actors whose roles have been obscured by stagnant high politics in the immediate postwar decades.

It is crucial to emphasize the transnational aspect of the stories being told in this study. Traditional understanding of *transnationalism* defines the term as "contracts, coalitions, and interactions across state boundaries."[1] This research reveals a plethora of boundary-crossing interactions between US and Vietnamese citizens, even during times of extremely restricted diplomatic relations between the two nation-states. British historian Patricia Clavin offers a fresh perspective on transnationalism. She argues, "Transnational history also allows us to reflect on, while at the same time going beyond, the confines of the nations. It sheds new, comparative light on the strengths and the fragilities of the nation-state and underlines the ways in which local history can be understood in relation to world history."[2] In this analytical framework, the study demonstrates how individuals or groups of individuals in the United States and Vietnam contested their national boundaries as well as reshaped relations between former enemies.

A pivotal work that serves as an inspiration and guiding framework for this research is Akira Iriye's *Cultural Internationalism and World Order*. Iriye defines cultural internationalism as "one idea of peace," in which "world order can and should be defined through interactions at the cultural level across national boundaries."[3] For him, viewing international relations through the cultural lens allows us to see beyond the geopolitical boundaries, for "the world is created and recreated as much by individuals from 'lesser powers' as by the great powers."[4] Opposing the common belief that cultural internationalism is idealism as compared to geopolitical realism, Iriye argues that cultural internationalists are realists. For these people, who strove for an alternative world order, human intellect and emotions are more realistic than armaments and national interests. Tracing the history of cultural internationalism from the 1890s to the post–World War II era, with examples from the idea for the International Committee of the Red Cross in the late 1850s, to the organization of the Chicago Parliaments of Religions of 1893, to the establishment of United Nations Educational, Scientific and Cultural Organization (UNESCO) in 1945, Iriye analyzes how cultural internationalism emerged as a response to the strong currents of geopolitical nationalism at the end of the nineteenth century and on the verge of World War I, then continued to develop during the interwar years and thrived in the aftermath of World War II. He asserts that the interchange among people across national boundaries effected change in governments' policies, an example of which is the creation of a cultural component in embassies.

Iriye's discussion illuminates the significance of nongeopolitical elements in international relations, calling for explorations beyond the traditional boundaries of diplomatic history. However, what he described as "cultural internationalism" seemed to fit the transnational paradigm. In fact, in his 2013 *Global and Transnational History: The Past, Present, and Future*, Iriye admitted, "Although I called the phenomenon [presented in the 1997 publication] 'cultural internationalism,' the term 'cultural transnationalism' might have been more appropriate."[5] In *Global and Transnational History*, he clarifies the distinction between "cultural internationalism" and "cultural transnationalism." Iriye asserts that internationalism indicates "cooperation among nations, whether in political, economic, or cultural affairs." He cited UNESCO as an example of cultural internationalism because it involves governmental policies in promoting cross-cultural understanding. Cultural transnationalism, on the other hand, refers to "collaboration among non-state actors in different lands in pursuit of cultural objectives, the nourishing of universal human aspirations and emotions, cultivation of mutual understanding among races, religions, and civilizations." Iriye also emphasizes that in practice, cultural internationalism and cultural transnationalism may intersect, as in cases of individuals or private organizations cooperating with governmental agencies to achieve cultural purposes.[6]

This book is an attempt to answer Iriye's call to examine "the relationship among the national, international, and transnational" through the lens of the "universal human aspirations and emotions." As Iriye points out, some emotions "are more adequately . . . seen as transnational because they are human, not national or international."[7] Underscoring that premise, this study explores US-Vietnam postwar relations through the transnational peace endeavors of ordinary US and Vietnamese citizens. In an attempt to understand how people transformed their negative emotions into positive actions, and how those acts helped reshape the relations between the two countries, the study chose as its subjects the lesser-known people who endured the effects of the Vietnam War. The subcategories of these people included Vietnamese refugees, children of US personnel and Vietnamese women, US and Vietnamese veterans and their families, relatives of fallen soldiers on both sides, and other civilians who experienced the impacts of war one way or another. The study also highlights the roles of nongovernmental organizations and individuals who strove for peace and mutual understanding through transnational humanitarian and cultural activities.

Bringing to center stage citizens' efforts to solve postwar individual and social problems, this book aims to bridge a gap in the scholarship on the US-Vietnam relations. While rich and voluminous, most Vietnam studies focus on wartime politics, combat memories, and veterans' homecoming experiences. In the past two decades, a number of scholars have explored postwar relations of the two countries, mostly at the governmental level and from US perspectives. They analyze the two nations' post-1975 political objectives, national interests, and diplomatic negotiations. To be sure, some scholars mention individual efforts in improving the relationship between the two countries, but the emphasis is still on governmental exchange, politicians, and a small number of US citizens. Vietnamese citizens hardly appear in the picture. As historian Edwin Martini points out, "Vietnam and the Vietnamese are rendered increasingly invisible in narratives of the war after 1975, either rendered outside the discursive construction altogether or dehumanized and marginalized to the point of invisibility and irrelevance."[8] While Martini was criticizing the absence of the Vietnamese in public discourse in general and in cultural products in particular, his comment aptly applies in scholarly works as well. Shifting the spotlight to ordinary citizens and putting Vietnamese people side by side with Americans in their postwar journeys, this research will be one of the first to fill in this gap in historical understanding.

The study's major argument is threefold. First, ordinary US and Vietnamese citizens were active historical actors in their changing environments. It would be erroneous to assume that underprivileged people remained traumatized in the aftermath of war and paralyzed by postwar domestic policies or by frozen diplomatic relations. Certainly, people on all sides of the conflict faced seemingly insurmountable obstacles in their quest for peace, but their determination, dedication, and creativity prevailed. Their abilities to move between and out of national and sociopolitical boundaries to reclaim or re-create their identities were illuminating. Transcending the obstructions imposed upon them, veterans, Amerasians, as well as humanitarian activists strove for peace, transforming their lives and their societies.

Second, it was ordinary citizens of both countries who laid the groundwork for US-Vietnam diplomatic normalization. Through nonprofit organizations, as well as cultural and academic exchange programs, trailblazers from diverse backgrounds promoted mutual understanding and acted as catalytic forces between the two governments. Both US and Vietnamese public discourse often credited President William Jefferson Clinton for normalizing US-Vietnam relations and promoting friendship between the two countries. For instance, historian John Dumbrell praises Clinton for "unilaterally end[ing]" the trade embargo against Vietnam despite opposition from veterans' organizations.[9] This observation oversimplifies the long road to normalization because it overlooks the foundational contributions of citizens from both sides since the late 1970s. The president's decision to end the trade embargo in 1994 and to normalize US-Vietnam relations in 1995 were but overdue actions grounded in citizens' quests.

Third, the "universal human aspirations and emotions" that Iriye mentioned played a significant role in US-Vietnam postwar relations. It was their shared experiences of a brutal war and desire for peace that connected strangers, even opponents, of two different worlds. Viewed from the traditional framework of state-to-state relations history, the relationship between the two countries was frozen, at least during the second half of the 1970s, and then slowly improved before normalization in 1995. However, upon an examination of their relations through the cultural transnationalism paradigm, especially with a focus on emotions, the interconnectedness between the US and Vietnamese people was striking. Even during times of governmental hostility on both sides, ordinary citizens vigorously developed cultural ties and promoted mutual understanding in unimaginable ways. In their pursuit of peace—for themselves and for others—these US and Vietnamese citizens realized that they had more in common than they had imagined. The label "enemy" that they had put on one another quickly dissolved; they were but men, women, and children who endured undeletable scars of a destructive violence. The pains that they shared served as a foundation for their aspirations for peace. This book presents a picture of vibrant interactions between the two countries in the postwar years.

Chapter 1 examines the initial transnational peace efforts of ordinary US and Vietnamese citizens, which included humanitarian aid and the Pacific-crossing phenomenon of the so-called boat people, against the backdrop of US-Vietnam governmental tensions in the immediate years after the ending of the war. While Vietnam was still listed as an "enemy country" by the US government, many US citizens chose to focus on humanitarian missions rather than politics and national interests, reaching out to those who were struggling in the aftermath of war, whether the people in need decided to stay in Vietnam or leave their homeland. Underneath the frozen diplomatic relations between the two nations were the transpacific material and human flow conducted by nonprofit organizations and human rights activists. In many cases, they circumvented laws and regulations and transcended political differences to accomplish their humanitarian endeavors. Simultaneously, the world was watching in horror as one of the most dramatic migrations in the late twentieth century developed. Common knowledge indicates that hundreds of thousands of Vietnamese people chose to leave their homeland for fear of the new communist government's revenge and its harsh rule. The study unfolds the complexity of postwar Vietnam, which is often overshadowed by critique of its communist regime. While the expatriates made radical moves by leaving their home country in risky manners, which resulted in untold suffering, they proved to be active historical actors who refused to submit to their circumstances. To an extent, they pushed both Vietnamese and US governments to work together and change their policies. They also prompted the United Nations to forge international cooperation. Both the humanitarian activists and the boat people transcended their boundaries, pursuing their aspirations and, to an extent, influencing high politics.

Chapter 2 explores the arduous quest for the identities of Amerasians — children of mixed US and Vietnamese parentage. Ostracized by their families and/or society, Amerasians' suffering was, and still is, immense. That commonly perceived image, however, obscures their historical role as a transformative force in postwar societies.[10] From the streets of Vietnam, Amerasians not only learned to fend for themselves but also found ways to get international attention. One way or another, they made the two hostile governments talk to each other to acknowledge their existence and accept their dual citizenship. In the US, whether enjoying newly found love or wounded by their fathers' rejections, or disillusioned by their "adoptive families," Amerasians refused to live as pitiful, voiceless, paralyzed victims. This chapter argues that Amerasians played dynamic roles in transforming their own lives as well as others'. It also examines Amerasians as a transnational community in which members found bonds in their shared nationless state, experiences of sociopolitical marginalization, and determination to thrive. Born out of war, Amerasians crossed boundaries with peace endeavors. They replaced the boundaries imposed by their maternal and paternal societies with love and compassion, privileges absent in their childhoods.

Chapter 3 presents the groundwork for normalization by ordinary citizens, with an emphasis on US veterans' contributions, from 1980 to 1994. This period of time witnessed the impact of a complex web of international politics on Southeast Asia. Despite the stalemate in governmental relations in the 1980s because of controversies over the peace settlement for Cambodia, numerous US citizens, especially veterans, diligently crossed the Pacific Ocean to help Vietnamese people, to promote cultural and academic exchange, and to advocate for diplomatic normalization between the two nations. Citizens' exuberant transnational activities in the 1980s and early 1990s stood in contrast with diplomatic constraints. In addition to humanitarian activities, cultural projects such as arts, literature, education, science, and tourism materialized. While they did not immediately change national policies, these cultural connections thawed the ice between the two governments, laying the foundation for diplomatic ties.

Chapter 4 discusses the US and Vietnamese people's peace efforts after the establishment of diplomatic normalization, including the continued returns to Vietnam of US veterans and/or their families for humanitarian as well as reconciliatory purposes. The chapter also brings to center stage the painstaking journeys of Vietnamese people in search of their families who had been missing because of wartime circumstances. Although these people's quests had never ceased, their stories emerged only in the past decade thanks to new developments in communication technologies. In the English-speaking discourse about the Vietnam War, narratives of Americans searching for their loved ones who died on foreign soil are not rare. Little do we hear about Vietnamese people who restlessly wondered what happened to their family members in those chaotic times. These heartbreaking searches, whether by Americans or Vietnamese, connect us as human beings and deepen our understanding of the impacts of war. The wounds of war are indiscriminative. Wherever a war broke out, it swept all on its path, whether one was choosing sides or staying neutral, whether one ended up winning or losing the conflict. This chapter reveals the reality of the lingering effects of war—how a war may never end for some people.

By no means does this book attempt to make generalizations of any group of people. On the contrary, it presents the dynamic of historical processes and actors. Each story of these historical actors adds dimension to our understanding of US-Vietnam postwar relations. It provides a different image taken from a different perspective to enrich the existing narratives of the subject. This is a study of human emotions in transnational relations. It is also a study of ordinary citizens whose journeys out of a war zone manifested into peace endeavors and transformative forces.

CHAPTER ONE

Turbulent Years of Peace

At the fall of Saigon in April 1975, Vietnam witnessed a dramatic human movement throughout the country as well as across the Pacific Ocean. The statement, "The war is over!" took different tones. For many, it was indescribable, overwhelming joy accompanied by inferences of homecoming, family reunion, and a normal life undisrupted by gunfire. For others, the statement was a horrific, humiliating defeat, a final blow to their hope, attached to the prospect of dislocation or even expatriation. This chapter examines the human and material flows between the United States and Vietnam in the immediate postwar years, from April 1975 to the end of 1979.

Three major components of the discussion include the governmental tensions between the United States and the Socialist Republic of Vietnam (SRV); the humanitarian aid carried out by US citizens in the context of limited, if not hostile, relations between the two nations; and the waves of Vietnamese refugees seeking safe haven outside the country. For the first time in decades, Vietnamese people were free from the noise of gunfire. Peace, however, did not return without a price; war heroes were not the best economists; noncombatants were not necessarily friends. Contrary to the US government's prediction, no bloodbath occurred in postwar united Vietnam. Reconciliation, however, seemed unobtainable. The second half of the 1970s proved to be a tumultuous transition for a weary people in a devastated country.

Governmental Tensions

In his speech to students at Tulane University in New Orleans, Louisiana, on April 23, 1975, President Gerald Ford said:

> Today, America can regain the sense of pride that existed before Vietnam. But it cannot be achieved by refighting a war that is finished as far as America is concerned.
>
> I ask that we stop refighting the battles and the recriminations of the past. I ask that we look now at what is right with America, at our possibilities and our potentialities for change and growth and achievement and sharing. I ask that we accept the responsibilities of leadership as a good neighbor to all peoples and the enemy of none. I ask that we strive to become, in the finest American tradition, something more tomorrow than we are today.[1]

During his flight back to Washington, DC, that night, however, the president "indicated to a few reporters that he might reassess his request for $722-million in military aid" in hope of halting the imminent collapse of South Vietnam.[2] The contradictions between President Ford's words and thoughts did not stop there; the discrepancies between rhetoric and reality continued to evolve in the years to come.

A few months after the fall of Saigon, President Ford toured China, Indonesia, and the Philippines. Upon his return to the White House, he announced the new Pacific Doctrine. The doctrine affirmed that "American strength is basic to any stable balance of power in the Pacific region (which includes all Asian countries facing the Pacific)." It also emphasized that the US partnership with Japan was "the pillar of the American strategy in East and Southeast Asia." Another highlight in the doctrine was "the need to normalize relations with China" and the intention "to remain actively engaged in the affairs of the region."[3] Journalist Harish Chanola commented in *Economic and Political Weekly*, "The significant point of Ford's New Pacific Doctrine is that the U.S. is going to stick around in Asia. It means that the U.S. will continue to manipulate the politics and try to influence the events in this continent—to further its national interests."[4]

Viewing the US perspective within the entanglement of international politics in the 1970s, it made sense that the United States wanted to "stick around in Asia." William Safire, President Richard Nixon's speechwriter and the Pulitzer Prize–winning political columnist for the *New York Times*, analyzed the driving force for the desire to enhance political ties between the United States and China. According to Safire, China perceived India and North Vietnam as the Soviet's potential puppets, while Japan remained the "economic battleground" of the two communist powers. Fearing Soviet encroachment, China shifted its interests to the United States, hoping to balance the political game.[5] The United States, on the other hand, saw the opportunity to regain China, a potentially significant partner it had "lost" decades earlier. In US calculations, Vietnam would not make a partner that was as important as China.

To be sure, President Ford mentioned that his overall policy in Asia was "peace with *all* and hostility toward *none*," and that "peace in Asia requires a structure of economic cooperation reflecting the aspiration of *all* the peoples in the region."[6] The president also said if "the new regimes" of Indochina "exhibit restraint toward their neighbors and constructive approaches to international problems, we will look to the future rather than to the past."[7] The doctrine seemed to indicate willingness of the United States to enhance its relationship with "all" nations in the Pacific world. However, the steps that the Ford administration was about to take in regards to Vietnam profoundly differed from "the responsibilities of leadership as a good neighbor to all peoples and the enemy of none" that he had announced.

First, immediately after Hanoi took over Saigon and ended the war in April 1975, Washington extended the 1964 trade embargo on North Vietnam to all of Vietnam and pressured US allies in Europe and Asia to avoid doing business with Vietnam altogether. The extended trade embargo not only restricted trade but also limited travel and humanitarian aid to Vietnam as well as blocked educational opportunities in the United States for Vietnamese students.[8] As Gareth Porter asserts, the policy "was explicitly aimed at hindering, even if only in small, symbolic ways, the recovery of Vietnam's postwar economy."[9] Second, the United States declined to recognize a reunified country renamed the Socialist Republic of Vietnam (SRV), and that decision served as the premise for the next step. Twice, in 1975 and 1976, the United States voted against Vietnam's application for membership to the United Nations. Reviewing the US policy toward Vietnam in the early postwar years, historian Edwin Martini comments, "Far from receding into isolation, the United States after 1975 remained in a position to shape the direction and contour of events in Vietnam and in Southeast Asia as a whole. The War on Vietnam continued; only the weaponry had changed."[10]

The leaders of the SRV, on the other hand, took a hard position in the nation's postwar relations with the United States. Initially, they maintained that the United States owed "reparations" to Vietnam. They soon realized that the term *reparations* was too harsh and decided to discuss "reconstruction and humanitarian aid" instead. They also talked about promises and commitment, holding the United States responsible for the $3.25 billion promised by President Nixon in a message to North Vietnam's Prime Minister Pham Van Dong dated February 1, 1973. The message also stated, "The Government of the United States of America will contribute to postwar reconstruction in North Vietnam without any political conditions."[11] In March 1976, in response to an American request for talks on the issue of Americans listed as missing in action (MIA), Vietnam's spokesman asserted, "Our position is clear. The United States Government must apply Article 21 of the Paris agreement [*sic*], under which the United States must fulfill its obligation to contribute to healing the wounds of war and the postwar reconstruction of Vietnam. On our side, the government of the [Socialist] Republic of Vietnam is prepared to apply Article 8-B of the agreement about Americans Missing in Action."[12] According to *New York Times* reporter Flora Lewis, in the same week of the Vietnamese announcement, the United States refused to attend a World Health Organization meeting to discuss medical and health needs in Vietnam.[13]

While presenting their firm position toward the United States on the aftermath of war, Vietnam's leaders made public their intention to expand the country's international relations beyond the communist bloc. At the conference of third-world nonaligned nations on August 17, 1976, Vietnam's Prime Minister Pham Van Dong stated that Vietnam was interested in normalizing diplomatic relations with the United States and establishing economic ties with capitalist countries. He asserted that Vietnam would adopt an independent approach for its international relations even though other communist leaders such as Prime Minister Pak Song-chol of North Korea and the Khmer Rouge leader Khieu Samphan of Cambodia were condemning the United States as an aggressive imperialist power.[14]

Nevertheless, the hardline position continued when Vietnamese Deputy Foreign Minister Phan Hien met with US Assistant Secretary of State for East Asian and Pacific Affairs Richard Holbrooke in Paris on May 3, 1977, to discuss diplomatic possibilities. Phan firmly claimed, "Without aid [normalization] is impossible." The negotiations failed. When addressing the issue to the press, Phan quoted Nixon's promise, revealing the classified letter to the world. As historian Edwin Martini observes, "The day of Hien's statement, the House voted 266–131 to further obstruct American aid to Vietnam." The

resolution, according to Martini, "specifically prohibited 'negotiating reparations, aid or any other form of payment to Vietnam.'"[15] The road to reconciliation turned into an impasse. Failing to find a negotiable range for their goals,
leaders of both countries frustrated and angered their counterparts.

Fueled by Hanoi's uncompromising stance, the United States continued to
play an active role in maintaining antagonism toward Vietnam. In June 1977,
the US Senate approved Senator Robert Dole's initiative, which required that
the Carter administration oppose the World Bank and other multinational
lending institutions such as the International Monetary Fund from providing
aid to Vietnam. According to the Dole amendment, if any institution provided
loans to Vietnam regardless of US disapproval, Washington would "deduct
its share of the aid from its next contribution to the institution." Simultaneously, the House of Representatives endorsed a foreign-aid bill that banned
assistance, direct or indirect, to Vietnam, Laos, Cambodia, Cuba, Angola, Mo-
zambique, and Uganda.[16] President Jimmy Carter nevertheless disapproved of
the blockade of indirect aid to Vietnam through international relief agencies
or the World Bank. In the same year, however, when the UN General Assembly's economic committee approved priority assistance to Vietnam, the
United States was the only one of the 149 members to refuse to participate
in the program, with the reason being that Congress had prohibited direct
aid to Vietnam.[17] US refusal to partake in UN economic relief revealed the
inconsistency in its policy, for its vote would have meant indirect aid via an
international organization.

Realizing that the United States was stiffening its opposition to Vietnam
and being desperate for financial aid, Hanoi's leaders softened their strategies.
When Senator Edward Kennedy's delegation arrived in Hanoi in August 1978,
Prime Minister Pham took the chance to express the Vietnamese desire to not
only reconcile with the United States but also develop friendship between the
two countries. The delegation brought with it nineteen Vietnamese-American
children and ten Vietnamese wives to the United States, the first to be reunited
with their American loved ones. The overall impression reported by American
representatives was that the Vietnamese had "a strong desire" to renew their
ties with the United States, noting that there was no criticism of past US actions
during their stay. Vietnamese leaders even emphasized that it was Vietnam's
"duty to act positively on legitimate family-reunion cases, including those of
the 'boat people.'"[18] Under their gloomy circumstances, which were significantly affected by US policies, the Vietnamese diplomatic adaptation was un-
derstandable. In addition, a long-term vision indicated that Vietnam would fare

better without depending too much on any single foreign force. With the complications of the Cold War and the internal competition between the communist powers of China and the Soviet Union, widening its circle of friends and balancing relations with both communist and noncommunist nations seemed essential to Vietnam. Yet the year 1978 turned tumultuous in Southeast Asia, adding obstruction to the expected improvement of US-Vietnam ties.

Since the mid-1970s, Vietnam's neighbor, Cambodia, had undergone an autogenocide carried out by its governing force, the Khmer Rouge. It is worth noting that the United States approved the Khmer Rouge's representation in the UN while disapproving that of Vietnam twice in 1975 and 1976. American hostility against Vietnam proved detrimental. The US accused Vietnam of illegally invading Cambodia while muting the fact that the ruling Khmer Rouge had been conducting a genocide of its own people for a few years and had crossed the borders of Vietnam in 1978. If anything, the Vietnamese occupation in Cambodia was similar to US "assistance" to South Vietnam in the 1960s, except for two major differences. First, North Vietnam, from which the United States wanted to liberate South Vietnam, was not a genocidal regime. In fact, North Vietnam won considerable popular support throughout the country. Second, North Vietnam did not invade the United States and kill its people, nor did it threaten to do so. On the contrary, the Khmer Rouge crossed its borders and killed approximately thirty thousand innocent Vietnamese civilians. Even though Vietnam defeated the Khmer Rouge regime in January 1979, the latter continued to enjoy direct Chinese and indirect US support while hiding near the Thailand border. Vietnam, therefore, had to maintain its armed forces in Cambodian territory to secure peace for both Cambodia and Vietnam despite enormous financial and human costs.[19]

In return, however, China and the United States labeled Vietnam as the "aggressor." On the one hand, the label provided a good excuse for China to "teach Vietnam a lesson" by militarily attacking six northern Vietnamese provinces in early 1979.[20] On the other hand, the United States added another condition to the possibility of diplomatic normalization with Vietnam: withdrawal from Cambodia. In his testimony before the Subcommittee on Asian and Pacific Affairs of the House Foreign Affairs Committee on June 13, 1979, Richard Holbrooke, assistant secretary for East Asian and Pacific affairs, stated:

We made clear that we were not taking sides in Vietnam's dispute
with Kampuchea, that we ourselves had long been at the forefront
of those nations denouncing the Pol Pot government for its terrible

human rights abuses, and that we were not supporting that regime. *We stressed, however, that even that regime's unparalleled crimes would not justify a Vietnamese military violation of Kampuchean sovereignty and replacement of the government by force.*[21]

If Pol Pot's genocidal regime and its intrusion into Vietnam's territory did not justify Vietnamese military intervention in Cambodia, how did the US government expect Vietnam to respond to the situation? Even if the United States was genuinely neutral in the Asian quarrel, criticizing the forces that overthrew a genocidal regime for doing just that is tantamount to supporting the maintenance of the genocide. As Senator John Kerry commented, "You know what Vietnam did? They did what nobody else was willing to do. They went into Cambodia and kicked the Khmer Rouge out and nobody in the world said thank you. We responded with an embargo. . . . Why is it that we are driven to treat Vietnam differently from Iraq, from China, from Chile and Pinochet, from countless of other governments?"[22] These policies against the restoration and development of Vietnam prolonged the suffering of a people who had already been battered by wars, leaving Vietnam with no choice but to strengthen its alliance with the Soviet Union.

Unlike the previous wars in the twentieth century, the United States did not see why it should help reconstruct the country that it had damaged, neither in terms of reparations nor humanitarian aid. Despite the SRV's interest in reconciliation and renewed connections between the two countries, the US government only agreed to discuss issues regarding twenty-five hundred MIAs, political prisoners, and the Vietnamese "invasion" of Cambodia.[23] The concept of *humanitarian aid* did come up in the discussions of politicians from both sides. Unfortunately, their definitions of the term differed. For US diplomats, it referred to the fate of the twenty-five hundred American MIAs, implying the possibility that Vietnamese authorities might be keeping them in prison. The term also referred to the thousands of Vietnamese political prisoners stationed in "re-education camps" set up by the Communist government since the end of the war. Vietnamese leaders, however, were concerned about their 1.4 million disabled veterans and civilians, five hundred thousand orphans, and three hundred thousand MIAs,[24] not to mention twenty-three million bomb craters scattered across their rice fields and 3.5 million landmines that continued to kill civilians throughout the country on a daily basis.[25] Thinking of humanitarianism in different terms, the stalemate in postwar relations between the two governments dragged on until the late 1980s.

The gap in US and Vietnamese understandings of humanitarianism, however, was not a cultural one; rather, it was a political construct to further isolate Vietnam. The United States' demand for complete information and/or the returning of all those listed as unaccounted-for service personnel was unprecedented and unreasonable. According to Bruce Franklin, the request was "bizarre" and "has no basis in international law." In comparison to the other major wars in which the United States had been involved, the percentage of US MIAs in the Vietnam War was the lowest: 4 percent in contrast to 15 percent in the Korean War and 22 percent in World War II. Yet the United States "has never asked for such a volume of information on its missing," and "there are no examples in world history to compare with the accounting now being requested."[26] To be sure, domestic politics significantly influenced the Carter administration's policy toward the SRV. Feeling that they were betrayed by their government and fellow citizens, many Vietnam veterans and families of those who were missing in action demanded attention and actions on the MIA issues. They feared that because the Vietnam War was not one that reinforced American pride, the US government was going to quickly forget the servicemen and servicewomen who were left in Indochina, alive or not. The establishment of the National League of POW/MIA Families in 1970, for example, was unprecedented. In fact, according to journalist Jay Price, the league "changed the way Americans think about missing troops and the government's responsibility for them."[27] Through painstaking effort, they brought their concern to the spotlight. However, the fact that the US government used MIAs as an essential condition in reshaping relations with Vietnam while ignoring the suffering of the Vietnamese people, including veterans and MIA families, caused many observers to characterize US politicians as unfeeling, arrogant, and using a double standard.

Humanitarian Aid

Despite governmental restrictions on both sides, in 1977, Martha Winnacker, codirector of the Indochina Resource Center, visited My Lai, a village in central Vietnam that bore the massacre conducted by Charlie Company in 1968. She shared her thought: "I had not really wanted to go to Son My—just as I still prefer not to look at that awful poster. Yet once I saw both the bitter past and the hopeful future of the people who have come back to rebuild their homes and raise their children, I realize that if we share in the building of their future, we Americans can learn to live with the memories we have tried so hard to deny."[28] Her comment implied an initial reluctance to face an unpleasant past, but only by facing the past, it seemed, can we see the future. Winnacker remembered the enduring, awkward moment when she met with two survivors of the slaughter, "who at first simply stared at us with bitter, tragic faces, as we looked, miserably, backed at them."[29] It is difficult to imagine what one can say in such a circumstance. They were strangers who claimed shared knowledge of a horrendous story. To an extent, their presence forced one another to relive the tragedy and to reactivate the pain of a time far passed. But it was at that awkward moment when words could not be found and tears quietly rolled that they felt the transformative power to step forward. Winnacker wondered, "If President Carter were to sit across that Formica table from Mrs. Doc [whose eleven direct family members had been murdered in the massacre], would he still claim Americans have 'no obligation' to help them?" Winnacker was referring to President Carter's response in a press conference on March 24, 1977. Although the President did not directly say that the United States had "no obligation" (to use Winnacker's words) to uphold President Nixon's promise of postwar reconstruction aid for Vietnam, he indicated that North Vietnam violated the Paris Peace Accords anyway. When pushed by another journalist who asked whether the president felt that the United States had "a moral obligation" to help rebuild Vietnam if the latter was willing to share information on American MIAs, Carter once again evaded the question by saying, "Well, the destruction was mutual."[30] For Winnacker, the president did not truly understand the impact of US military involvement on the Vietnamese people. She maintained that the $3.25 billion promised by President Nixon was "a pittance compared to the $150 billion the United States spent to destroy it."[31]

Individuals such as Martha Winnacker were groundbreakers for the postwar transnational network of US and Vietnamese citizens who worked tirelessly for peace and the betterment of people's lives. Emphasizing humanitarianism, these people crossed not only geographic but also cultural and political boundaries. For them, the shared human experiences and emotions were far more significant than national interests. The path they took was challenging, but their determination prevailed.

To be sure, they were not the first Americans to have traveled to a country listed as an enemy by their government. Numerous antiwar activists had visited Hanoi during wartime. Their activities varied from getting to know the reality of war to providing medical aid for civilian victims. Some groups negotiated with North Vietnamese officials, managing to send care packages to American prisoners of war (POWs) and even successfully pressing Hanoi to release twelve of them well before the two governments agreed upon a POW exchange.[32] To borrow historian Mary Hershberger's words, these people inherited "a long, still-seldom-heralded tradition of American travel to 'enemy' territory during times of crisis."[33] Hershberger traces the history of people-to-people diplomatic work back to 1763 when some white settlers journeyed to Native American towns seeking peaceful solutions to racial conflicts. She refers to this phenomenon as "a stream of citizen-based efforts to rise above national interests."[34] Even though the subjects of the study reached out to Vietnam in the postwar era, their journeys were not necessarily easier. In some cases, the otherwise law-abiding Americans risked their own freedom upholding compassion for other human beings.

Despite tensions among top leaders of the two countries, nongovernmental humanitarian efforts continued to flourish. Several organizations that had worked in Vietnam during wartime resumed their activities after a brief pause because of the political transition. Nevertheless, they soon found their road even bumpier than it had been under fire. In June 1975, barely two months after the fall of Saigon, the US Internal Revenue Service announced that contributions to the Bach Mai Hospital Emergency Relief Fund were no longer tax deductible. In July, the US Department of the Treasury denied the American Friends Service Committee a license to ship agricultural and fishing equipment to Vietnam.[35] Bach Mai was the largest civilian hospital in North Vietnam, which was severely damaged during the twelve-day Christmas bombing of 1972. Contributions from US civilians to rebuild the hospital had been tax exempt while the war moved on. According to journalist Eileen Shanahan, shipment of agricultural and fishing equipment to areas under communist control had also been allowed in 1973. For Stanley L. Sommerfield, director of the Foreign Assets Division of the Treasury Department, policy did not change; only the label did: assistance to Vietnam before April 1975 was considered "humanitarian aid"; now it became "economic aid."[36] United States citizens, of course, would not be permitted to provide "economic aid" to communist countries. Elinor Ashkenazy, a former staff member of the American Friends Service Committee, voiced her dissent: "Quite literally, the Friends face prosecution for taking the plow, instead of the sword, into Vietnam."[37]

The American Friends Service Committee, however, did not give up. In response to the license rejection in July 1975, Wallace T. Collett, chairman of the organization's board of directors, announced that the shipment of fishing nets and hospital repair tools worth $325,000 would go forth anyway, and that he and other officials were prepared to face fines, penalties, or jail time if they had to.[38] Between late July and early November 1975, the agency was repeatedly denied licenses to send other shipments to Vietnam, among them 16.5 tons of yarn to be made into children's sweaters and two hundred and twenty tons of powdered milk also for children. On November 11, Collett and Executive Director Louis Schneider led a quiet protest outside the White House. While the Quaker leaders were seeking a discussion with President Ford, two hundred and fifty supporters filled the length of the White House's north fence, carrying pictures of Vietnamese children and signs that read, "Are Vietnam's children the enemy?" They did not get to talk to the president but left at the White House twenty-five hundred copies of donor forms with the donors' signatures certifying their acknowledgment that the donation "may be interpreted as a violation of the law."[39] A few days later, the agency received permission to send self-help supplies to Vietnam. Nevertheless, the main reason for their gain was not the protest; rather, it represented the US Department of State's response to Hanoi's release of nine US prisoners a month earlier. Most of these prisoners were missionaries who remained in Vietnam after the collapse of Saigon and the final withdrawal of US forces in April 1975.[40] The fact that the US government responded to the SRV's behavior rather than the American Quakers' humanitarian efforts exemplified a big gap between the American leaders' thinking and their citizens'. While the Quakers saw only human beings in need of food, essential supplies, and self-help tools, the government officials saw communists, enemies, and power struggles. Politics must have obscured the officials' human eyes.

The American Friends Service Committee was determined to convey its peace and reconciliation message to top US leaders. In 1976, together with southern Quakers, the agency organized a Christmas prayer vigil for peace and reconciliation in front of the newly elected president's home in Plains, Georgia. The vigil fell on the fourth anniversary of the Christmas bombing in North Vietnam. According to the plan, approximately fifty people would silently stand in line facing the Carters' home, emphasizing to the president the significance of reconciliation with Vietnam and de-escalation of US military power.[41] In their letter to the president informing him of the vigil, the agency's representatives wrote:

We come in the belief and hope that you share our faith that together we can resolve the outstanding issues of the Vietnam War and take the next steps toward reconciliation and peace. . . . We WELCOME your statement that you will appoint a commission to meet with the Vietnamese, Cambodians, and Laotians in the belief that such actions can be an important step toward resolving the outstanding issues of the war including obtaining whatever information may exist about the missing in action, normalizing relations and providing humanitarian assistance to help the people of Indochina in the awesome task of post-war reconstruction. We believe steps you can take early in your presidency will help assure a positive future in relations between our two peoples.[42]

The Quakers' efforts were impressive. Their genuine desire for peace dictated their initiatives. They spoke truth to power and stood up for their call, peacefully but fearlessly.

It is worth noting that religious organizations played a prominent role in paving the way for humanitarian aid to the Vietnamese people. Soon after the war ended, US churches and civic groups came together on October 2, 1975, under the name Friendshipment, and announced a campaign that collected funds and relief supplies for Vietnam. The campaign particularly called for donations of blankets, children's clothes, antibiotics, and farming tools.[43] Friendshipment was a coalition of thirty to forty religious and other civic groups actively involved in helping the war-torn people in Vietnam in the late 1970s. Between May 1975 and May 1976, Friendshipment generated $1.34 million worth of medical supplies, clothing, and other materials.[44] The coalition also raised its voice against the trade embargo, which it saw as a major harm to economic development in Vietnam. Through its words and actions, Friendshipment presented a convincing success of "people-to-people" relations. It upheld humanity against political, religious, and racial boundaries.

In March 1976, a group of religious leaders representing Friendshipment planned a two-week trip to Vietnam with these individuals' personal expenses to evaluate reconstruction needs in the country. Members of the delegation included president of the Methodist Board of Church and Society, an executive of Lutheran World Relief, the executive director of Church World Service, former president of Disciples Peace Fellowship, and staff members from Clergy and Laity Concerned, the Indochina Mobile Education Project, and News Service Indochina. Their host was the Vietnamese Committee for Solidarity with the American People.[45] Upon their return, they urged the US government to lift the trade embargo, normalize diplomatic relations, and provide reconstruction aid to Vietnam. James Armstrong, the United Methodist

Bishop of North Dakota and South Dakota, appealed to the US government to carry out its "moral obligation" by assisting the devastated country. He also encouraged individuals to contribute their share as a gesture of "friendship and reconciliation."[46]

The desire for peace and reconciliation of Friendshipment's members was also mentioned in the media. In a letter to the editor of the *New York Times* on December 6, 1976, its coordinator, Cora Weiss, wrote: "Thousands of Americans have already given privately to heal the wounds of war. Mr. Carter will find wide support for a policy of reconciliation. The Americans who are building the My Lai hospital are helping to keep the door to negotiations open. He needs only step in."[47] In fact, by March 16, 1977, Friendshipment had received donations from 12,852 Americans for the construction of a hospital on the My Lai massacre site. The coalition presented the sum of $150,000 to a Vietnamese representative on the ninth anniversary of the incident. The gift also included a plaque to be hung in the hospital with inscriptions in Vietnamese that read: "Friendshipment Hospital—A gift of friendship from the American People." Speaking at the ceremony, Cora Weiss emphasized the US people's good will: "We hope this gesture of helping to rebuild what our government destroyed will serve as a demonstration to the President and the Congress that the American people will support a government move to help heal the wounds of war."[48] The idea of turning a massacre site into a hospital vindicated a profound symbol of reconciliation. A massacre is the utmost brutal human act, and its victims represent ultimate powerlessness. A hospital, on the other hand, is synonymous with caring and healing. A hospital always gives people a sense of hope—the hope to transform pain and suffering into strength and wholeness. The My Lai hospital, founded on blood stains of a dishonorable past and built by the compassion of borderless hearts, upholds the ideal that reconciliation is always possible.

One of the most long-standing nongovernmental organizations in Vietnam is the Church World Service (CWS). Born in 1946, following the end of World War II, CWS's mission was clear and straightforward: "Feed the hungry, clothe the naked, heal the sick, comfort the aged, shelter the homeless."[49] CWS staff came to Vietnam in 1954 to assist refugee resettlement. Throughout the 1960s and the early 1970s, it operated through the Vietnam Christian Service (VNCS) and partook in peace and reconciliation initiatives through the World Council of Churches Fund for Reconstruction and Reconciliation (FRRI). From 1976 to 1990, CWS provided Vietnam with more than $8 million in project assistance while continuing its activity through FRRI in helping with emergency relief funds as well as health care and economic recovery. In 1990, five years before US-Vietnam diplomatic normalization, CWS established its office in Hanoi and has continued its activity in remote areas of Vietnam.[50]

Despite bureaucratic difficulties in the immediate postwar years, Church World Service strove in its humanitarian efforts. In November 1977, CWS announced its fundraising program, aiming for a February shipment of ten thousand metric tons of wheat to be distributed in schools and hospitals in Vietnam. That would be "the first food shipment sent directly from the United States to Vietnam since the war's end."[51] The fundraising mission was achieved, and the ship carrying the said amount of wheat left Houston, Texas, on April 2, 1978, but the agency failed in persuading the US government to assist in the $800,000 shipping expenses, which were normally reimbursed in humanitarian aid to other countries. As the director of the United States Agency for International Development explained to CWS, the shipping cost request was rejected "in view of the expressed opposition of Congress to the provision of food aid to Vietnam."[52] The shipment, operated under the American National Council of Churches, arrived in Vietnam on May 22, 1978. The council's seven-member delegation reported their impression of the Vietnamese cordiality during their three weeks in the country.[53]

Before that first direct shipment of aid from the United States, Church World Service assisted the Vietnamese in need by circumventing the restrictions imposed by the US government. In 1976, for example, together with Friendshipment and Lutheran World Relief, CWS sent thirteen hundred tons of rice to Hai Phong, a northern Vietnamese city that shouldered the Christmas bombing with Hanoi in 1972. These agencies had to carry out their mission through the United Nations with the rice bought and shipped for them from Thailand by UNICEF. Paul F. McCleary, executive director of CWS, stated, "It has been four years since the Christmas bombing of Hanoi. This Christmas, Americans are sending food, recognizing that the war is over and the time for reconciliation is here."[54] Marian Wright Edelman, director of the Children's Defense Fund, shared a similar observation: "I have always believed that Americans would not object to purely humanitarian shipments to Vietnam, so I have been perplexed at Congressional [sic] actions that, perhaps unintentionally, have had the effect of denying such aid, including food and medicine."[55] Edelman referred to the Vietnamese children as "the unwitting victims of differences between our two countries."[56] They truly were.

Visions of reconciling with Vietnam and of transcending political boundaries for humanitarian efforts like those of McCleary and Edelman, unfortunately, did not reflect general American sentiments in the late 1970s. However, that a small number of individuals stood up and did what they believed to be the right thing was an admirable phenomenon. These people knew that they were going upstream, but for them, that was the only way. They refused to follow the path paved by their government and to listen to the rhetoric that made little sense to them.

On the other side of the Pacific Ocean, ordinary Vietnamese citizens were also journeying upstream in response to dramatic changes in their society. The revolutionaries who triumphed in their struggle for national independence and reunification proved to be much better wartime fighters than peacetime managers. The new government's poor policies combined with damages resulting from decades of military violence and international political developments caused many people to discover their homeland was too hostile to stay. Desperation prompted them to become historical actors, forming an unprecedented wave of transpacific migration. These individuals' efforts to find peace and stability for themselves turned into catalysts that forged transnational endeavors as well as international cooperation.

Drifting Expatriates

In the immediate years after the war ended, the sheer numbers of Vietnamese refugees were appalling. Between April 1975 and June 1979, approximately three hundred thousand people resettled in another country as refugees.[57] According to other statistics, by August 1979, an estimated 675,000 people had left Vietnam at an average rate of nearly 12,500 people per month, with the peak number of refugees arriving in first-asylum countries (countries that temporarily admit refugees and provide them with basic assistance while waiting for permanent resettlement or repatriation) between June 1978 and July 1979.[58] These statistics included only those who left *and* survived their journeys; there were no official records of lives lost because of boat accidents, hunger, sicknesses, and pirates' attacks. For many people, the chaotic scene of Saigon during the final days of the war in late April 1975 was unforgettable, with powerful images of panicked civilians jamming the United States Embassy and Tan Son Nhat (or Tan Son Nhut) International Airport, struggling to board final flights for the United States. Many of those people had no more than a vague idea of their destinations—somewhere in the Western world, somewhere across the Pacific Ocean. Regardless of the viewer's politics, the scene was heartrending.

Those so-called first-wave refugees, however, would be considered much luckier than the expatriates who followed, the "boat people." Unlike the evacuees of April 1975, whose panic and desperation soon ended once they got on an airplane, the boat people's suffering persisted even after they arrived in first-asylum countries. The human flow out of Vietnam continued in the years following the end of the war, and it magnified into a movement—the ocean-crossing movement as it is referred to in Vietnamese—in the late 1970s.[59] According to researcher Milton Osborne, the number of Vietnamese leaving Vietnam before May 1978 was "relatively small" compared to the number during the period of 1978 to 1979. For many reasons, thousands of people found their homeland increasingly hostile and decided to venture into an unknown future outside their national boundaries.

The dramatic plunge into the sea of Vietnamese boat people is often interpreted as a reaction against the communists' harsh control. In Vietnam, people often use the terms *trước giải phóng* (ante-liberation) and *sau giải phóng* (post-liberation) or *hồi giải phóng vô* (when the liberators came) to imply dramatic changes in their lives since April 1975. Common sentiments among those who had had better lives before 1975 indicate that "liberation" meant the end of the "good old days": liberation was the cause of their suffering—losses of jobs, incomes, and assets. Simply put, liberation brought with it adversity, so they sought their own solution: leaving. However, the driving force behind this life-risking decision is complex and manifold. Other than fear of political punishment and revenge, major causes of the Vietnamese expatriation in the late 1970s included the collapse of an unsustainable economy, cultivation of the American dream, and reactions to new policies of the SRV.

First, underpinning the refugee flight was the inevitable collapse of an unsustainable economy relying on foreign support and the war machine. When the US government started pumping aid into South Vietnam in the 1950s, it created an American- and war-dependent economy, especially in urban areas. From 1955 to 1961, South Vietnam received $1.65 billion from the US government.[60] In the early 1970s, US aid was approximately $700 million a year, with almost all imports financed by the US government.[61] In total, from 1961 to April 1975, the United States spent more than $141 billion in South Vietnam.[62] Little of that money, however, was spent on the nation's economic development. One way or another, financial aid benefited mostly urban elites and black marketers. Meanwhile, the intensification of the war dislocated people, causing serious overpopulation in major cities. Political scientist Samuel P. Huntington estimated that South Vietnam's urban population had increased from 15 to 20 percent in the early 1960s to about 40 percent in the mid-1960s. Huntington pointed out that apart from approximately one and a half million refugees relocated in cities, many peasants found opportunities in the "wartime urban boom," in which they could earn incomes five times what they used to make in the countryside.[63] With the increased arrivals of US personnel, urban economies mainly focused on the service sector and heavily depended on imports for food and consumer goods. Upon American military withdrawal and budget cuts following the Paris Peace Accord in 1973, South Vietnam's economy significantly declined.

On the other hand, agricultural production, which was the country's economic foundation, was severely disrupted because of military confrontation, bombing, and shortage of manpower caused by casualties, dislocation, and military recruitment. As the Provisional Revolutionary Government took over the Republic of Vietnam in April 1975, it inherited "a near famine condition among the poor; the collapse of the economy followed by speculation, hoarding and inflation; the concentration of hundreds of thousands of soldiers and other personnel of the former regime in the cities, exacerbating already serious problems of unemployment, order and security; and urban over-population, the symptom of an artificial distribution of population in this basically agrarian economy."[64] The wretched living conditions fell on everybody, regardless of politics. For those whose livelihood had relied heavily on the US dollar and opportunities made possible by war, the conclusion of the war meant the end of their businesses and incomes. As economist Robert S. Browne indicates, American aid during wartime had created "good life" for many people, thus "[they were] not prepared to work so hard" when times changed.[65] Therefore, it is notable that a large number of these early refugees were not necessarily victims of the war; on the contrary, they were well-off people unaccepting of imminent hardships in postwar reconstruction. In fact, it was reported in July 1975 that Vietnamese at refugee camps in California, Florida, Arkansas, and Pennsylvania sold gold worth millions of dollars. The US Silver Corporation of Van Nuys, California, and Deak-Perera International, Inc., of New York State bought 2.3 million in gold at one camp alone at Fort Indiantown Gap, Pennsylvania.[66] As economist Arjun Makhijani observes, "Any reform . . . will necessarily cause some discomfort for those who derive excessive benefits from the existing arrangements."[67] The "reform" in this case was a general political, social, and economic transition. For those who had benefited from wartime developments, the seemingly insurmountable ordeals during postwar reconstruction made their homeland a hostile place, urging them to look for an alternative elsewhere.

Second, the two decades of US presence in Vietnam also caused many locals to cultivate the American dream. The money flow and show of technology presented by the United States created a fascinating image of the Western world. In addition, the flow of information and the import of cultural and consumer products enriched the Vietnamese imagination of a wonderland. Considering Vietnam's history of continuous political turmoil and war-torn economy, the dream of living on the soil of a significant world power is not surprising. For supporters of the US alliance, immigrating to the United States upon the fall of Saigon seemed legitimate. Furthermore, Vietnamese people's desire to get out of the war-torn country was boosted by the media, specifically Voice of America (VOA) and the British Broadcasting Corporation (BBC). These two companies had (and still do) broadcast in the Vietnamese language, a program staffed by Vietnamese overseas. The general theme in their Vietnamese programs was, understandably, anticommunist. In a congressional hearing before the Subcommittee on Asian and Pacific Affairs of the Committee on Foreign Affairs in December 1979, Representative Charles H. Wilson from the state of California expressed his concerns:

> One of the most significant things I think that was mentioned to me on the trip [to Asia] was that the United States has a peculiar foreign policy. We do not understand why Voice of America is beaming into Vietnam and encouraging people to leave that country because if they do the United States will have ships to pick them up and to save them and to put them into some sanctuary where you can get some freedom.
>
> I will just say that I am as sympathetic as anyone else to refugees but I question what the capacity of our country is and I question the philosophy of the Voice of America and the British Broadcasting Company, who are the two outfits who are encouraging people to leave their countries, that they will find some refuge some place if they do.[68]

Saving people's lives on the high seas is a humanitarian act, but encouraging them to venture into an unknown future is something else. Poverty stricken and desperate for solutions to the puzzles of their lives, these people must have felt as if they were drowning, and the VOA or the BBC threw out some lifelines that seemed within easy reach. Many Vietnamese people answered the call, believing American (or Western) ships were awaiting them just offshore of Vietnam. As journalist Martin Woollacott describes in the *Guardian*, "Refugee officials and diplomats call them 'the boat people.' Some are indeed fishermen, but most are city folk who, before they slipped away from their homes in Saigon and other towns with hearts knocking, and gold and dollars sewn into their clothes, they knew nothing of the ocean or its dangers."[69] Woollacott also quoted the Australian minister of immigration, "The potential is there for large numbers of people to reach Australia in small boats now that the trail has been blazed."[70] Confirming the minister's concern, Woollacott pinpoints the role of the media: "Given the care with which Vietnamese apparently continue to listen to the BBC, the Voice of America, and Radio Australia, the new 'trail' to Australia will already be general knowledge back in Vietnam."[71] The call for Vietnamese expatriation might have stemmed from the goodwill of the broadcasting companies, and, in truth, it did bring many people to safety. Nevertheless, its simplistic vision and misleading information contributed to the venturesome decision-making that led to untold suffering of many others.

The third major cause of the Vietnamese exodus was a reaction against the new policies of the Socialist Republic of Vietnam. One of the most controversial postliberation policies was the New Economic Zone of 1975. When the communist victors took over Saigon, the city shouldered a population of nearly four million, of which approximately one and a half million were jobless.[72] Other urban areas throughout South Vietnam faced similar problems of overpopulation and unemployment resulting from wartime migration. Therefore, one of the most urgent tasks of the new government was to balance the rural and urban population in order to reduce the unemployment rate among city dwellers and to restore agricultural production. Approximately three million volunteers and "forced evacuees" were transferred from urban to rural areas to develop the New Economic Zones throughout the country. On average, between July 1975 and June 1976, about twenty-two thousand people moved from Saigon to rural areas each month. The resettlement program seemed like a well-intended initiative, with promises of governmental assistance—three months of food supply for people with some agricultural background and six months for those without it.[73] However, the ambitious movement met great obstacles because of the lack of materials, personnel, and management experience. The biggest problem was the lack of agricultural backgrounds of the settlers, which subsequently led to crop failures and further impoverishment. Furthermore, in the Vietnamese culture, urban residency is often associated with modernity, high class, and "high culture." Moving to rural areas, therefore, was a demotion in social status, especially for forced evacuees. Hence the New Economic Zone policy caused dissatisfaction among many people, even though it achieved encouraging results in reducing urban population and unemployment, as well as recovering and developing new areas for agricultural production.[74]

While the resettlement program had shortcomings and unintended consequences, to claim that the New Economic Zone policy was a communist doctrine aimed toward eliminating trade and urban development is to oversimplify the issue. Representative Benjamin A. Gilman from the state of New York condemned the policy: "By forcing large segments of their urban population to rural areas, they have sought to reduce the size of their cities and to virtually eliminate the business and professional classes."[75] What Representative Gilman saw was only the surface of the issue without understanding the need for population resettlement and the complexity of postwar problems. In truth, the South Vietnamese government and its US ally had planned in 1973 a similar postwar plan of relocating a number of urban residents to rural areas for the same purposes of balancing the population, reducing unemployment, and recovering agricultural production.[76] The differences between the South Vietnamese government's postwar reconstruction plan and that of the Socialist Republic of Vietnam were that the former's included only South Vietnam with continued financial aid from the United States while the latter's absorbed both North and South Vietnam without the American dollar on top of other economic obstacles caused by the trade embargo imposed by the United States. As Professor Michael Lang, an expert in urban studies and community development, asserts, "It is clear the policy decisions [on the New Economic Zone] made by Vietnam had little to do with ideology or politics."[77]

It is also worth noting that farming in the immediate years after the war ended was extremely difficult, not only for new rural settlers but also for "real" experienced farmers because of the environmental damage caused by defoliants and B-52 bombing. An estimated 72 million liters of defoliant was sprayed on approximately 10 percent of South Vietnamese landmass during the war.[78] Yet the effects of the chemicals are not limited to the sprayed areas. As scientists Gordon H. Orians and E. W. Pfeiffer pointed out in 1970, "Significant quantities of defoliants are regularly carried by the wind over broad areas of cropland in the Republic of Vietnam."[79] Pfeiffer, in another article, indicates that "soil nutrients lost after spraying will not be restored for at least 20 years."[80] Orians and Pfeiffer also estimated that in South Vietnam alone, about 848,000 bomb craters were formed in 1967 and 2.6 million in 1968, with craters as large as forty-five feet across and thirty feet deep.[81] According to scholar Joseph P. Hupy's "conservative estimates," the Vietnam War left behind about twenty-six million bomb craters littering the country smaller than the state of Montana in land area.[82] Farming in such an environment, and with deadly encounters of unexploded landmines and ordnance, became a horrendous task. Although settlers to the New Economic Zones had justifiable reasons to dislike the program, the economic policy should not be politicized as communist oppression.

Another policy that caused frustration among many upper- and middle-class people, contributing to their motivation for expatriation, was the Anti-Bourgeoisies Campaign of 1978. The common complaint was that these people found themselves empty-handed overnight as their assets were confiscated during the campaign. To an extent, the claim was true. According to historian Turley's analysis, the target of the campaign was the "comprador bourgeoisies," defined as "big businessmen who had made their fortunes in contract work or commerce in support of the US-RVN war effort and who used the economic power thus obtained to establish monopoly control over certain markets."[83] After the war, these comprador bourgeoisies continued to control the market by speculating and hoarding goods as well as trafficking gold, diamonds, narcotics, and currency "to such an extent that they had made stabilization of the economy impossible."[84] During the campaign, a number of commercial "kings" were arrested, including the "kings" of rice, fabric, coffee, scrap iron, barbed wire, and the "tigers" of textile, transportation, real estate, banking, and shipyards. Their assets were seized and their businesses shut down. Many of the arrested comprador bourgeoisies were Chinese-Vietnamese merchants who had a stronghold in Saigon's market.[85] This well-intended economic policy aimed at stabilizing the chaotic economy resulted in the upper class and Chinese community's resentment against the new government.

On the other hand, corruption was a reality as well. A number of cadres abused their power, seizing bourgeoisies' and petite bourgeoisies' property without reporting. Class-based animosity existed among some weathered warriors who became authorities and those who had enjoyed the comfort of urban life. Thus, these corrupt authorities ruined the image of the "liberators." One common phrase in the tales of former soldiers was, "When we were in the jungle," which literally meant the time they were hiding and fighting in the woods. Antirevolutionary urbanites often referred to former soldiers, especially those who became corrupt cadres, as "the jungle men" who knew only "the law of the jungle." Widespread wrongdoings stained the picture of economic change to a large extent. For many, coping with the new regime seemed impossible. On top of the economic struggle, the country was at war *again*. Border conflicts with Cambodia in the south and with China in the north further squeezed human and financial resources out of a land already crippled by decades of war.[86] The country had become too inhospitable.

Under any circumstances, Vietnamese refugees' escapes from adversity did not necessarily bring them to "the promised land." The ordeals that they underwent were immeasurable. Even the "luckier" ones who were evacuated from Saigon on its final days by US planes or navy ships did not simply find a friendly haven on their ally's soil. Upon their arrival, the first evacuees were met with "wide hostility" (to use journalist Douglas Kneeland's term) across the United States. Kneeland reported that in 1975, the city council of Seattle, Washington, voted 7 to 1 against a resolution that would have welcomed Saigon evacuees. Residents of Niceville, Florida, petitioned that the Indochinese refugees be sent elsewhere rather than Eglin Air Force Base, which is eight miles from town.[87] According to a Gallup poll that asked 1,491 people in three hundred locations whether the South Vietnamese evacuees should be permitted to live in the United States, 54 percent said "no," 36 percent said "yes," and 10 percent had no opinion. The article also reveals unfriendly comments from random interviews: "Charity begins at home. Keep the Vietnamese in Vietnam. Send funds to help them in their own country"; "They are a burden on this society. We have enough problems without carrying more unemployed persons"; "They can't speak English, and they will be on welfare before they get off the airplane. And who pays for that? We do"; and, "Am I going to have a choice whether my taxes are going to support those unfortunate people? If I don't have a choice, I don't want them coming. If they are going to up my taxes, I would rather it were to help some Detroit auto worker."[88]

Seeing the arrival of an overwhelming number of Indochinese refugees, Californians reacted strongly. Governor Edmund G. Brown Jr. "protested loudly that he did not want [the refugees] taking jobs from Americans in his state."[89] Clyde Taylor, an African American lecturer at the University of California, Berkeley, published an article in the *Los Angeles Times* entitled "A Black Teacher's Agonized Message to the Vietnamese Refugees." Taylor asserted that black resentment against the Asian refugees was higher than that of whites, explaining that underpinning the hostility was racial bitterness. He said, "The bigots in this country object to your presence because they think you are beneath them. Not so with blacks. We are not overjoyed by any new immigrants because, we know, wherever you come from and for whatever reason, the forces in American life have a place reserved for you—*ahead of us*."[90] Saigon evacuees, it seemed, were running from one adversity to another.

To be sure, not all Americans turned a cold face to these refugees, and the resentments against the Vietnamese evacuees were not a new issue either. Throughout history, immigrants to the United States always faced some kind of hostility. Mostly job insecurity and tax increases were the sources of animosity against newcomers. Racial and cultural differences, however, still underscored the enmity against immigrants in the late twentieth century. Many South Vietnamese people simply believed that because the United States had fought with them side by side for nearly two decades, finding safe haven in their ally's territory should not have been a problem. In reality, Indochinese refugees were far from being welcome. In an empirical study conducted by sociologists Alden Roberts and Paul Starr, while 40 to 81 percent of the people from nine towns and cities across the United States that were asked agreed "it was a good idea to have people from different countries in the community," only 15 to 45 percent (of the same people) said they would be willing to have an Indochinese refugee as a guest in their home, and a slim 7 to 43 percent would approve of a family member marrying an Indochinese refugee.[91] The participants of the study did not represent all Americans, but their opinions proved the complexity of race relations in American society. As Taylor puts it, "The melting pot warms for only the select," and for him, American diversity was but "a rainbow of multiethnic pain."[92] Emma Lazarus's words carved on the pedestal of the Statue of Liberty represented an ideal, not yet a reality:

> Give me your tired, your poor,
> Your huddled masses yearning to breathe free,
> The wretched refuse of your teeming shore.
> Send these, the homeless, tempest-tossed to me,
> I lift my lamp beside the golden door!

Resettlement in a foreign country is never an easy task. Language barriers, cultural differences, and employment issues are but a few common obstacles that most immigrants face. An article in the *New York Times* reported that while many US sponsors generously assisted Vietnamese refugees to settle and adapt to their new environment, "a good number" of sponsors "exploited the Vietnamese as coolie labor or simply left them to fend for themselves."[93] A lack of language skills and desperation for jobs often turned new immigrants into easy targets for exploitation. Unless they had US friends or families, the refugees had nowhere else to turn if problems occurred.

Apart from the difficulties that these refugees faced on a daily basis, the struggle to make sense of what was going on was, in many cases, even greater but often obscured by practical needs. Honest former officers of South Vietnam learned an ironic lesson that "the worst and most corrupt of the former officials have the best lives in the United States."[94] The story of Colonel Nguyen Be illustrates telling detail of the seemingly monolithic picture of Saigon's evacuees. A prominent figure in the mid-1960s, Nguyen was known for his pacification program under Lieutenant Colonel John Paul Vann in which he was training South Vietnamese cadres to win the hearts and minds of remote peasants. According to *New York Times* reporter Frances FitzGerald, Nguyen was "unlike most of his fellow officers. . . . He was honest, dedicated and, at least for a time, sincere in his belief that the Americans could support a nationalist movement and help his poor, underdeveloped country."[95] A decade later, he was an expatriate living in poverty, cheated at his job, and laughed at by his former colleagues as a fool. Leaving his wife and six children behind in a desperate escape while he was working far away from home, he added guilt and loneliness to his economic burden.[96]

Another man, who also left his wife and children behind, showed severe symptoms of depression. He kept asking, "How can I work here?" "Who would I work for?" "Who would I raise?" It was reported that during his stay at Fort Chaffee, Arkansas, he would walk around by himself all night long.[97] People like this young man and Nguyen tasted the bitter end of the war. Their suffering might have been clandestine, but it was definitely corrosive.

The journeys to the "free world" of the first wave of Vietnamese refugees were strenuous, but their struggle would seem trivial compared to that of the boat people in the peak years of the movement, from 1977 to 1979. The *Los Angeles Times* defined the boat people as follows: "They put to sea in small, overcrowded boats that are easy prey for storms, pirates, and the hostile naval forces of Vietnam and Cambodia. If they survive—and many haven't—to reach a foreign shore, they may be interned or turned away and forced to try their luck elsewhere. They are the 'boat people.'"[98] The definition sums up quite accurately the exodus of hundreds of thousands of Vietnamese in the late 1970s. There is no record of the numbers of those who set offshore but never saw another shore again, carrying their free world dream with them into the Pacific Ocean. Those who survived the horrors at sea endured hardships in first-asylum countries for several months before resettlement in a third country.

The most horrendous stories of the boat people were their encounters of pirates; mostly the Thai, but there were also Malay, Cambodian, and Burmese raiders. Originally, Thai pirates were armed fishermen who made easy money by raiding other fishing boats. It was reported that in a six-month period, one gang captured twenty-six fishing boats and killed four hundred and fifty fishermen in the Gulf of Thailand.[99] Then, rumors of Vietnamese refugees carrying gold shifted the pirates' attention, and it turned out that the rumors were accurate. The pirates not only stole gold and jewelry from their victims, they also raped and killed and, in many cases, burned or sank the refugees' boats. If the pirates were "merciful" enough to not destroy a boat, chances were the victims might be raided again by other gangs. Thomas Barnes, head of the US refugee office in Thailand, claimed that he knew of some boats that were robbed five times before landing in a refugee camp. As some relief agency workers pointed out, rape victims included girls as young as eleven or twelve years of age.[100]

Many of those who survived the journey lived with gruesome memories for the rest of their lives. Nguyen Ngoc Ngan, a well-known writer and master of ceremonies for Thuy Nga Productions' *Paris By Night*, shared his story in one of these shows. In late 1978, together with his twenty-six-year-old wife and four-year-old-son, Nguyen boarded a crowded boat of nearly three hundred people. The men were jammed in the lower deck that was soon flooded, while women and children remained on the upper deck. After six days, they encountered a violent storm near a Malaysian coast. At dawn on the seventh day, Nguyen heard his wife whisper through a small vent that the crew members had abandoned the boat for their lives. He climbed onto the upper deck and realized that the boat was not too far from the coast, but they could not come in because the bright light beam was scanning the shore, accompanied by cannon shots. He only had enough time to tell his son and wife that each should hold on to an empty soda bottle to stay afloat in case the boat wrecked. In a matter of seconds, the boat listed, throwing everything on the upper deck into the cold, dark water. Nguyen was quick enough to grab a rope nearby and remained on the deck when the boat returned to its upright position, only to be destroyed minutes later. Ngan remembered seeing women and children drowning around him, within an arm's reach. One or two days later, Nguyen woke up, lying prone atop a pile of corpses. Somebody must have thought that he was dead and piled him up there. He found his four-year-old son's body but not his wife's, and he buried him in a mass grave of ninety-seven people.[101]

The Rev. W. Stanley Mooneyham, president of World Vision International, told another horrid story of ninety-three Vietnamese refugees on one of the many boats that he saved. On June 12, 1979, 289 people boarded a boat to leave Ca Mau, the farthest southern tip of Vietnam, for the Gulf of Thailand. Two days later, they encountered Thai pirates who were "quite out of character" and left them alone after the robbery. The boat drifted ashore at Dungun, Malaysia, where "the Vietnamese begged for sanctuary on their knees" with a bribery of gold and jewelry that some had managed to hide from the pirates earlier. The Malaysian military held them in a barbed wire compound on the beach for eighteen days without food for the first week. On July 3, they were told that they would be taken "to a beautiful island in the south" in four fishing boats. After twenty hours being towed toward the South China Sea, their tow ropes were cut, and they found out that their boat engines would not work. When Mooneyham's rescue ship *Seasweep II* spotted and saved one of the four boats, his crew found ninety-three people aboard, "close to death by dehydration." All that the refugees had were a few pounds of rice and a half gallon of rainwater collected from the night before.[102]

One detail of the distressing scene did not escape Mooneyham's eyes: a lonesome man "sitting and staring blankly into the ocean." This refugee's wife, children, and other relatives had been aboard the other boats that were towed off the Malaysian coast, and nobody saw any sign of their survival. It is worth quoting Mooneyham's comments in full:

> He was alone; he had nobody left. He was caught between a past to
> which he could never return and a future that was very uncertain. He
> was the world's total victim with absolutely no recourse to help himself.
> He had been victimized by his government, victimized by Thai pirates,
> victimized by the Malaysian government when he sought refuge, and will
> be victimized by Western governments who are unconscionably slow in
> dealing with his problem. He was totally powerless and the microcosm of
> this world problem.[103]

Mooneyham did not exaggerate when he said the mentioned refugee was "the world's total victim." To be sure, the boat people made their own decisions to leave their home country and to test their luck, but they weighed their decisions within the economic and political forces of push and pull. They made choices out of fear and want, thus easily falling victim to multiple elements.

First, in fear of political and economic change, those who wanted to leave

Vietnam were conveniently lured into scam businesses. With the vast numbers of boat people landing in first -asylum countries, it should be recognized that the ocean-crossing movement was also a highly profitable business. There were boats to be built, gold to be paid, and multilayered contacts to be made before a load of people could be shoved offshore. Common knowledge in Vietnam was that each adult had to pay between two to ten taels of gold (one tael equals 37.80 grams or 1.33 ounces). One refugee spoke of paying twenty-five ounces of gold "to be smuggled out of Saigon."[104] In many cases, it was a scam business, for the boat owners or organizers were not leaving Vietnam. They simply took the gold and jammed the victims-to-be on hastily built or old fishing boats with a small amount of food and supplies that were not meant to last until any coast came in sight. Often the boat captains, equipped with some old map clipped from an American magazine, had no ocean experience prior to the trip. They did not even know how to use a compass or a nautical chart.[105] If a boat owner finally decided that he or she had made enough money and it was time to flee, the voyage would be much better prepared.

Secondly, the boat people fell victim to corrupt government officials, either in Vietnam or in first-asylum countries. Bribery was not uncommon. In Vietnam, some bribed to get on board; others did it when arrested. Corruption was especially bad when the Vietnamese government wanted the Chinese-Vietnamese to leave. In some situations, police officers even arranged the boat for their "clients."[106] Once their underqualified and poorly equipped boats were seaward, they became victims of the Pacific storms and easy prey of pirates. Then, if they arrived in any other Asian country, especially Thailand or Malaysia, sometimes boat people had to exchange gold and jewelry for sanctuary in refugee camps. Overwhelmed by the numbers of refugee arrivals, Malaysia planted soldiers along its coasts, and patrol boats offshore received "orders to shoot across the bow of incoming refugee boats." In cold blood, one Malay security agent stated, "If I get orders I will shoot every one of the refugees. I do not have such orders. I obey."[107] In Thailand, some patrolling policemen robbed refugees at gunpoint, raped women and young girls, and then ordered the boats to leave Thai waters.[108] Similar to encounters in Malaysian coastal areas, Thai police also dragged refugee boats back into the ocean even though they had managed to get ashore.[109]

Life in refugee camps, however, was another ordeal. After his visits to some of the camps in Thailand and Hong Kong in 1979, Representative Dan Marriott from Utah remarked, "The suffering is unbelievable. The whole situation was enough to eat my heart out, seeing what these people have gone through."[110] According to Marriott, camp Loei, situated sixty hundred and fifty kilometers (403.8 miles) northeast of Bangkok, Thailand, was overloaded with a population of thirty-five thousand at the time of his visit. From 1975 to 1979, the camp saw a total of 276,955 arrivals by both land and sea and 101,728 departures for resettlement. Among these, the numbers of Vietnamese nationals were fairly low, with 33,167 arrivals and 23,987 departures. Laotian and Cambodian land refugees made up the majority of camp residents. Marriott reported that malnutrition at the camp was "appalling," medical care also "appalling," and sanitary conditions "poor."[111] His observations concurred with a report conducted by a US Public Health Service team in June and July 1979. According to the report, the general impression of approximately forty camps in Asian countries of first asylum was overcrowding with limited medical care and sanitary conditions.[112] The bleak picture, however, should not undermine the efforts of the host countries and the camp workers. They simply were underprepared for the overwhelming waves of arrivals.

The Vietnamese boat people, together with Laotian and Cambodian escapees, created one of the greatest waves of refugees in modern history. Individually, they were unknown people, but together they captured the focal point of attention for several years. Their individual acts combined into formidable collective strength, pushing governments to change existing policies or create new ones to accommodate the urgent situations that dismayed international communities. Not only did refugees play an active role in determining their own fates, they also pushed governments, organizations, and individuals to take up new tasks and to incorporate international efforts for humanity.

The boat people would probably not consider themselves historical actors who heated debate in Washington and moved top leaders of the United States. In reality, they did. In 1978, as a response to the escalating numbers of Indochinese refugees, the Subcommittee on Asian and Pacific Affairs of the US Congress conducted three hearings on May 17, June 8, and August 15. The subcommittee's chairman, Representative Lester L. Wolff, referred to the refugee crisis as "a time bomb . . . waiting to explode."[113] In January 1979, the subcommittee members visited refugee camps in Thailand, Malaysia, and the Philippines. In June 1979, it issued House Resolution 321, urging President Jimmy Carter to request that the United Nations convene an emergency session of the General Assembly. Consequently, on July 20–21, 1979, the UN held a conference on the Indochina refugees in Geneva with the participation of representatives from sixty-five countries.[114] During a visit to Bangkok, Thailand, Vice President Walter Frederick Mondale asserted, "There is no more profound test of our government's commitment to human rights than the way we deal with these people who deserve our admiration for their courage and our deepest sympathy and support."[115] The seemingly powerless and vulnerable refugees were indeed testing the leadership of the free world.

Time and again, the boat people occupied US leaders' minds, posed questions, and modified their political moves. On June 23, 1977, Secretary of State Cyrus Vance sent a memorandum to President Carter seeking authorization to request the attorney general "use his parole power on an urgent basis to admit 15,000 refugees into the U.S." According to Vance, approximately eighty thousand people were jammed in refugee camps in Thailand at the time, and none of them were eligible to enter the United States under existing immigration laws.[116] One week later, on July 1, 1977, National Security Adviser Zbigniew Brzezinski sent a memo of similar content to the president, urging him to approve Vance's request. The two memos circulated for comments among White House staff, with the deadline stamped "Immediate Turnaround."[117] In the revised version of Brzezinski's memorandum for the president on July 15, he presented four arguments supporting the State Department's request. First, it was a "sure and swift remedy." Second, the United States had a "moral obligation" to act fast, and in so doing, it acted accordingly with its "human rights stand." Third, by setting a good example, it would be easier for the United States to persuade other countries to share responsibility in solving international problems. Finally, "failure to go this route would result in strong media and Hill (Senator Kennedy) condemnation."[118] President Carter authorized the request on the same day.

Soon State Secretary Vance had to send the president another memorandum, for the floods of Vietnamese boat people sweeping ashore on other Asian countries of first asylum had reached over fifteen hundred persons monthly. In a memo dated December 6, 1977, Vance wrote: "I believe that the boat refugee situation has become as acute that we cannot await the formulation of a long term policy with Congress which could take several months before implementation. If we do nothing in the interim, lives will be lost." He was asking for authorization of another attorney general's parole to admit seven thousand more boat people to the United States.[119]

On December 19, 1977, Brzezinski once again sent the president a similar memo. This time, however, he recommended a higher number than Vance's: ten thousand persons.[120] Again, the national security adviser's memo was circulated for "immediate" comments within the day. The speed at which Washington leaders worked in dealing with the emergency of the boat people showed that ordinary citizens' actions had an impact on decision makers. While the refugees' actions were radical, the act of putting their lives at risk underpinned political and social change.

The increased numbers of Indochinese refugees, especially the Vietnamese boat people, not only consumed the time and effort of US leaders, it also incorporated international efforts. In mid-December 1978, cabinet and subcabinet officials from thirty-eight countries participated in a Geneva conference. Although this UN conference achieved modest results—an increase of yearly quotas of all receiving countries from nearly eighty thousand to 82,250, the event was the first of its kind in raising awareness of the Indochinese refugees as an international problem.[121] The second UN conference, held on July 20–21, 1979, was much more fruitful by comparison. Sixty-two out of sixty-five participating countries pledged a total of two hundred and sixty thousand resettlement places and $290 million in aid.[122] Other outcomes of the second UN conference included Vietnam's agreement to a moratorium on unorganized departures and the orderly departure agreement between the United Nations High Commissioner for Refugees (UNHCR) and Vietnam. The British writer and broadcaster William Shawcross, however, criticized Western countries for being too slow in responding to refugee issues. He claimed that between February and June 1979, Malaysia turned away approximately forty thousand boat people, and it was unknown how many among these unfortunate people would make it to safety. "But until June, the sense of crisis in the West was not as urgent as such figures and such palpable suffering demanded," he complained.[123] He made a good point that five months were indeed too long considering the daily numbers of lives lost in the Pacific, and it took that long for the UN to convene an international conference on the emergency. He also pointed out that the United States treated these refugees as immigrants, not as refugees, when they applied quotas and prioritized those who had worked for the US war effort or had relatives living in the United States.

Meanwhile, nongovernmental organizations were also actively involved. On June 28, 1979, Catholic, Protestant, and Jewish leaders announced a joint appeal to international communities to assist Indochinese refugees, especially the boat people who were in danger of drowning in the South China Sea. Addressing what they called "the greatest humanitarian crisis of this decade,". the interfaith leaders urged President Carter to double the refugee admission to the United States to fourteen thousand. They pleaded for additional asylum opportunities outside Southeast Asia, the establishment of transit camps, and the use of US military transport to speed up the relocation of refugees cleared for entry to the United States.[124] Prior to the second UN conference, the International Council of Voluntary Agencies held a conference on July 18–19, 1979, attended by more than fifty voluntary agencies to discuss the refugee crisis. A few days later, the World Council of Churches convened a meeting on July 24–25, with representatives from approximately forty international churches, national councils of churches, and church aid and relief agencies. Both of these conferences took place in Geneva.[125] It should be noted, however, that long before these announced acts, those nongovernmental agencies had quietly assisted Indochinese refugees in various ways. Devoting both human and financial resources either independently or through UNHCR, they rescued boats, helped in refugee camps in both first-asylum and resettlement countries, and sponsored newcomers in their communities.

Taking their individual journeys in search of a better world, the refugees unintentionally connected people and organizations of differing beliefs and politics. To an extent, they made governments, organizations, and individuals work together on a common cause of human dignity despite their differences. As political scientist Barry Stein observes, the most "striking feature" of the World Council of Churches' conference is its statement, "We recognize that within the ecumenical family, we differ among ourselves in the interpretation of the events which have led to the flow of refugees." Stein stresses that the statement appeared "to illuminate much of what had occurred at all three conferences."[126] He points out the existing antagonism between the United States and Vietnam at the time, and that opponents on the causes of the refugee crisis based their arguments either on the US or Vietnamese sources of information. Nevertheless, they put aside their political differences and worked together to save human lives.

After almost a hundred years of colonization and decades of war, Vietnam eventually obtained national independence and reunification. Peacetime, however, was smeared with lingering animosity among former foes. Vietnam walked a bumpy road during her postwar reconstruction, as reconciliation among all sides seemed unattainable. Yet, against that backdrop of political tensions were ordinary US and Vietnamese citizens who crossed boundaries to forge changes.

The American people's genuine kindness manifested in their actions and stood in contrast with their leaders' political calculations. Those calculations, however, were not the best. In fact, by refusing friendship with Vietnam, the United States pushed Vietnam closer to the Soviet Union, which ironically had been a US fear and the main reason for the US intervention in Indochina decades before. Displaying their faith in an ideal—the American tradition of humanitarianism and democracy—these individuals exercised their citizen power in the most practical way. On the one hand, they were idealists. On the other, they were true realists, for they dealt directly with the urgent needs of human beings.

Similar to the Americans, the Vietnamese people, while acting out of desperation and enduring significant risks, refused to accept the boundaries imposed on them. Unwittingly, the boat people became the link between antagonistic governments. From a powerless status, they made their voices heard, occupied the spotlight, and pushed governments to work together. Although they started their journeys as individuals seeking peace for themselves or an opportunity to improve their living conditions, they ended as a collective force that affected change in governmental policies and even international relations, which in turn would benefit many others. When US leaders decided to intervene in Vietnam in the late 1950s, they probably thought that their mission of containing communists in North Vietnam would be completed in a short time, and once the business was done, the United States would have nothing to do with Vietnam. Perhaps they could not imagine that the Vietnamese would make up a considerable count in the US population later.

CHAPTER TWO

Derelicts of War and Their Metamorphoses

After the war father returned to his homeland
Leaving behind his misfit children,
Children of two different bloods,
To face ostracism and debasement

After the war, everything was gone.
Father, nothing was left but suffering for mother
Who to blame? Who can I blame?
Together with animosity I grew up

Gone you were, disappearing into the horizon
Mad at life, I befriended orphanhood
Aimlessly roaming the streets
Quietly getting by with private pain

Father, oh father, where are you?
Why don't you return for me?
Of father's love I know nothing
I wonder why life is full of suffering.

After the war father returned to his homeland
Mother choked up over misery and desperation
Night after night, holding me she sobbed . . .
Father, have you truly forgotten your love?
      —Randy Trane, *After the War*

The above song, written by Randy Trane, portrayed one of the thorniest issues that concerned Americans visiting Vietnam in the late 1970s and early 1980s: the sight of American-Vietnamese children being treated as social outcasts.[1] While poverty struck the entire nation, those who had had connections with Americans during wartime faced a more arduous reality, and American-Vietnamese children like Randy Trane were easy targets because of their skin color and peculiar features. These Amerasians, children of US personnel and Vietnamese women during the Vietnam War, underwent multilayered discrimination.[2] Politically, they were children of the enemy. From the perspective of the victor of the conflict—the new government of Vietnam—there was a clear line between those who fought for the reunification of the country and those who favored a divided Vietnam, especially the Americans. Thus, any association with US military personnel would be considered traitorous, and these innocent children were evidence of that forbidden alliance. Socially, Amerasians were considered bastards because of the absence of their fathers. For the majority of Vietnamese people, having children born out of wedlock meant staining the family's name. Single mothers and their children, therefore, suffered not only from social but also familial abuse. Certainly not all Amerasians were born out of wedlock, but disconnection with their fathers and the faint prospect of reunion placed them all in a monolithic category. Culturally, xenophobia caused many Vietnamese people to be racist against descendants of interracial parents. Although Vietnam consists of more than fifty ethnicities, few interactions happened among them. Vietnamese city dwellers in particular tended to look down upon ethnic minorities, viewing them as backward and uncivilized. Little exposure to diversity made people intolerant to differences. Consequently, Amerasians fell victim to political, social, and cultural prejudice.

Like other marginalized groups, Amerasians employed self-help and self-empowerment as effective tools to improve their conditions. The bleak picture of their circumstances often overshadowed their ability to cope and thrive. Forced to be aware of their "otherness" from the early years of their lives, most chose self-isolation for a little peace when they were coming of age. "Imprisoned in their own skin" (to borrow Amerasian poet Kevin Minh Allen's words) and excluded from social gatherings, Amerasians seemed absent from the discourse of community.[3] At best, they appear in the media and studies as a group of like conditions. However, there came a time came when Amerasians decided to stand up as a community, bound by shared pasts and common goals for the future.

According to political scientist David J. Elkins, ethnic communities fall into three categories: the concentrated, the dispersed, and the virtual. By his definition, the Amerasian community fit into the dispersed type because its members scattered widely across geographical territories. Elkins emphasizes an important feature of the dispersed ethnic community that he calls "isolation together," such as the formation of ghettos in urban America.[4] To some extent, Amerasians were also isolated together, as they lived in oases within larger American or Vietnamese communities. In light of Elkins's discussion, the formation of the Amerasian community was a historical process of "unbundling" the concepts of boundaries and national-territorial hegemony. To borrow Elkins's words, Amerasians were "repackaging their identities," untying themselves from mainstream notions of single identities and embracing multiple identities. That process of repackaging identities may not be comfortable at times, but there are certain "compensations" to it. As poet Gloria Alzaldúa describes: "Living on borders and in margins, keeping intact one's shifting and multiple identities and integrity, is like trying to swim in a new element, an 'alien' element. There is an exhilaration in being a participant in the further evolution of humankind, in being 'worked' on."[5] Being unbound from the boundaries of a single identity, many Amerasians made good use of the flexibility offered by their mixed heritage. This chapter explores the ordeals Amerasians underwent, stretching from traumatic experiences in their mother's land to new struggles in their father's land, and their transformation into transnational forces that influenced national policy and reshaped their identities.

Pathway to the Father's Land

With almost no diplomatic ties between the United States and Vietnam, the prospect of Amerasians reuniting with their biological fathers seemed unimaginable. Above all else, their poverty, social status, and lack of education shut them off from opportunities for change. Because their Western appearance was a visible reminder of foreign invaders, Amerasians were forced to live invisible lives. But many did not; instead, they sought out allies, appealed for attention, and made their way into international news. In early 1980, a television team consisting of a cameraman, a technician, and a reporter embarked on a trip to Vietnam to do a follow-up story on the effects of Agent Orange. The reporter, Bill Kurtis, had been to the country before; he was a wartime reporter and anchorman for the Chicago station WBBM-TV. During their brief stay in Saigon, Kurtis and his associates took notice of the American-Vietnamese street children. Hardship showed in the children's eyes and their tiny, bony bodies. Despite their language barrier, these children and their mothers made an effort to communicate with the Americans, telling them how they were struggling as social outcasts. Since few foreigners came to Vietnam at the time, the Americans' presence was noticeable and word quickly spread. After just a few days, despite their efforts to avoid causing a commotion, the team received close to a hundred letters, including personal identification information such as birth certificates, addresses, and pictures. Having been watched by local authorities, the Americans were asked to turn those letters in. After long discussions on ethics and the safety of the parties involved, the television team decided to photograph the letters, which they did secretly in their hotel bathroom, and to turn in two letters without specific personal information. Unaware of the number of letters, the Vietnamese official in charge was happy with what he received. Kurtis then arranged to meet in secret with a foreign consular official, who listened to the story and agreed to keep the letters and send them to the United Nations and to a US embassy.[6]

We do not know how those letters directly contributed to the promotion of American-Vietnamese children's chances to immigrate to the United States, but these Vietnamese mothers and the American television crew helped make their stories more noticeable. Risking their security, they brought a reality to light and reclaimed the undeniable existence of the war's aftermath. Those Vietnamese mothers and children acted out of great desperation and faint hope, unaware that they were helping to change life for themselves and for many others. Bill Kurtis and his crew had traveled to Vietnam with one particular task but ended up doing something that they had never considered. To an extent, they became inadvertent historical agents.

The efforts made by Vietnamese mothers and their Amerasian children to reach the outside world with the hope that they could eventually reunite with a US family member and have a better life were not unique to Bill Kurtis and his colleagues' experience. *New York Times* reporter Colin Campbell described a similar scene: "While the delegation from the Vietnam Veterans of America was discussing the problem [of immigration] in a closed meeting with Do Duy Lien, deputy chairman of the Ho Chi Minh City People's Committee, dozens of [children], some on bicycles, began gathering at the end of Nguyen Hue Street outside the meeting place."[7] On another occasion, a mother of three approached a US reporter, telling him that she had applied for immigration visas for her and her children but had heard nothing in return; she wrote down her and her children's names and their case number in the reporter's note-book.[8] Evidence of individual efforts can also be found in a testimonial letter in the congressional hearing on the Amerasian immigration proposals in June 1982. The long, handwritten, ungrammatical English letter, dated December 20, 1981, appealed for the US government's consideration of the desperate situation of ten Vietnamese women and their Amerasian children. The letter started, "We are Vietnamese women, and we have an [*sic*] American halfbreed children." After explaining their circumstances in Vietnam, the writers stated, "We send to you our petition to the [*sic*] US Government assistance[;] please intervene with the government of Vietnam in order that we would be permitted to leave for [*sic*] Vietnam and immigrate to the United States to live."[9] They carefully included the names and addresses of the women, headshots of them and their children, and their immigration application numbers issued by the US immigration office in Thailand. Despite their circumstances, these disadvantaged people played an active role in making a change in their lives.

On the other side of the Pacific Ocean, Americans were touched by news stories and images of Amerasians being maltreated in their mothers' lands. In US media, Vietnamese Amerasians were often referred to as the "dust of life" or "children of dust," which was translated from the Vietnamese term *bụi đời*. This was a misunderstanding, however. In Vietnam, *bụi đời* is a slang term referring to street life. For example, *trẻ bụi đời* means "street children"; *đi bụi đời* means to "(leave home and) live in the street." Therefore, not all children of dust are Amerasians, and vice versa—not all Amerasians are children of dust. Nevertheless, images and stories of Western-like children living like the "dust of life" in the streets of Vietnam were disturbing to many Americans. Some started discussing the issues, others worked toward adoption, and many more appealed to authorities to effect change. Senator Carl Levin from Michigan quoted from a letter sent to him by an adoptive mother of two Amerasian girls: "America owes these children a chance to become good citizens in the country of their fathers."[10] Another couple, Kris and Annie of Grand Rapids, Michigan, who adopted several Amerasian children, touched Senator Levin's heart as they wrote:

Culturally, financially and practically we have the ability to help the Amerasian children and young people. There are many tragic situations in the world that we can do little about. But in this situation we can do something and we should feel especially compelled since this involves our own children. How can we as a country speak about human rights if we turn our backs on the rights of the American-Asian child? We do not believe that America will continue to ignore these children and young people.[11]

Efforts to bring Amerasians to the United States both by individuals and by nongovernmental organizations effected change in US immigration policy. As Senator Edward Kennedy acknowledged in his opening speech at a congressional hearing, "I think all of us must recognize that it has been the voluntary agencies that have been knocking on the doors of Congress."[12] In fact, Representative Stewart McKinney's Amerasian bill, HR 808, stemmed from the appeal of Fr. Alfred Keane who was working for the St Vincent's Home for Amerasians in Incheon, South Korea.[13] In his testimonial address to the congressional Subcommittee on Immigration, Nationality and International Law, Keane defined an Amerasian as "a child forgotten and abandoned by his father and the country that sent his father to Asia." He further explained the significance of the father's role in Asian cultures and the ordeals that Amerasians underwent:

In Asia, children belong to the father. A child is from the father. It is from the father that the child receives his/her name, nationality, ancestry, clan and family relationship—all of which determine schooling, marriage and obtaining a job and social position in Southeast Asia.

For the Amerasian, those forgotten American children of Asia, life is a misery—a tragedy that is full of misery. Every day brings them stares of others. The endless questions about their origin. Constant ridicule from adults as well as from their playmates. The harassment never seems to end. Sometimes they are beaten, stoned, kicked and reduced to a subhuman status in ways I could never begin to describe. The cruelest abuse of all is ai-ee-no-koo—person in between who belongs to no one.[14]

Concerns for American-Koreans' alienation in their mother's land resonated with stories from Vietnam, Laos, Cambodia, and Thailand. Testimonial information from Vietnamese mothers and their children made its way to US media and authorities. Stanley Karnow, a former foreign correspondent for the *Washington Post*, reported in March 1981 that the office of the UN High Commissioner for Refugees in Saigon was "inundated with letters from these women."[15] Karnow and other journalists such as Bill Kurtis and Colin Campbell contributed their parts, not only by informing the US public of the Amerasians' circumstances but by also calling for action. Karnow argues, "These offspring would not exist unless American soldiers had been sent here. They are, therefore, a burden that America ought to bear." He suggested that the US government "assume the responsibility for these children," modeling French policy toward Eurasians born in its former colonies in Southeast Asia.[16] In response, humanitarian agencies and many Americans did more than provide immediate assistance to those in need; they lobbied for an additional immigration law that would affect thousands of lives.

Although the Orderly Departure Program, which granted some Vietnamese legal immigration to the United States, had started in 1979, reunions among American men and their Vietnamese partners and/or children were infrequent. Not until October 1982, seven years after the last American personnel left Vietnam, was the first group of eleven Amerasians united with their US families. These children were among the ninety-one Amerasians who had obtained US citizenship thanks to their fathers' acknowledgement of biological paternity.[17] The arrangements for these reunions, however, involved tremendous effort of nongovernmental organizations. Representatives of the Church World Service, for example, met with Vietnam's Minister of Foreign Affairs Nguyen Co Thach, requesting permission to bring more than sixty Amerasians to the United States. Other agencies joining the effort included the Pearl S. Buck Foundation, Vietnam Veterans of America, American Council of Voluntary Agencies for Foreign Service (an organization of forty-seven private groups), American Friends Service Committee, Holt International Children's Services, Americans for International Aid, and Operation California. The UN High Commissioner for Refugees and the Intergovernmental Committee for Migration also contributed their part.[18] These organizations' successful attempt to bring the eleven Amerasian children to their fathers' land marked a milestone in their efforts, giving hope to many others. Nevertheless, bureaucratic roadblocks due to the lack of official diplomatic relations between the United States and Vietnam remained a major obstacle. By 1982, the American embassy in Bangkok, Thailand, had piled up approximately four thousand cases of American-Vietnamese children out of what were really tens of thousands.[19] Of those four thousand children in their files, many had to wait several more years before they could board a plane for the United States.

It took Congress four years to discuss and finally approve Senator Stewart B. McKinney's proposal, approval of which would allow unmarried Amerasians to move up to the first preference category and married ones to sixth preference under the existing Immigration Reform and Control Act, regardless of their American fathers' acknowledgement. Meanwhile, nonprofit organizations worked tirelessly to help the children of denial. One such organization was Holt International Children's Services, which was founded in Eugene, Oregon, in 1956 by Harry Holt and his wife Bertha. Concerned for the disadvantaged mix-raced children of the Korean War, the couple adopted eight American-Korean children. Realizing that they could assist more children by calling for collaborative efforts, they founded Holt International Children's Services. Although the organization started with a specific interest in mix-raced children in a war-torn country, it soon recognized the desperate situations of children of all races worldwide. By 1982, Holt had assisted more than thirty-five thousand abandoned and otherwise endangered children in Korea, Bangladesh, Vietnam (from 1972–1975), the Philippines, Thailand, Nicaragua, and India with both temporary, emergency needs and stable, permanent homes. In July 1982, before Senator McKinney's bill was approved, Holt sent a "proposal for participation" to the Vietnamese government, asking for its representative's permission to enter Vietnam to conduct needs assessment. In fact, Holt had submitted a visa application for a staff member to the Vietnamese embassy in Bangkok, Thailand, in October 1981. The proposal emphasized that Holt's representative was prepared to travel to Vietnam "as soon as Vietnamese authorities permit."[20]

On the other hand, Holt also raised his voice for Amerasians by discussing the proposal to amend the existing immigration law. David Kim, Holt's executive director, wrote to Congressman Peter W. Rodino, urging Congress to change the language in the bill so that Amerasians' mothers and siblings would be permitted to accompany them to the United States. Kim also asked Congress to reconsider the three-year time limit proposed for registration and the restriction of immigration to Amerasians of twenty-one years of age and under. He argued that registration may take longer than three years because of "the complex and diplomatically sensitive work" that needed to be done to execute the law.[21] Kim was probably thinking about the limited relations between the US and Vietnamese governments and the difficulties that Amerasians and other applicants for immigration were facing without embassies and consulate offices in both countries. In proposing the deletion of age limit, he maintained, "The problems Amerasians face do not cease when they become adults. In fact, it is in the early adult years that discrimination regarding employment and marriage become most evident."[22]

In addition to Holt, organizations such as the Mennonite Central Committee, the American Friends Service Committee, and the Church World Service also played an active role in the discussion of pending legislation regarding the benefits of Amerasians. On August 11, 1982, leaders of these three organizations sent a joint letter to Senator Carl Levin expressing their concerns that "the legislation appears to exclude provisions for birth mothers and siblings to accompany the affected children" to the United States and recommended that the aforementioned people be moved to the first-preference immigrant category.[23] On September 2, 1982, these three NGOs sent a memorandum to several other organizations, encouraging them to write to members of Congress in support of Representative McKinney's initiative to bring Amerasians to the United States and to propose changes to the pending legislation that would further benefit Amerasians.[24] Advocacy continued for years until Congress finally approved HR 808 and President Ronald Reagan signed it into the Amerasian Immigration Act on October 22, 1982.

Although the act was a significant policy that offered Amerasians an opportunity to immigrate to the United States with first or fourth visa preference (respectively applied to single and married applicants) regardless of their fathers' acknowledgement, disagreements between the US and Vietnamese governments continued to hinder the immigration process. Prior to July 1984, only 3,244 out of an estimated twenty thousand Vietnamese Amerasians immigrated to the United States.[25] On June 25, 1984, a Vietnamese consular official complained that the United States' quota of one thousand refugees a month caused the backlog of immigration applicants, among them Amerasians. He claimed that approximately twenty-nine thousand Vietnamese people who had been granted exit visas were waiting for entry visas to the United States.[26] American staff processing Amerasian immigration in Bangkok, Thailand, also confirmed that strict standards of proof and refugee quotas imposed by the US government contributed to the sluggishness. Leo Dorsey, a member of the nongovernmental US Committee for Refugees and Immigrants and director of aid programs for the Unitarian Universalist Association in wartime South Vietnam, stated that it would take eight years to complete the resettlement of Amerasians at the current speed. According to journalist Barbara Crossette, the two governments "continue[d] to accuse each other of obstructing or delaying the movement of these children." While Vietnamese officials complained about the long list of Amerasians waiting for US-entry visas, their American counterparts criticized Vietnam for holding back exit visas of other applicants.[27] However, root causes of the delay in Amerasians' immigration were, according to journalist Carol McGraw, "entangled in international politics."[28] In fact, the issuance of Amerasians' exit and entry visas, to some extent, depended on solutions for the MIA and Cambodia issues.

As a result of the political games the two governments were playing, numerous Amerasians continued to suffer. They continued to roam the streets of Saigon, trying to reach Western visitors with a faint hope that somehow these visitors could help speed up the immigration process so that they could resettle in their fathers' land. Even Amerasians who had received sponsorship from their American fathers faced significant delays in their immigration. One such case was Nguyen Thi Dan Thao, daughter of a former adviser with the US Agency for International Development and a Vietnamese schoolteacher. Nguyen was born in 1971, four months after her father, Don Burges, returned to the United States. Burges lost contact with his Vietnamese family until 1981, when he ran into an old acquaintance who happened to be married to a cousin of his Vietnamese partner. The following year, Burges completed the paperwork to obtain US citizenship for his daughter. Nevertheless, they had to endure six years of "bureaucratic nightmares" (to borrow Burges's terms) before Nguyen finally arrived in California in June 1988.[29]

The slow motion of Amerasians' resettlement seemed to go unnoticed until October 1985 when *Newsday* photographer Audrey Tiernan captured the image of Le Van Minh, a homeless fourteen-year-old Amerasian moving around "like a crab on all four limbs" on the streets of Saigon. The image of the skinny, polio-ridden youngster holding up an aluminum cigarette-wrapper flower in his hand and looking up at the photographer with immense sadness in his eyes broke viewers' hearts. A few months later, four students of Huntington High School on Long Island, New York, decided to act. They wrote a petition to bring Le to the United States for medical care, collected twenty-seven thousand signatures, and convinced their congressman Robert Mrazek to help.[30] Mrazek took the students' initiative seriously, circulating in the House of Representatives a letter requesting humanitarian exemption for Le. The letter obtained 306 signatures in the House and was sent to State Secretary George Shultz on March 6, 1987.[31] On March 25, upon receiving a positive response from Shultz, Mrazek made a visit to the residence of Dang Van Quang, first secretary of the Vietnamese Mission to the United Nations, to request exit permission for Le. After the Vietnamese representative promised to push for Minh's immigration, Mrazek remarked, "I am sure that this little boy could be an important symbolic gesture between our two countries. He is a reflection in human terms that we're reaching out for a more positive relationship. This goes beyond the case of one little boy—it could be the first step to removing some of the roadblocks."[32] Less than three months later, Le arrived in New York State in Mrazek's arms; the congressman had traveled to Vietnam to bring the Amerasian teenager home.[33] The Huntington High School students' act of compassion brought a happy ending, but the best was yet to come.

Representative Mrazek's experience with Le and his encounters with other Amerasians in Vietnam inspired him to author a bill that would help speed up the immigration of thousands of Vietnamese Amerasians. A few months after his trip to Vietnam to bring Le to the United States, Mrazek introduced the Amerasian Homecoming Act to Congress on October 28, 1987. Signed by President Reagan on December 22, 1987, the act allowed for the admission of those fathered by American personnel during the Vietnam War to the United States as immigrants (instead of being admitted as refugees as indicated in the Amerasian Refugee Act of 1982). The new legislation also granted immigration opportunities to spouses, children, and mothers or guardians of Amerasian applicants. *Newsday* photographer Tiernan probably could not imagine the ripple effects of her photo, and neither could the Huntington students. Their good intentions started with a desire to speak for one particular person but ended effecting change for thousands of lives.

Old Ordeals in a New Home

Escaping from adversity in their mother's land, young Amerasians crossed the Pacific Ocean with hopes and dreams. After years of destitution and social marginalization in Vietnam, they were "coming home" at last. Many boarded airplanes believing their hardship was over. In contrast to their expectations, transition was not easy, and the "home" they were searching for remained unobtainable for many. Like most refugees and many other immigrants, Amerasians faced the inevitable obstacles of language barriers and cultural differences. Their low levels of literacy, which resulted from poverty and social discrimination in their mother's land, made it even more difficult for them to learn English and to get an education or vocational training in the United States. With limited English and job skills, they became vulnerable in the job market. Even with the refugee benefits from the federal government and adjustment assistance from nonprofit agencies, some had difficulty adjusting to their father's land, continuing to live on the margins of society. Those difficulties, however, seemed common among refugees and immigrants. The distresses uniquely applied to Amerasians and their family members were continued social ostracism and abandonment in their father's land.

The good intention of resettling Amerasians in Vietnamese communities throughout the United States was problematic. The idea stemmed from concerns for language barriers and cultural differences. Resettling in a place where one can communicate in their mother tongue is an unquestionable desire for new immigrants. Authorities and volunteer agencies probably assumed that Amerasians and their family members would feel more comfortable living among their compatriots, especially because of their shared culture and animosity toward communist rule. When the US public discussed the social prejudice and discrimination that Amerasians faced in their mothers' closed, homogeneous countries, they thought the problem would end once the children found refuge in their fathers' open, heterogeneous society.

Resettlement decision makers seemed to believe that the maltreatment of Amerasians and their mothers was simply a postwar issue. The truth is they had *always* been mistreated by other Vietnamese people. During wartime, many Vietnamese women who had relationships with American personnel suffered familial punishment and disownment; some were even forced to abandon their children. Many Vietnamese people on all sides of the political boundaries despised biracial children and their mothers because of their "impurity." In these people's eyes, Amerasians' mothers were lowly, "loose" women, regardless of the nature of their relationships and circumstances. Living in the United States, it seemed, did not necessarily change their perspectives on cross-boundary relationships and biracial children. When Amerasians arrived in Vietnamese communities in large numbers in the late 1980s and early 1990s, animosity prevailed. Journalist Pamela Constable observed that even refugees struggling to survive on a daily basis considered themselves more respectable than Amerasian families.[34] A former military officer of South Vietnam stated, "In the eyes of the community, there are two groups. The [political refugees] were people with rank and education. The Amerasian families were generally poor, and they did not have a good foundation to succeed here. . . . The [political refugees] got a lot more respect."[35]

In Vietnamese culture, at least for older generations, a woman's past was very important, especially in terms of marriage and relationships. Once she broke social norms, she and her children would have to live with disrespect for the rest of their lives. A woman in her seventies, desperately looking for her Amerasian son whom she had left in an orphanage in 1971, spoke of her untold suffering:

The pain and humiliation that a mother having biracial children like me has to carry are ten times as much as what her children undergo. Please forgive and sympathize with mothers like me. Women whose pasts are not so great can easily hide them, simply by not mentioning them. For women like me, their children are living testimonies to their past actions. Ironically, our children are our love, our shoulder to cry on, but they are also a disgrace, a shame of our pasts, even if our neighbors do not speak their minds.[36]

After more than forty years, this woman still grieved and suffered anguish over the abandonment of her son. Her wartime lover, an African American soldier, returned to the United States upon the end of his military tour when she was pregnant with her first child. Even though she was disowned by her family, she decided to keep the baby. A few years later, she was pregnant again, with another African American soldier's child. Facing dire poverty, she brought her seven-day-old son to an orphanage, asking for help in raising the child because she needed to work to support herself and the older son. She returned to the orphanage several years later, only to find out that her son had been adopted by a family. In an interview, she said that she did not expect her son to forgive her, but she wanted to let him know that she, too, endured pain over the decades.[37] Mothers of Amerasians faced double condemnation—the first for having biracial children, the second for abandoning them—regardless of their circumstances. Ostracism seemed inevitable for Amerasians and their mothers, whether they lived in Vietnam or in America.

Unable to fit in their communities, some Amerasians resorted to street life. An FBI agent in Atlanta, Georgia, remarked, "They don't fit in the Vietnamese community. They don't fit in the American community. They seem to be outcast from both."[38] For some Amerasians, especially those without loved ones accompanying them to the United States, the gangs they joined became their "family, bound by common pasts, [shared] memories of gang life on the Vietnamese streets, problems in the Philippines, and a hostile American and Vietnamese culture in the US."[39] For these Amerasians, obtaining entry visas to the United States did not equate the ending of their misery. As required by the US government, Amerasians and their accompanying relatives spent six months in the Philippines for English and vocational training as well as cultural orientation before entering the United States. While the program meant well, understaffing and overcrowding resulted in chaos, and even violence. Many of these gang members started as lost, lonely youngsters looking for companionship. Without a strong foundation—family, education, and a sense of belonging in their community—they easily drifted onto the wrong path, beginning with minor thefts to supplement their meager incomes, then evolving into serious, violent crimes. Marge Flaherty, regional director of the International Rescue Committee, an agency that helped settle Vietnamese immigrants in Atlanta from 1979 throughout the 1990s, commented, "When you grow up with no values, no direction, no bearing, what you see in [federal] court is the result. It was a very brutal existence."[40] To be sure, not all orphans or Amerasians became gangsters, but understanding their high-risk circumstances is crucial in deconstructing the stereotype of Amerasians as lawbreakers.

Another tragedy that many Vietnamese Amerasians underwent was abandonment, sometimes multiabandonment. Most were abandoned by their fathers, some were abandoned by their mothers, and still others were abandoned again by their adoptive families. The first and second cases usually happened during wartime; the third one arose after the Amerasian Homecoming Act of 1987 took effect, when the "dust of life" suddenly became the "dust of gold." Since the Amerasian Homecoming Act allowed Amerasians' family members or guardians to accompany them to the United States, which was a good intention and a significant improvement compared to the Amerasian Refugee Act of 1982, several Vietnamese people sought to "adopt" or "marry" Amerasians in order to obtain immigrant visas. In some cases, the deal was a mutual agreement with a price paid to the Amerasian and a limited time set for their "bonds." On average, it cost between $300 and $1,000 to "adopt" an Amerasian to obtain immigrant visas for the whole family.[41] With others, the Amerasian did not know of the scheme because most of those who were approached were orphans longing for familial bonds. Under such circumstances, the Amerasians developed emotional attachment to their "adoptive family" only to discover soon after they arrived in the United States that they would be betrayed again. In any case, Amerasians were victims of exploitation.

Stories of fraudulent Amerasian families were common knowledge in Vietnam and among Vietnamese communities in the United States in the 1980s. Yen Do, editor of the *Nguoi Viet* newspaper in Westminster, California, stated, "[The Vietnamese] understand buying the ticket to America through an Amerasian child. The practice is popular."[42] According to the US State Department's records, approximately 10 percent of applicants applying for visas to the United States as accompanying relatives of Amerasians were rejected. There are no data on how many people entered the United States on the basis of falsified relationships with Amerasians, but the department confirmed that the percentage of such cases is "extremely low."[43] However, Peter Daniels, coordinator of St. Anselm's, a private refugee resettlement agency, estimated that approximately 20 percent of the Amerasians that arrived in Orange County, California, were sponsored by fraudulent families.[44] Rene Shakerin, director of the Amerasian program at Catholic Charities in San Jose, California, remarked on those cases, "Once they come here, they do break up. There is no natural bond between the family that 'adopts' them and the Amerasian. They get here and they may live together for a while and then sometimes the families just throw them out."[45] According to a resettlement official of Lutheran Family Services in Phoenix, Arizona, more than 40 percent of the Amerasian families arriving in Phoenix broke up within six months because they were not related. Reports of abuse and abandonment of Amerasians were not uncommon to resettlement centers. In some cases, the Amerasians moved out because their adoptive families started to treat them like servants as soon as they arrived. In others, the "families" simply told them to go away. In "married" cases, the "spouses" just left the Amerasians to join their relatives elsewhere. One reason why fraudulent relationships with Amerasians persisted was because the Amerasians involved did not tend to report their cases for fear that the fake family would not take care of the Amerasians' relatives in Vietnam as promised. On the other hand, according to journalist Jeffrey Brody, the US government was "reluctant to deport the Vietnamese" because deportation would involve complicated legal and diplomatic processes.[46]

The abuse of Amerasians often caused devastating effects, and even catastrophic dramas. In 1991, Do Kiem, an Amerasian, was arrested and charged with murder just four days after he arrived in Garden Grove, California, from the Philippines. Do had been put in an orphanage and adopted by a woman when he was six months old. After four or five years of formal schooling, Do dropped out and moved in with his adoptive mother's brother. He developed bonds with the family and fell in love with the adoptive uncle's daughter. When he applied to immigrate to the United States, the uncle's ten-member family accompanied him while his adoptive mother remained in Vietnam. Two days after their arrival, the uncle and his wife told Do that they did not want him to marry their daughter because they wanted someone with more money and more prestige to be their son-in-law. The mother also asked her daughter, who was in love with Do, to tell him that there would be no marriage. Betrayed and lost, Do stabbed his sweetheart to death. Arrested about an hour later, he expressed deep regret and said that he really loved her. In his pocket was a letter he and his girlfriend had written together, pleading for help in going off to live together on their own. Do's act of revenge destroyed his dream of reuniting with his father, living a normal life with his love, and working as a tailor in the United States.[47]

Of all their ordeals, perhaps the greatest one that Amerasians faced upon arriving in the United States was the shattered dream of a family reunion. Whether they came with other family members or alone, many hoped to reconnect with their long-absent fathers. However, few fulfilled that dream, and many ended their journeys of hope with a cold, bitter reality. To many American fathers who had settled down with new families by the time they learned about the arrival of their foreign children, these Amerasians were children of the past. They did not want their pasts to interfere with their present lives. According to an article in the *Washington Post*, of 244 Amerasians who requested help from the American Red Cross in searching for their biological fathers during a period of three years, only twenty-one found their fathers. Unfortunately, fifteen out of the twenty-one identified fathers asked the Red Cross not to reveal their addresses to their Amerasian children. One father, who was living in Connecticut at the time, wrote to officials of Catholic Charities after being informed of his two Amerasian children, "Let me tell you one thing right now. Never, and I mean never, will you call any member of my family concerning any item involving or in reference to events in my past. You will not ask questions or pressure anyone to accept responsibility for my past life."[48] In another case, an Amerasian medical student sought help to locate her father, who was a US Army chaplain during wartime. The father, still a minister, acknowledged that she was his child but announced that he did not care about her and did not want anything to do with her.[49] These may have been rare occurrences of extreme denial, but it was common for Amerasians to never have an opportunity to meet their fathers. Approximately 3 percent of some twenty-six thousand Amerasians who resettled in the United States found their fathers.[50]

Even long-term relationships between their parents would not ensure Amerasians a reunion with their fathers. Considering the US military's one-year tour during the Vietnam War and the nature of wartime mobilization, one or two years of togetherness would be considered a stable relationship. In a rare exception, Nguyen Quoc Bang's parents had a family together for eight years—they were married and his birth was registered at the US consulate. When the last US personnel evacuated from Saigon in 1975, Nguyen's mother decided to stay, for fear of "not [knowing] what to do with herself" in the United States. Nguyen came to Little Saigon in Orange County, California, in 1989, with his mother, wife, and two daughters, one of whom was Elizabeth, named after his father's mother. Nguyen maintained a relation with his American grandmother, who had sent him a package of clothing when he was still in Vietnam. His father also sent him about $200 a year from 1985 to 1987. Nevertheless, when he arrived in Los Angeles, and even after he had met his grandfather and uncle in San Jose, Nguyen's father refused to see him. When Nguyen called his father, a woman answered, "Please don't call anymore." Nguyen's dream was shattered. His mother was helpless. She respected his father's privacy and did not even allow her picture to be taken for a news story, fearing her appearance might disturb the man's life, but the rejection was too much to bear for her son. To quote from journalist Dianne Klein, "*Devastated* may not be a strong enough word to describe how he feels."[51] While the story sounded extreme, it was not uncommon. Many veterans were not ready to deal with their pasts; they were still adjusting to a civilian society, trying to forget their Vietnam experiences.

Although having a father waiting in their adoptive homeland would make one's resettlement much easier, it would be erroneous to think of Amerasians' search for their fathers as a demand of responsibility for past actions. Rather, it was a quest for identity. Klein remarks, "Almost all of the Amerasians hope to be reunited with their fathers some day. They want to see how they look, how they move, and maybe connect with something inside them that will make them whole."[52] The social stigma of being bastards denigrated these men and women; it plundered their confidence, urging them to disprove their fatherless status. In Vietnamese culture, one's father is his or her root, and rootlessness is one of the greatest misfortunes. Children without a father's acknowledgment are referred to as *con hoang*, literally translated to "children of the wilderness," which is synonymous to "misfit." Amerasians simply wanted to be "normal"—to be able to talk about their fathers, like anybody else. As Klein puts it, "All the Amerasians do [ask about their father], with words or with just a feeling that swells in their hearts."[53] In truth, some decided not to search for their fathers for fear of rejection, a risk too high to take. Others delayed the inquiry, waiting until they could speak English and be "somebody" so that their fathers could be proud of them if they ever met. Uttered or not, the question never faded away.

Amerasians' quest for identity was an arduous mission, but it was a lingering desire too strong to bypass. Nguyen Thanh, who had arrived in Garden Grove, California, in 1988, wrote to journalist Dianne Klein after four years of hope and desperation: "When I came to [the] United States I hope I searched my father, but four years from now I still don't know how to look for him and who can help me to search [for] my father. I'm very sad and very disappoint[ed]." He shared his feelings, "I always [*sic*] thinking about him. When I was in Vietnam, I thought I would find him. I want to know how he look [*sic*] like. I don't know why, but I have a feeling that I love my father." Nguyen Thanh's father was an army sergeant. Briefly before he left Vietnam in late 1968, he told Nguyen's mother that he had been married with two children. His mother tried to forget her US lover; she later remarried and had three more children. Despite his limited education from Vietnam, Nguyen Thanh managed to finish high school with a B average after only four years in America. He wanted to join the military to be just like his father. Unfortunately, he failed the English test. He commented on his enduring quest: "I just want to know him. I think he is just like me. I don't want the whole of my life to go by without my real father. I don't want anything from him. But I want to know him." Nguyen Thanh, however, did not fantasize about a reunion with his father. He understood that he might face rejection but believed he would survive; he would rather have the experience than not know who his father was.[54] Even for accomplished middle-aged Amerasians, the absence of their fathers still bored an unbridgeable hole in their soul. As forty-six-year-old Tran Trinh from Houston, Texas, remarked, "I need to know where I come from. I always feel that without him, I don't exist."[55]

Unable to connect and identify with their communities in Vietnam, Amerasians believed they would fit better in American society. The day he arrived in Minneapolis, a young boy cried with joy, "I'm in America and I look like everybody else. I look like everybody else. I'm in America. I'm home."[56] That simplistic belief was not uncommon among Amerasians. Excited to fit in their new "home," they thought they had found their long-lost identities. However, becoming American was not necessarily easier than being Vietnamese. Nguyen Anh Dung, who arrived in Utica in 1983, spoke of his experience three years later: "In Vietnam, they curse me because I am American. They tell me [to] go to America where I belong. I come to America but I don't feel like I belong. Here I find out I am more Vietnamese than I thought. I find out black or white, we Amerasians have much to learn about being an American."[57] Another nineteen-year-old Amerasian echoed a similar observation after living in the United States for two years: "In Vietnam they called me American. Here they don't know what I am."[58] Being trapped between the two cultures was a perpetual Amerasian dilemma.

A significant part of the Amerasians' quest for identity was their legal status. Although Amerasians and their family members automatically obtained permanent residency upon their arrival in the United States, until 2003, more than 60 percent of the twenty-three thousand Amerasians who came to the United States under the Homecoming Act of 1987 were still legally aliens.[59] Another estimate in 2008 indicated approximately 50 percent of Amerasians did not have US citizenship because they did not pass the English language and civic tests.[60] Having lost their Vietnamese citizenship and unable to obtain American citizenship, these Amerasians became nationless. Even an "imagined community" seemed out of reach for them.[61]

Fulfilling the Amerasian Dream

Forgotten Pasts Remembered

Reflecting on his past journey, a US veteran wrote to a Vietnamese woman whom he dated more than thirty years before: "I remember the last night I was with you. I put my hand on your stomach and felt our son kicking and moving. I did not write you as I should have done. I was young and immature in 1968 and I am sorry I was not there to take care of you."[62] He was a nineteen-year-old soldier, and she was a bar girl. Seven days after their farewell, as he ended his tour in Vietnam, she gave birth to a son, and they permanently lost contact. While this story was not necessarily typical of wartime love affairs between American GIs and Vietnamese women, it presented some common facts about Amerasians' parents. First, they were young and mostly immature. Second, the geographical distance and political relations of the two countries favored forgetfulness, but third, not all fathers would forget the seemingly dormant memories of a time long past. Although many veterans chose to forget their children, stories of the other few are illuminating.

Among the very first US fathers who searched for their children in Vietnam was Gary Tanous, a resident of Washington State. Coming to Saigon as a civilian communications advisor, Tanous met and married a Vietnamese girl in 1966. They had a daughter, and he brought his family back to the United States in 1968. However, his wife and daughter returned to Vietnam later, following which the couple divorced. The mother left the baby with her relatives and fled to the United States in 1975. In 1980, Tanous received a letter from his daughter in Vietnam and a phone call from the mother. Learning about his daughter's loneliness and hardship, he quit his job to solve the problem. He started knocking on the doors of Congress and the State Department to ask for assistance. Two years later, Tanous located his daughter. Before the Amerasian Immigration Act was passed, he flew to Vietnam to pick up his daughter, Jean Marie Tanous. Holding his fifteen-year-old girl in his arms after fourteen years of separation, the father said, "I have never been happier in my life. . . . I just feel sick at all the important years of her life I missed." In 1982, his daughter was among the first eleven Amerasians flown to the United States.[63]

Tanous's undertaking to reunite with his daughter prompted him to be vocal for the Amerasian cause. In fact, he became "one of the most visible spokesmen for Amerasian children" of the early 1980s.[64] Part of it was because of the bureaucratic problems that he faced. He remembered, "I still burn because when I wrote Ronald Reagan, he referred me to the refugee program, knowing that she was an American citizen, which referred me to a Post Office box in San Francisco, which turned out to be the Orderly Departure Program, which was where I started two years before."[65] Tanous's experience revealed the confusion of the time. Both governmental officials and fathers hardly knew where to start and how to categorize Amerasians in legal terms. Were they refugees, immigrants, or citizens? Tanous's devotion to the rescue of his daughter, however, transcended the distress. Not only did he lobby the US government, he also met with Vietnamese officials in Thailand and England to advocate for vulnerable children. Following the reunion with his daughter, Tanous established the Jean Marie Foundation in Vancouver, Washington, to help US fathers relocate their children in Vietnam.

Army veteran Jim Edward Wilder was not as lucky as Tanous despite his well-documented fatherly love. Wilder married Nguyen Thi Kim Hoa in a Vietnamese ceremony a year after he landed in Cam Ranh Bay in 1968. Their marriage, however, was not recognized by the US government because his commanding officer disapproved of it. According to Wilder, the officer tore up the marriage application in front of him, declaring it "immoral, unjust and just not right."[66] Wilder became a father the following year but had to return to the United States two months after his son's birth, unable to obtain exit visas for his family. Once in the United States, he worked hard to earn his GED and tried for two years to get help from Congress, but his efforts were in vain. He and his wife stayed in touch for two and a half years, but then his letters were returned unopened. During the chaotic months of the collapse of South Vietnam, he contacted the Red Cross for help in locating his son. When the Red Cross informed him that it had found the child in a Saigon hospital, Wilder went to Oakland, California, planning to help with the evacuation efforts as an escort for World Airways. Upon his arrival in California, however, he learned that the Red Cross had made a mistake—it could not find his son. Disappointed, he returned to Maryland and started drinking heavily. A few months later, he abducted a child, whom he released the same day, and received a ten-year prison sentence.[67]

In prison, Wilder formed and became president of a chapter of the United States Junior Chamber, or Jaycees, which attracted inmate enrollment from three-quarters of the Upper Marlboro Detention Center in the first year. His Jaycees chapter organized unprecedented activities in prison, including a steak banquet for fellow inmates and community leaders with funding from doing haircuts and photography services for prisoners. Wilder's leadership earned him the title Jaycees Outstanding President, an honor only twenty-five people enjoyed nationwide. Released in 1980, Wilder proposed a plan for an "Amerasian center" in Maryland to help prepare children for adoption and adaptation to American life. He hoped his center would be able to shelter Amerasians for three to six months, during which they would learn basic English and survival skills in the United States. His initiative inspired other veterans to step up for Amerasians. Sam Fain, a former Vietnam vet wishing to help Wilder with the Amerasian center, shared his concerns: "I might have children in another place going through pure hell. We did bring all those children into the world. They are our children, and we have an obligation."[68] Wilder's "project of love" (to borrow journalist Tom Vesey's words) stemmed from the caring heart of a father. Time, space, and politics could not diminish his love. In his perilous journey to reclaim his son, Wilder erred but then made remarkable efforts to fix not only his problems but also that of others.

Another touching example of US veterans' personal ties in Vietnam was Joseph Crotty's case. Crotty was serving in the First Naval Construction Brigade in Da Nang in 1969 when he met a young Vietnamese woman. By the time his tour ended, he learned that his Vietnamese girlfriend was pregnant. Nevertheless, they parted ways, and he did not hear from her again until several years later. The Vietnamese woman included a picture of their son in her letter. Crotty and his American wife, Velda, wanted to bring the boy "home" to the United States. Velda patiently wrote to the address "once a week, then once a month and finally, after six years had passed with no word back, just once every six months or so."[69] Her efforts were not in vain. After more than a decade passed, Crotty finally heard from his son again. They exchanged photos and letters and started the son's immigration application. Their long road to reunion came full circle when Crotty flew to Saigon in 1988 to meet his now-eighteen-year-old son to bring him to California. Crotty described the moment they met: "I was trying to fill out my customs forms, and I looked up, and there he was. I don't cry much. I'm not like that. But I started bawling. I could hardly see the customs forms. I just wanted to go grab him."[70] Crotty was among the few luckier veterans, not only because he succeeded in finding his son but also because he had his wife's significant support. In some cases, the father-and-child reunion led to the father's divorce, which caused other veterans to be even more reluctant to acknowledge their "other" children.

Amid the entanglement of Vietnamese and US governments' intensification over postwar issues and the emotional surge among the US public about the ill fates of Amerasians, John Rogers stood out as an extraordinary link between the two countries. In 1969, Rogers met a woman twenty years his senior at a beach resort. Their brief affair brought his daughter into existence. Later, he married another Vietnamese woman who he brought back to the United States. Before he left Vietnam in 1972, he saw his daughter, Gloria Jean Rogers, a few times. In 1988, he returned to the coastal town to look for her. "I had thought about my daughter all those years. I felt it was my responsibility all that time to take care of her," said Rogers in an interview. Witnessing the Amerasians' adversity in Vietnam and personally undergoing the emotions of an overdue reunion, Rogers decided to devote his efforts to helping Amerasians. One year after reuniting with his daughter, Rogers established the Foundation for Amerasian Children's Emergency Support (FACES) based in Honolulu, Hawaii. FACES was the first private US charity authorized to operate in Vietnam since 1975, with permission to shelter, examine, treat, and immunize homeless Amerasians in Saigon. According to a FACES medical doctor, 76 percent of the examined children were suffering from medical problems and/or malnutrition.[71] While FACES was Rogers's initiative to meet the emergency needs of Amerasians and most of its funding came from him, the project called for collaborative efforts from multiple parties. It confronted the Vietnamese government with an unpleasant reality and, one way or another, got local Vietnamese people involved in solving the problem. FACES started out with US staff but gradually trained Vietnamese health workers to carry out its missions. Furthermore, Rogers encouraged US veterans to support the project and inspired other philanthropists to aid Amerasians.

The American fathers' search for that missing piece of their youth—and blood—went on for decades after the war's end. For many, the scant memories of their children resurfaced even more forcefully over time. Thirty-two years after he left Vietnam, Clint Haines returned to the country's Central Highlands "with the same stomach-churning, heart-pounding thrill of mission he felt every morning he boarded his helicopter in 1971" to look for his child who he had never seen. His military tour had ended when his fiancée was pregnant. He left the country with a promise to return and marry her, but his extension was denied. Through a fellow soldier, he received one letter from her and wrote back, adding one hundred dollars. Their communication, however, ended there since the intermediary finished his tour and returned home.[72] Haines eventually found his fiancée in 2005 and learned that he had fathered a son, but by a twist of misfortune, he also discovered an ultimate pain: his son was given away, and Haines remained clueless about the son's circumstances.[73]

Haines's personal despair urged him to take up a transnational mission. While searching for his child, he found Brian Hjort, the Danish founder of Father Founded, a nonprofit organization that, since 1995, had helped reunite American fathers and their Amerasian children, and Rich Collins, a California-based Amerasian looking for his biological parents. With the assistance of Hjort and Collins, Haines created the Amerasian Child Find Network in 2002. Within six months, approximately two hundred veterans signed up in hope of finding their children. In less than a year, Amerasian Child Find Network helped twenty-nine fathers reunite with their long-lost children.[74] It was not known how many reunions the network facilitated altogether, but Haines devoted his efforts to the cause until the end of his life in 2012.

Earl Hicks from Michigan was one of the veterans who owed his miraculous reunion with his children to Haines. "Almost every day for four decades," Hicks was "haunted" with "guilt" for abruptly leaving his lover and their two children. He was suffering from a skin rash and was flown out of the country unexpectedly in 1972. His son was one year old; his daughter was three. Then one day in 2009, the sixty-three-year-old veteran found a post about him on his former military unit's website, the army's 504th Military Police Battalion. The message read,

I'm looking for a Sgt. Hicks who worked as a mess sgt. in 68–69. . . . He was reported to have worn . . . a MP helmet and sidearm. He was in Pleiku and then in Saigon . . . both times with an MP company. [It] was reported that he was assigned to pick up the KPs and drop them off at night. . . . Anyone who knew him or has old company rosters or orders with his name on them, please e-mail your phone number.

Hicks dialed the number provided. On the other end was Haines. It was a lucky day: within twenty-four hours of the post, Haines got in touch with the person he was looking for. Hicks's children had been searching for him since they came to the United States in the early 1990s. His son even studied the names on the Vietnam Memorial in Washington, DC, the result of which reinforced his belief that "Sgt. Hicks" was still alive. The father-children reunion was filled with "a lot of crying, smiling, and hugging." Hicks was finally at peace, knowing that his children were "doing so well" and that they simply wanted a father to be whole.[75]

Sometimes miracles happened thanks to social media that seems to be of little use other than for time-consuming entertainment, such as Facebook. Jerry Quinn, who became a missionary and lived in Taiwan later in his life, was among the last US soldiers withdrawing from South Vietnam in 1973 as a result of the Paris Peace Accords. Quinn and his pregnant girlfriend were in the process of acquiring permission to get married. For a year, Quinn sent her a hundred dollars every month but was uncertain if she received the money. In his possession were three photos from his girlfriend: a portrait of her, one of her and their son, and another of her and the midwife who delivered their baby. Unsettled with the separation for forty years, Quinn sought help from Father Founded and traveled to Saigon, looking up and down every corner of the neighborhood where his girlfriend lived during wartime. The drastic changes in the city, including those of street names, housing, and residents, combined with faded memories over decades, made the trip seem hopeless. Quinn showed everybody in the neighborhood the three photos, and finally one person recognized the midwife. Coincidentally, the midwife's daughter was in town—she was visiting from the United States. The daughter immediately recognized Quinn's girlfriend and remembered helping her mother deliver Quinn's son, but nobody knew where his family was. The best guess was that they had moved to the United States, just like most Amerasians' families. Quinn was desperate but arranged to meet with the woman who knew his son. Hopelessly holding back tears, Quinn asked the woman, "May I hold your hands? Because these hands held my baby. There is so much emotion in my heart right now. I may never see him or touch him. This is as close as I may ever get to my son."[76] With faint hope, Quinn posted the photos on Facebook, noting that he was looking for a forty-year-old son, whose Vietnamese last name was Bui. From Albuquerque, New Mexico, Gary Bui recognized the photos—the same copies that he had always kept.[77] The one-time orphan's story concluded with a happy ending.

While the majority of Amerasians could not, and may never, reunite with their fathers, the number of happy cases increased over the years thanks to multiple underlying factors. The most obvious reason was the advances of communication and transportation technologies. The internet enabled networking, enhancing transnational and interorganization communication. International travel also became more affordable, and local transportation in Vietnam had improved significantly compared to that of the 1980s. Another factor that eased perilous journeys was the improved diplomatic relations between the United States and Vietnam, which sped up the visa process and enhanced freedom to travel around Vietnam. Bureaucratic hassles of the 1980s in both countries might have been discouraging for some people. Finally, the passage of time contributed to growing searches for Amerasian children. Many veterans in the 1970s and 1980s were not ready to deal with anything related to Vietnam. They needed a break from an unpleasant past and tried to start their lives over. They did not want their Vietnam experiences to interfere with their postwar life. The cushion of time filtered their memories and preserved what seemed important to them. For both Amerasians and their fathers, the reunion fulfilled an obligation they owed to themselves. In their quest for inner peace, they bridged the distance between the two countries. They were also transnational historical actors who refused to bury what seemed to be unpleasant pasts. By enlivening unwanted memories, they deepened our thoughts about the aftermath of war. For those Amerasians who were not fortunate enough to find that missing link of their lives, the burning question about their identity persisted, more privately for some than others but equally painful.

From Nationless State to Transnational Community

Amerasians undoubtedly underwent enormous ordeals, both in Vietnam and in the United States, but the portrayal of Amerasians as a monolithic group of paralyzed victims is an incomplete picture. While some of them gave up and continued to live in the margins of society as voiceless misfits, others strove to reclaim their voices. Not only did they overcome difficulties to stabilize their lives, they also crossed boundaries to assist others. Despite the lack of love in their childhoods, many Amerasians nurtured the seeds of tolerance and compassion to effect change. Born in circumstances of hostility and growing up with a plethora of hatred, they deeply understood the thirst for love. Their experiences of animosity transformed them into peaceful, loving individuals. Some even used their nationless state as an advantage to advocate borderless love.

One significant transformation among the Amerasian community was a newfound answer to its members' enduring question: "Who am I?" Growing up with social (and sometimes familial) humiliation because of their birth-roots, Amerasians were constantly forced to confront that identity question. The stigma of otherness imposed upon them often led to self-pity and shame. As grown-ups and within a community, however, they celebrated their biracial origins and embraced their multicultural heritage. In fact, many referred to themselves as "proud Amerasians." Tara Linh Leaman, an Afro-Amerasian abandoned by her birth mother and adopted by an American family, elaborated in an Amerasian Voice newsletter, "I have discovered that, because of my background, I can move in and out of contrasting spaces, frequently acting as an interpreter between distinct cultures. Now that I am an adult, I identify with more than one characteristic. I am not just an adoptee, not just African American and not just Vietnamese. I am a diverse human being, like all of us."[78] The embrace of cultural flexibility that Leaman described speaks volumes of the metamorphoses undergone by Amerasians. Their postwar journey began with hatred and confusion but evolved into love and pride. From children belonging nowhere, they transcended rejection to belong to multiple cultures.

One outstanding Amerasian was Jenny Do, an attorney, artist, and philanthropist in San Jose, California. Like many Amerasians, she grew up in poverty and never met her father, but luckier than some, she had the security of her mother's love. Arriving in the United States with her mother and brother on her eighteenth birthday in 1984, Do started a new chapter of her life by learning the alphabet of the English language. Thirteen years later, she became an attorney. In addition to her legal profession, she relentlessly fought for the disadvantaged—among them Amerasians, victims of human trafficking, underprivileged children in Vietnam, and low-income families in San Jose. Practicing "humanity through arts," a concept of employing arts to effect social change, Do founded the Green Rice Gallery in 2006 to promote Vietnamese American artists' work and raised awareness of social concerns. The exhibition *Humans for Sale*, for instance, toured the United States as a photo documentary about human trafficking in Southeast Asia. In 2011, Green Rice Gallery changed its name to Green Rice Foundation, which continued its activity for the same purposes. Do also created San Jose's biannual Ao Dai Festival, which celebrated Vietnamese women's traditional dress, for multiple purposes. The festival enhanced the cultural pride of Vietnamese Americans, a nexus of values and beliefs that needed to be forwarded to younger generations of Vietnamese overseas and introduced to the American cultural tapestry. The event also invited artists, performers, volunteers, and philanthropists to work together to raise funds for Friends of Hue, a nonprofit organization sheltering forty disadvantaged children in central Vietnam.[79]

Do's contributions to society were widely recognized. In 2007, she received the Lifetime Achievement Award from the city of San Jose and a Woman of the Year award from the California Legislature of District 23. In 2011, she achieved the Congressional Award bestowed by US Congresswoman Zoe Lofgren. In 2015, she ran for San Jose City Council in District 8. Unfortunately, she withdrew from the race in October to battle a returning breast cancer that threatened to shorten her life to a few months. In a television interview after the shocking diagnosis, she shared her four-item wish list in a calm, positive voice: (1) for the Friends of Hue Foundation to continue its activities in the advancement of underprivileged children, (2) for the Ao Dai Festival to carry forward its cultural and humane missions, (3) for more people to contribute to the cause of Fr. Pedro Opeka to help improve children's living conditions in Madagascar, and (4) for a Vietnamese-American Community Center to be established in San Jose. She also called for humanity acts without borders, emphasizing that human needs should not be overshadowed by political differences.[80] Miraculously, two years after the shocking diagnosis, Do completely recovered from cancer. She continued her charity work and added to her agenda the establishment of a support group to help cancer patients. Do's compassion, devotion, and achievements stood in contrast to the "typical" tale of Amerasians. Not only did she successfully adapt to US culture, she also effectively advocated for social change in both her father's and mother's lands and beyond. Her childhood disadvantages did not block her path. On the contrary, they inspired her to reach out to vulnerable populations across boundaries.

By a twist of fate, some Amerasians grew up as Americans, and for much of their young adulthood, they paid little attention to their Vietnamese heritage. Nevertheless, their bicultural backgrounds still shaped the paths they took. Trista Goldberg, founder of Operation Reunite, shifted the course of her life in such a manner. Adopted by an American family when she was four years old, Goldberg had significant advantages adapting to her fatherland compared to those who came to the United States a decade or more later. As Goldberg turned twenty-five, her adoptive mother gave her the adoption file, which inspired her to learn more about her birth culture. She started studying the Vietnamese language and its history, then decided to find her birth mother. Luckier than most, within three months, Goldberg reunited with her birth mother and other relatives. That journey to find the missing piece of her life inspired Goldberg to create Operation Reunite in 2003. As its name indicated, the operation aimed to help Vietnamese adoptees worldwide reconnect with their birth families through DNA tests. In 2008, Goldberg came back to Vietnam, collecting eighty DNA samples in the hope of using potential DNA matches to advocate for approximately four hundred Amerasians applying for immigration to the United States. In 2010, in a trip organized for fifty Vietnamese adoptees from the United States, the United Kingdom, and Australia in order to help them learn more about their birth culture, Goldberg carried with her to Vietnam two hundred DNA samples.[81] Her diligent collaboration with Amerasians and/or adoptees worldwide, as well as with agencies in Vietnam, paid off, and successful DNA matches encouraged more participants. Goldberg's dedication to the reunion cause brought joy and hope for many people across the globe. She transformed the personal journey to her roots into a transnational endeavor to answer the seemingly dormant but burning questions that were decades overdue.

Several Amerasians established their names through a singing career, among the most famous was probably Phi Nhung, "diva" of Vietnamese traditional and folkloric music. Phi Nhung was born an unwanted child in a Buddhist pagoda in the Central Highlands of Vietnam in 1972. Because she was fathered by a US soldier, her maternal grandmother beat her mother and insisted on an abortion. Phi Nhung's mother stubbornly kept the child by taking shelter in a pagoda. After birth, however, her grandmother gave in and allowed mother and child to come home. A few years later, her mother married a Vietnamese man and moved out. Phi Nhung stayed with her grandmother. Loneliness turned her into a shy girl. She remembered not having the courage to come close to her mother on her rare visits; she would often be startled even upon hearing her mother call her name. Not until she was six years of age did she come to live with her mother. However, that happy time was short-lived. A traffic accident ripped her mother out of her life when Phi Nhung turned eleven. Soon her stepfather abandoned the children—Phi Nhung and five of his own. As the oldest child, she started working to help her grandmother and other relatives support her siblings. Less than a year later, her grandmother died; Phi Nhung quit school to be the breadwinner of the family. She would go to the market and did whatever people would hire her for. Later, she learned to work a sewing machine and started making money as a seamstress. With some relatives' assistance, she applied to immigrate to the United States under the Amerasian Homecoming Act. In 1989, she arrived in Tampa, Florida, alone and empty-handed. She remembered begging for food at the airport, as she had too little money to buy anything. Deeply concerned about her and her siblings' destitution, the seventeen-year-old girl resolved to work day and night.[82]

An opportunity of a lifetime happened to Phi Nhung when a famous Vietnamese singer accidentally discovered her talent in a community show at a pagoda in Florida and encouraged her to take up singing seriously. With the singer's guidance and support, Phi Nhung moved to California in 1993. She started by sending her recording to Vietnamese music production companies, including Thuy Nga Productions, whose *Paris By Night* was the most popular Vietnamese show worldwide. Despite her sweet voice, Phi Nhung received only rejections because she lacked professional training. She did not give up. She contacted the companies that rejected her, asking for specific suggestions to improve her performance. She took their feedback seriously and trained herself. Her perseverance paid off. Within a couple of years, her expressive voice and distinct Mekong Delta accent started winning the audiences' hearts in the category of sentimental folkloric songs. Later, she succeeded in acting and singing *cai luong*, southern Vietnamese traditional theater.[83] Realizing a Vietnamese soul was hidden behind a Western face, the audience was awestruck. It was a combination that few could imagine, but Phi Nhung proved it was a perfect match. Her beauty and talent diminished racial boundaries.

Phi Nhung's talent brought her fame, but it was her gentle heart that made her a legendary Amerasian. After completing her role as a big sister in helping her siblings stabilize their lives, Phi Nhung extended her compassion to other underprivileged people. She sang at Amerasians' fundraising events to help other Amerasians who remained in Vietnam. She sponsored the construction of charity nursing homes in remote areas in Vietnam. Most admirably, she adopted twenty-one disadvantaged children in Vietnam.[84] She translated her memories of childhood adversity into actions of compassion. In an interview, she shared, "When I see those [underprivileged children], I think of my unhappy childhood. I was an orphan, but I was fortunate to have met kindhearted people who took me in and helped me. I am blessed to have an opportunity to become a singer and to be favored by the audiences. I have received a lot; now it's time to give back."[85] With her perseverance, Phi Nhung transformed her life and helped improve that of others. Despite being unwanted, she evolved into an icon of love and compassion.

Another remarkable Amerasian was Randy Trane, who transformed bitter life experiences into tolerant, loving attitudes. Abandoned in a Vietnamese orphanage, Randy Trane began his sorrowful journey when he was just one month old. Born on January 25, 1971, he was brought to an orphanage in Da Nang on February 26 of the same year. In retrospect, however, he considered the years living at the orphanage as the happiest time in his life. On November 15, 1975, he was adopted by a family, which marked the beginning of his endless misery. Randy Trane remembered being so abused by the family that he would isolate himself by roaming the country roads after finishing farm work. He would come "home" late in the evening and sleep in the barn together with the cows, covering himself with hay to stay warm. Then, when Amerasians could apply to immigrate to the United States under the Amerasian Immigration Act of 1982, his adoptive family sold him to a Chinese-Vietnamese family for three taels of gold in 1983. At first, the new family treated him "decently"; they even sent him to school, starting first grade at age twelve. The mother, however, would refuse to eat at the same table with him. After the third grade, they decided he should work instead of going to school, and from then on, their relationships worsened. When they finally entered the United States in 1990, Randy Trane realized that he was not considered a member of the family. They did not care about him, even when he was very sick. The mother started to complain that he ate too much and that he was draining the family's tight budget. Randy Trane demanded that government subsidies be equally divided among the five family members and he would take care of his food. Consequently, each month he received forty dollars in food stamps and $180 in cash, but he had to pay the family $100 to sleep on their couch. He started going to school and found jobs at a laundromat and a garment factory. After nearly two years, he decided to move out. It was not an easy decision because they were the only family he knew in the United States, and as he put it, "They were so much part of my life even though they were never really very good to me." Despite their maltreatment, Randy Trane did not express any hard feelings toward these two "families." He just couldn't understand why they did not love him.[86]

Unable to share his sorrow with anyone, Randy Trane conveyed his emotions in the songs he sang. Some acquaintances recognized his singing ability and encouraged him to participate in karaoke contests in Vietnamese communities. In 1992, he did and won a small prize. A few months later, he participated in another contest. This time he won first prize. One of the examiners, also a musician, recommended him to a recording company. His very first album sold well, prompting him to continue his singing career. Randy

Trane quickly won the audience's hearts, especially because of the songs about orphans, mothers, and Amerasians. His success as a singer profoundly transformed Randy Trane from a "nobody" into a "somebody." His growing popularity boosted his confidence and dignity. Over time, he became less sensitive when somebody called out "black American" or "curly hair," phrases that had scarred his early life. Now that he was "somebody," the "endless nightmare" of verbal abuse that he had suffered in childhood did not matter anymore.[87]

Childhood disadvantages and abuse transformed Randy Trane into a forgiving, loving person. He envisioned his mother as a loving, tender woman, and he believed that abandoning him must have been a heartbreaking decision for her. He believed that perhaps she could not afford to keep him; orphanages must have been the best solution available to her and she trusted he would be cared for by the nuns. Burning with a desire to find his birth mother, Randy Trane returned to Vietnam for the first time in 2007 and many more times after. Several women contacted him, but DNA tests disproved their connections. Randy Trane did not give up and continued his search, even though there was word that his mother might have died. He visualized how he would look after his mother and longed for the simple joy of making her a cup of tea every morning. He also imagined that his mother was a good cook and that she would cook him his favorite foods when he came home. Randy Trane's hunger for love prompted him to help with charity causes, from visiting nursing homes and singing to raise funds for disaster victims in Vietnam to helping Amerasians across borderlands.[88]

Randy Trane's quest for love was also revealed in the songs he composed. His signature songs "Sau Cuộc Chiến" (After the war) and "Mẹ" (Mother) spoke volumes about his enduring loneliness and hunger for love. The song "Mẹ," born out of his bottomless solitude while he was watching Mother's Day commercials, contained the words that he hoped would reach his mother:[89]

> Mother, you left when I was an infant
> Wonder where you are now
> Here am I lonely
> Nobody to love or care for
> Facing all the ordeals by myself
>
> Where are you, mother? I'm waiting for you.
> Do you know how I miss you so?

My beloved, gentle mother, the pain is endless
Nothing is more sorrowful than losing one's parents

Oh . . . nobody to sympathize
Nobody to teach me about maternal love
Lonely I walk in my own shadow
Nobody understands my thirst for love
Nobody understands my need for you

Mother, you left when I was an infant
Years passed by . . . still don't know who you are
My beloved, gentle mother,
How could you understand my anguish?
Nothing is more sorrowful than losing one's parents.[90]

Although the song stemmed from Randy Trane's personal thoughts and feelings, it also depicted the hitherto unspeakable inner self of many Amerasians. Both "Sau Cuộc Chiến" and "Mẹ" brought forgotten Amerasians to the spotlight, waking society to a reality it had chosen to ignore. Gently but deeply, the songs pricked the conscience of those who held prejudice against Amerasians. Trane turned a taboo subject into an appeal for love and forgiveness.

Randy Trane also joined other Amerasians in their fight for Amerasian causes, including helping those who remained in Vietnam file immigration application to the United States and requesting automatic citizenship for Amerasians living in the United States. In July, 2008, Randy Trane and twenty-one other Amerasians traveled to Washington, DC, to lobby for the Amerasian Paternity Recognition Act, HR 4007, introduced the previous year by Representative Zoe Lofgren from California. The passage of HR 4007 would grant automatic citizenship to Amerasians holding permanent residence status in the United States. Until that point, it was estimated that more than ten thousand Amerasians living in the United States had been unable to obtain citizenship because they could not pass English tests.[91] Despite their language barrier, these representative Amerasians made an effort to speak up about their alienation. The journey that Randy Trane and his associates made to Capitol Hill was a quest for identity—to obtain both legal status and a sense of belonging. While their journeys were not yet triumphant, Amerasians were no longer invisible.

Many other Amerasians also achieved popularity through their talents.[92]

Among the best known was Phuong Thao, Vietnam's pop diva of the 1990s. Unlike her counterparts, Phuong Thao established her name in Vietnam before reuniting with her father in the United States. The first part of her story, however, was typical of Amerasians—growing up in poverty, bullied by classmates, and silenced by her mother when questions about her father arose. Phuong Thao's victory in a singing contest paved her career path. At nineteen, she quit her job selling rice snacks in a little town in the Mekong Delta and moved to Saigon to sing in night clubs and small shows. Two years later, she rose to stardom. By that time, her mother had twice obtained immigration visas to the United States, but twice she refused to go, fearing she would "feel lost" in the strange land. In 1992, she met journalist Thomas Bass, who came to Vietnam to study the situation of Amerasians, and she asked him to help her trace her father. Bass interviewed her mother, who at first was reluctant but eventually released identification information about her wartime lover—an army sergeant. Phuong Thao was the result of their brief love affair, and he did not know about his daughter's existence, even though she was born before his tour ended in 1968. Three years after her discussion with Bass, Phuong Thao received a letter and photos from sixty-year-old James Marvin Yoder—her long-lost father. In November 1996, Yoder flew to Vietnam. Phuong Thao, accompanied by hundreds of curious fans, greeted him at the airport with twenty-eight roses—each representing a lost year between father and daughter. Choked with emotion, she finally uttered the word "Dad" for the first time in her life.[93]

Phuong Thao's story was an unusual piece in the Amerasian tapestry, but it reflected the dynamics in human conditions and historical processes. Like singers Randy Trane and Phi Nhung, Phuong Thao conquered people with her talent and determination. As her popularity grew, acceptance replaced the ostracism that she had endured. Although she never directly raised her voice against social prejudice, she proved her ability to challenge class and racial boundaries.

Starting in the early 2000s, several Amerasian organizations came into existence, among them the Amerasian Voice, Amerasian Foundation, Amerasian Fellowship Association, Vietnamese Amerasian Society, and Amerasians Without Borders. While varied in structure and activities, these organizations generally shouldered common causes such as helping members find their birth families and advocating for Amerasian automatic citizenship and immigration visas for Amerasians in Vietnam. They also served as support networks and social spaces where members could share a sense of belonging. They often organized fundraising dinners, especially to help Amerasians remaining in Vietnam. Even though some of the organizations were short-lived, their existence revealed Amerasians' efforts and capability to stand up together as a community for social change.

Amerasians' worlds were filled with ironies. They came into existence as the result of love amid a violent conflict. They were generally denied by both of their mothers' and fathers' societies, for their presence reminded people of unpleasant wartime memories. Marginalization and oppression, however, could not mute their voices. Suppressed to the bottom of society, they bounced back in creative ways, shaking the conscience of others and making politicians work harder. Subjected to hatred, they transformed into loving social activists. Their historical agency was uniquely nurtured by paradoxes. Their ability to transcend the boundaries imposed upon them, to move from statelessness to binational identity, and to metamorphose from "nobody" to "somebody" illuminates our understanding of the power of the powerless.

CHAPTER THREE

Groundwork for Diplomatic Normalization by Ordinary Citizens

Peace starts from within and flows out into the world. Peace doesn't happen at a negotiating table. It happens inside people's hearts, and then spreads and makes it safe for politicians to sign pieces of paper, when enough of us learn to trust and love one another.

—Danaan Parry, quoted in Gay-Wynn Cooper, "Peace Trees, Vietnam," *Yes! Magazine*

Despite continued governmental talks between the United States and Vietnam on issues such as immigration, MIAs, and Amerasians, the 1980s also witnessed hostility between leadership of the two countries. Discussions were repeatedly interrupted because of their disagreements, particularly because Vietnam was at war with the Khmer Rouge in Cambodia and with China on its northern borders. International politics once again fueled the friction between the United States and Vietnam. The Khmer Rouge's genocide, the Sino-Soviet power struggle, and US interests in the region posed great challenges for Vietnam's postwar reconstruction and economic development. The US trade embargo against Vietnam remained in effect for another decade, and Vietnam continued to be listed as an enemy nation throughout the 1980s. In addition to political complications in the region, the United States continued to demand a full account of American MIAs as a precondition for diplomatic normalization with Vietnam. While this demand sprang from both a humanitarian impulse and a governmental obligation to US personnel serving in the war, it ignored the tremendous suffering of Vietnamese victims of the war. The Socialist Republic of Vietnam's (SRV) government made an effort to meet US demand because of its need to improve relations with the world's most powerful nation, but from the Vietnamese perspective, searching for American MIAs, or any MIAs, was not perceived as the most urgent task at the time. The country was preoccupied with issues that needed immediate attention, including national security and a desperate economic crisis. The absence of mutual understanding was obvious, and the road to normalization remained at an impasse.

On both sides, however, ordinary citizens diligently advocated for normalization and initiated transnational peace-building activities. While well-established nongovernmental organizations (NGOs) continued their humanitarian missions, new organizations were emerging, exploring paths to promote mutual understanding. Most noticeable was the participation of America's Vietnam veterans. In efforts to heal the wounds of war—for themselves and for Vietnamese people—many US veterans returned to Vietnam. Together with their former enemies, they built schools, medical clinics, and houses for the disabled. They organized cultural and academic exchanges, thus creating channels of communication that helped bring Vietnam out of isolation under the effects of the embargo. Some simply visited Vietnam to make peace with their inner selves, hoping to end the lingering wartime memories that still plagued them. Other Americans, especially academics, also played an active role in transpacific interactions, despite the lack of governmental diplomacy. Not only did they take action in their fields of expertise to help reconnect the two countries, they also raised their voices in the realm of politics to effect policy changes. This transnational undercurrent of interconnectedness among ordinary citizens laid the groundwork for US-Vietnam normalization. Without these ordinary citizens' peace endeavors, diplomatic ties between the two countries would have been even harder to achieve.

The Long Eve before Normalization

David Lamberston, deputy assistant secretary of state (with special responsibility for Southeast Asia), summarized the US policy toward Vietnam throughout the 1980s: "No trade, no aid and no normal relations except in the context of a political settlement and an end of Vietnam's occupation of Cambodia." He asserted that the policy did "not reflect any lingering animus toward Vietnam resulting from the war," and that it was "not a function of what Vietnam did in 1975, but of what it is doing right now—occupying militarily a once sovereign neighbor."[1] Lamberston's statement was out of context and misleading. Without providing background as to the causes of Vietnam's military occupation of Cambodia, he implied that Vietnam was politically aggressive and that there was absolutely no reason for Vietnam to remain in its neighbor's territory. With this simplified version of the story, one may wonder why Vietnamese troops were still in Cambodia, even after they had ended the Khmer Rouge genocide several years before. Lamberston, however, answered that unasked question almost immediately after his statement about the US policy: "To achieve genuine peace and stability in Cambodia, any settlement reached must ensure that the withdrawal of Vietnamese troops will not lead to the return to power of the Khmer Rouge. Crafting such a solution will not be easy, inasmuch as the Khmer Rouge remain probably the most militarily powerful of the Cambodian factions."[2] Unwittingly, he acknowledged that Vietnam had made and continued to make an effort to stop the Khmer Rouge. A similar position prevailed in Representative Stephen Solarz's response in a press briefing following his trip to Asia in 1989: the United States would consider normalization with Vietnam only after the latter withdrew its troops from Cambodia "in the context of a political settlement." The briefing minutes read, "If Vietnam simply withdraws its troops without providing for a negotiated settlement, the US conditions for normalization will not have been met. The main obstacle at the moment to a political settlement in Cambodia lies with [Cambodia's prime minister] Hun Sen and [Vietnam's foreign minister] Nguyen Co Thach."[3] Again, Americans had simplified the complex political entanglements in the region in such a way that it seemed Cambodia's fate was solely in Vietnam's hands. Both Lamberston's and Solarz's comments also revealed a contradiction: Vietnam had to end its occupation, but it could not "simply withdraw."

It is worth reviewing the background of the political entanglement in Cambodia. According to Jeremy Stone, president of the Federation of American Scientists, Vietnam "did nothing more to Cambodia than the US did to Japan when, in response to Japanese attack, the US overthrew the government of Japan, established an occupation regime in which it called every shot and reshaped the Japanese Government into one less antagonistic."[4] Vietnam did not simply invade a "once sovereign neighbor" as mentioned in Lamberston's accusation—similar versions of which prevailed in US media as rhetoric to pressure Vietnam's withdrawal. The "sovereign neighbor" that Lamberston mentioned was suffering from autogenocide that claimed approximately two million lives out of a population of less than eight million between 1975 and 1979.[5] Furthermore, starting in January 1977, under the Khmer Rouge regime, that neighbor attacked Vietnam's border provinces, brutally killing Vietnamese civilians. One of the most horrifying massacres occurred on September 24, 1977, in Tan Lap town, Tay Ninh Province. Within three hours, 592 people were murdered and most houses turned into ashes.[6] As Jeremy Stone notes, in April 1977, the Khmer Rouge leaders issued a directive calling for the killing of all ethnic Vietnamese living in Cambodia as well as all Khmer people speaking Vietnamese or having connections with the Vietnamese. Vietnam first responded with mediation through the Chinese, followed by a request for a special session of the UN Security Council and proportionally retaliatory military attacks inside its borders. However, Pol Pot, the Khmer Rouge's leader, escalated the conflict with his plan to exterminate all the Vietnamese and revealed his calculations on Radio Phnom Penh on May 10, 1978: "In terms of numbers, one of us must kill thirty Vietnamese . . . that is to say, we lose one against thirty. We don't have to engage 8 million troops to crush the 50 million Vietnamese, and we would still have six million left."[7] The calculations indeed bolstered Khmer Rouge soldiers in their killing fields. When raiding Vietnamese villages, they killed indiscriminately. Babies, even unborn babies, counted toward their victory.

For national security reasons, Vietnam launched a massive counterattack and successfully overthrew the Khmer Rouge regime in January 1979. Subsequently, Vietnam helped install the government of the People's Republic of Kampuchea (PRK), led by Hun Sen. The Khmer Rouge retreated to the jungles near the Thai border. With Thai sanctuaries and Chinese supplies, the Khmer Rouge tried to rebuild its army and continued to launch guerrilla attacks against the PRK. According to journalist Nate Thayer, an expert on Pol Pot's regime, until 1989, the Khmer Rouge always won in their attacks, and the few occasions in which the PRK army won were because of Vietnamese assistance.[8] While Hun Sen desired to expel foreign forces, Vietnamese troop withdrawal seemed premature, specifically because his opponents still enjoyed outside support.

American foreign policy toward the countries involved in the Cambodian predicament was ambiguous. For years, the United States vocally opposed the Vietnamese occupation of Cambodia despite Vietnam's major role in stopping the Khmer Rouge genocide. Meanwhile, US leaders ignored China's and Thailand's known support for the Khmer Rouge. In June 1982, the

Khmer People's National Liberation Front (KPNLF) led by Son Sann and the National United Front for an Independent, Neutral, Peaceful, Cooperative Cambodia (known by the French acronym FUNCINPEC) led by Prince Norodom Sihanouk joined the Khmer Rouge to form the Coalition Government of Democratic Kampuchea. It is worth noting that Prince Sihanouk had been Cambodia's king (1941–1955), prime minister (1955–1960), and head of state (1960–1970). He was house arrested during the Khmer Rouge's rule and was released in 1979. Attempting to recover his power and opposing Hun Sen's Vietnam-backed regime, Prince Sihanouk advocated a new "neutralist" government that would include the Khmer Rouge. Son Sann was prime minister under Prince Sihanouk. He lived in exile in Paris after Prince Sihanouk was overthrown in 1970 and returned to Cambodia to establish KPNLF in 1979 with the purpose of ending Vietnamese occupation and influence. He reluctantly but in desperation joined the Coalition Government of Democratic Kampuchea for international financial assistance because the United Nations recognized Democratic Kampuchea under the Khmer Rouge at the time, and international aid could only be given to that government. Nevertheless, the coalition benefited the Khmer Rouge.[9] According to a 1988 report by the Congressional Research Service, China was the key supporter of the Cambodian resistance coalition against the Vietnamese occupation, and "the bulk of the Chinese assistance has gone to the Communist Khmer Rouge guerrillas" who made up "over half" of the coalition.[10] In the aforementioned press briefing, Solarz said he believed that China was supplying some materiel to the Non-Communist Resistance (NCR), "although supplying more to the Khmer Rouge," and he "hopes that China will shift its aid from the Khmer Rouge to the NCR."[11] In a 2004 interview, Lamberston admitted, "Our friends, the Thai were certainly facilitating supplies, the flow of supplies to the Khmer Rouge from China. It was a messy situation to say the least." At another point, he added, "We know that the Thai army had regular and friendly contacts with the Khmer Rouge leadership."[12] Evidently, US politicians were well aware that Vietnam's intervention was the main reason the Khmer Rouge was not in control of Cambodia in the 1980s and that the genocidal force's ability to maintain its considerable military strength largely depended on "friends" of the US: China and Thailand. More disturbingly, the State Department decided not to accuse the Khmer Rouge of genocide because that accusation would justify Vietnam's invasion. As the scientist Jeremy Stone observed, the accusation would also force the United States to take part in bringing the Khmer Rouge to justice under the international convention on genocide, which in turn would complicate US support for Prince Sihanouk who wanted to incorporate the Khmer Rouge into the new government intended to replace the PRK.[13] Choosing to ignore the Khmer Rouge's crimes, the State Department proved loyal to its national interests at the price of truthfulness and other values for which the United States claimed to strive. All things considered, from US politicians' perspectives, since Vietnam was still responsible for the region's chaos, it did not deserve normal relations.

Not only did the Reagan and the Bush administrations vehemently condemn Vietnam's occupation of Cambodia, they also provided financial support to factions that opposed Vietnam's intervention and the Vietnam-backed government of Cambodia. The problem was that by choosing to strengthen the two factions led by Prince Sihanouk and Son Sann, the United States risked the chance of indirectly aiding the Khmer Rouge, for these were the three components of the anti–PRK coalition. Senator Alan Cranston pointed out that the United States had "since at least 1986, if not since 1975, squandered opportunities to construct a viable, non-communist, pro-democratic Cambodian political force and wasted millions of American tax dollars to fuel a civil war that has only benefited the genocidal Khmer Rouge." He made that conclusion based on the US General Accounting Office's report in 1990, which also revealed that there was "no control over the aid . . . once inside Cambodia" and that "no one can testify whether or not this aid is benefiting directly or indirectly the Khmer Rouge." According to the report, the aid program "wasn't designed with any clear goals and objectives."[14] However, the mystery of whether or not US aid slipped into the hands of the Khmer Rouge was not so mysterious. Prince Sihanouk was quoted as claiming that all three factions "assist[ed] one another in every circumstance and cooperate[d] with one another on the battlefield."[15] The link was apparent. That the United States politically and financially supported Prince Sihanouk, who cooperated with the Khmer Rouge, was illogical and absurd.

After his visit to Asia in early 1989, Representative Solarz urged the US government to strengthen the NCR with lethal aid so that if the proposed political settlement failed, the NCR could be "the 'last, best' hope we have in preventing the Khmer Rouge from returning to power." In an effort to justify his support for the NCR, Solarz observed that if the settlement fell apart, neither the United States, nor China, nor Thailand, nor any of the Association of Southeast Asian Nations (ASEAN) would come in to stop the Khmer Rouge, just as they had failed to do in the late 1970s. He added, "And Vietnam will not return so soon after leaving."[16] By June 1989, Solarz suggested that, "for starters," the United States should supply the two factions of the NCR with weapons worth "somewhere between $20 million and $30 million."[17] The George H. W. Bush administration welcomed the recommendation and pushed for continued large-scale military aid to the NCR in 1990. However, the Senate voted to end the government's known "covert" support for noncommunist factions in the same year.[18] The moves made by Solarz and the Bush administration did not look as though they were preparing for a peaceful settlement of Cambodia's civil war. The fact that the United States was aware of a possible gruesome outcome resulting from Vietnam's complete withdrawal *and* still imposed the withdrawal as a principle precondition for US-Vietnam reconciliation revealed the ambivalence and absurdity in US foreign policy.

The US policy toward Southeast Asia, however, did not proceed without dissent. Republican Senator Mark O. Hatfield from Oregon maintained, "It is a disgrace that Pol Pot and his murderous cohorts have escaped justice, and I believe the US has been a guilty bystander by pretending we could back a well-intentioned twin resistance front in a corrupt partnership with the Khmer Rouge." He condemned US "inaction" and "acquiescence to questionable regional strategies" that allowed the Khmer Rouge to be "nursed back to health by the Chinese." He also opposed the idea of a peace settlement that included the Khmer Rouge as a "constructive" component of a new Cambodian government, criticizing its proponents for having "forgotten the nature of the Khmer Rouge beast" and for "contemplating a pact with the devil." Hatfield regarded the policy of making the Cambodia settlement a major condition for normalization with Vietnam as "a diplomatic double standard," "inconsistent," and "arguably the most hypocritical of our current foreign policy positions." He contrasted the way the United States treated Vietnam to its postconflict policies toward Japan, Germany, and the Soviet Union. Citing how the United States maintained diplomatic relations with the Soviet Union while the latter was occupying Afghanistan, Hatfield stated that the United States "used the Vietnam occupation of Cambodia as a pretext to punish Vietnam."[19]

Similarly, Edmund S. Muskie, former senator and chairman of the Center for National Policy, remarked that the problem with regard to US policy toward Indochina was "a lack of concrete, first-hand information." In his congressional testimony, time and again he emphasized that "everyone" should go to Cambodia and "take an honest look." After a two-week trip to the region, Muskie observed that "the Cambodians would be irrational if they had not preferred the results of the Vietnamese invasion to what had gone before." Refuting the common rhetoric that Hun Sen's government was but Vietnam's puppet, Muskie asserted that Cambodia "is not a country run by Vietnam." He credited the PRK for its efforts in rebuilding the nation and noted that reconstruction "occurred in large part while the Vietnamese were still there." He underscored that Vietnam was preoccupied with economic development, not military adventures, and that the US embargo was affecting Vietnam's struggle. Muskie questioned the reasoning behind the demand to dismantle the functioning PRK before elections and criticized the big five (the United States, the Soviet Union, China, France, and the United Kingdom) in Paris for maintaining silence about the Khmer Rouge's crimes. He contended, "As long as we continue to support China's wish to bring back the Khmer Rouge, we are on the *wrong side* in Cambodia."[20] Nevertheless, even influential voices such as Muskie's and Hatfield's could not engender a significant turn in the Bush administration's policy.

While issues such as MIA/POW identification and immigration for Vietnamese re-education camp detainees remained in the background as other conditions for the improvement of US-Vietnam relations, the four-stage roadmap to normalization devised by US leaders in 1991 was dependent on the peace settlement of Cambodia. According to this plan, the first stage required Vietnam's and the PRK's signatures on an international peace agreement, which would earn Vietnam the "rewards" of US permission for group travel of American veterans and businesspeople to the country as well as the abolition of the existing twenty-five-mile confinement of Vietnamese diplomats in New York City. In phase two, the United States would end the embargo against Cambodia and *start to lift* the embargo against Vietnam after United Nations officials arrived in Cambodia and arranged a ceasefire among the Khmer factions. Phase three was expected to occur six months later. Once all Vietnamese troops and advisors had withdrawn from Cambodia, the United States would end the embargo and relax its obstruction against international lending to Vietnam by institutions such as the World Bank or International Monetary Fund. The United States would then also consider having diplomatic offices in the two countries' capitals. The final stage would have to wait until the success of Cambodia's elections and establishment of a new national assembly. *If* that happened, the United States would be open to full diplomatic and economic normalization. The plan's architects also added that during each phase, Vietnam had to make progress in accounting for American MIAs to satisfy the conditions for normalization.[21] Considering the complications in Cambodia at the time, the United States' plan to make peace with Vietnam was based on distrust and antagonism. Even though Vietnam had withdrawn most of its troops by 1990, the road to normalization still seemed far too long.

Warriors' Efforts to End a War

Throughout the 1980s, American veterans of the Vietnam War played a significant, dynamic role in accelerating reconciliation and peace-building during a time of restricted, somewhat hostile, communication between the two governments. Transcending personal ordeals and political roadblocks, veterans created an exuberant transnational flow of goods, people, and ideas that helped reshape US-Vietnam relations. Through humanitarian endeavors, cultural exchanges, and peace tours, former enemies transformed themselves and their societies in profound ways. Often overshadowed by the stereotyped image of the tragic, numbed Vietnam vet, stories of American and Vietnamese veterans working side by side to rebuild their shattered worlds remained little known.

The interconnectedness and the bonds between US veterans and their Vietnamese counterparts developed in a unique way. Being former warriors on opposing sides of a prolonged, highly destructive conflict, these veterans seemed to have little in common, and their reconciliation was unthinkable for many. Nevertheless, it was their shared pasts that drove them closer to one another. In their postwar struggles to adjust to their societies and to redefine themselves, these former adversaries realized they had more in common than they did with some of their compatriots. Their shared memories of the war and unpleasant emotions resulting from it underpinned their peace endeavors to transform themselves and their societies. Crossing boundaries, veterans from both sides eagerly worked together to replace the landscapes of war with the foundations of peace.

When Rifles and Tools Changed Places

On a cold December afternoon in 1981, four American veterans landed at Noi Bai International Airport. Awaiting them were high-ranking Vietnamese officials and a group of young soldiers. At the sight, one veteran "swiftly returned to the plane, trembling"; he was thinking of canceling the whole trip. It took the veteran several minutes to recompose himself and to digest what was going on. Then, together with the other three, he proceeded in astonishment toward the friendly salute of their former enemies.[22] The four veterans—Robert "Bobby" O. Muller, Thomas A. Bird, Michael R. Harbert, and John F. Terzano—were making a historic trip on a mission of their own design. Representing the Vietnam Veterans of America (VVA), an organization founded in 1978 and originally known as the Council of Vietnam Veterans, the group was the first of its kind to cross the Pacific seeking reconciliation with its erstwhile adversaries. Upon their return to the United States, the trailblazers faced accusations by some Americans, including veterans, of perpetrating "fraud," and of "serv[ing] Vietnamese propaganda purposes."[23] Some people expressed disappointment because the veterans did not bring home specific information about MIAs. Countering the antireconciliation attitude, VVA associate director Harbert argued, "If nobody is talking to the Vietnamese, no one will find those Americans. You ought to support us."[24] For the group's members, the trip was fruitful on different levels. Collectively, they won Vietnamese leaders' trust, which reinforced their faith in VVA's peace mission. Vietnam's Foreign Minister Nguyen Co Thach asked them to work as a liaison with his government over the issue of American MIAs. Frustrated by the Reagan administration's continued distrust of the Vietnamese government, the Vietnamese minister wished to work with the former combatants instead. Furthermore, Nguyen also promised to develop a cultural exchange program, prompting the VVA representatives to plan a second visit early the following year.[25]

On a personal level, the veterans found a sense of peace, a long-lost feeling for which they were yearning. Thomas Bird spoke of his experience: "The war finally stopped in my mind. The other day I told some Vietnamese officials in Hanoi that I killed some of their people. I needed to tell them. They said they understood."[26] Bird's brief comment speaks volumes about how the act of killing affected combat soldiers. Despite the fact that soldiers are trained, prepared, and paid to kill, overcoming the thought that one actually killed a fellow human is not always easy. Bird's first killing had haunted him for more than a decade, for it was an act of "depriving somebody of everything you want for yourself." He remembered searching his victim's wallet and being shocked when he found the photos of the communist's children and wife. That moment, Bird realized he had killed a fellow human. Those images lingered in him over the years, undeletable.[27] Now Bird "needed to tell" his former enemy what he had done, and their "understand[ing]" was comforting. Similarly, Harbert expressed his feeling: "The war is over, really over for me." Harbert had joined the US Air Force and was assigned bombing missions in North Vietnam during his military tour. Before arriving in Vietnam in 1981, Harbert was "nervous as hell," imagining that he might be imprisoned for his wartime actions. To his relief, the Vietnamese people that he met were not concerned about the past as much as he was.[28] As historian Julia Bleakney observes, "For many veterans, returning to Vietnam is the final and most important step toward recovery from their traumas of the war."[29] Venturing into their former foes' land to find an answer to the question of MIAs, these trailblazers unexpectedly found closure to their personal struggles. Their positive experiences opened a new communication channel that would benefit politicians and veterans on both sides.

Vietnam Veterans of America, the organization that these veterans represented, played a significant role in improving US-Vietnam postwar relations. VVA's delegation arrived in Vietnam during the stalemate of initial governmental interactions over MIA issues in 1981. Bobby Muller, VVA's cofounder and first president, asserted, "We are not trying to substitute for the U.S. Government. The Vietnamese did not invite us. We asked to go because the US Government is not talking to them."[30] VVA's interests in humanitarian causes such as MIAs, Amerasians, Agent Orange, and cultural exchanges, convinced the SRV's authorities, prompting the latter to continue domestic work on MIAs despite governmental disputes. While agreeing to the Vietnamese government's suggestion that VVA function as a liaison, VVA members requested that the SRV reopen talks with the US government. One month following the group's visit, Vietnam informed VVA of its agreement to reconnect with the United States, "pursuant to VVA's requests."[31]

Quarrels occurred again in 1983 when Secretary of State George Shultz commented to ASEAN leaders that Vietnam was "brutal and unhumanitarian." Governmental coordination on MIAs halted once again, compelling Vietnam to ask that VVA receive the newly recovered US soldiers' remains on behalf of its government.[32] In February 1984, VVA communicated with the US government, requesting the participation of governmental representatives at the repatriation ceremony to ensure honors and dignity for the soldiers who died for the country. In his letter to Secretary of State Shultz, VVA President Muller wrote, "We believe this matter requires your immediate attention. . . . In the absence of advance planning by the Department of State and other involved agencies, it may be that repatriation would occur without the presence of official representatives of the United States Government. In our view, this would be unfortunate and would work against further resolution of the MIA issue." Muller emphasized VVA's expectation that "the United States Government will continue to do everything possible in its power" to bring home the identified remains.[33] The request put the State Department back in discussion with Vietnam. VVA's intermediary role was evident in the response from the State Department, confirming that the Vietnamese "had promised to turn over the remains" to VVA and that they "did not wish to break their promise" to the organization. The letter indicated that now Vietnam would also be willing to work directly with the US government on this matter if VVA affirmed its *"willingness to allow* the governments concerned to coordinate a proper turnover in the customary, exclusively government-to-government manner."[34] Once again, VVA succeeded as a catalyst for action between governments.

While VVA's humanitarian endeavors moved the Vietnamese and inspired some fellow Americans, its work was "both difficult and lonely," as described by Gregory Kane, director of VVA special programs.[35] In fact, some Americans condemned VVA for working with communists, regardless of the nature of its agenda. Among the most vocal opponents of VVA was Clifford G. Olson Jr., national commander in chief of the Veterans of Foreign Wars. Upon learning about the possibility that Vietnam may turn over the three soldiers' remains to VVA, Olson publicly asked VVA "to step aside" and accused VVA of being "a hindrance to speedy recovery of remains and resolution of the POW/MIA issue." He wrote to the VVA president, "It is shamefully dishonorable for an organization representing veterans of that conflict to be dealing directly with the communist government of their former enemies. Such activity dishonors the brave men and women who endured that conflict."[36] Olson also wrote to Congress to oppose the establishment of a VVA federal charter, claiming that "our Vietnam veterans have been disgraced and dishonored by the VVA's shameful relationship with the communist governments of Vietnam and Kampuchea."[37] Politics, it seemed, obscured humanitarian concerns. Almost a decade after the end of the conflict, hostility still lingered, and VVA's vision for peace was unimaginable for many.

Striving for reconciliation and mutual understanding, VVA extended its activities beyond humanitarian causes. Its delegation to Vietnam in 1984 dedicated its efforts to a wide range of issues, including MIAs, Amerasians, and Agent Orange. The members of the delegation also visited orphanages and hospitals, which they ranked "from poor to dismal," and discussed potential aid for the underprivileged.[38] In 1985, VVA proposed to send to Vietnam a delegation consisting of a cultural group of six and a tourist group of twenty. While the tourist group wished to travel freely to see the real Vietnam, the cultural ambassadors hoped to meet with Vietnam's minister of cultural affairs to discuss potential exchange programs. Among members of the delegation were representatives of CBS-TV and *New York Magazine*, whose mission was to see Vietnam with their own eyes and provide the US public with images of Vietnam as a country instead of Vietnam as a war. Greg Kane, VVA spokesman, explained: "Americans now see Vietnam through the cloud of war. We need a new view of Vietnam, its people and culture. When veterans can go to Vietnam and see it now, they will see a side of Vietnam they were not able to see before. This can be the start of a real people-to-people bridge that can generate support for continued progress."[39] This vision of promoting cultural exchange for sustainable world peace persisted throughout VVA's course of action. At its 1991 national conference, VVA President John F. Terzano emphasized the organization's core belief: "These people-to-people exchanges shatter the time-frozen images of war that still remain as a haunting for many veterans. . . . There should be a clear and open exchange of ideas between citizens of different nations. It is through the free exchange of information and ideas that tremendous changes in the world can take place."[40] Terzano's words reflected the experiences of those who reconnected with Vietnam as well as a vision of peace and mutual respect, regardless of national interests. While the idea had stood the test of time, its supporters still faced obstacles in their path.

VVA as an organization was productive in its mission to reconstruct world peace through cultural and humanitarian efforts. Its members, as individuals, also effectively contributed to the cause in unique ways. Among VVA's most accomplished members was Thomas A. Bird, whose peace endeavors lasted a lifetime. In 1979, Bird founded the Vietnam Veterans Ensemble Theater Company (VETCo) as "a means for healing" for him and fellow veterans in New York City. VETCo created plays about the reality of war that US soldiers experienced in Vietnam, and its actors consisted of Vietnam veterans. The theater served as a venue for Bird to exorcise his war-inspired demons. It was a place where he could "deal with what was bothering me the most, which was being a Vietnam veteran in America, and with what I think is bothering America most, which is the Vietnam War, which they're being silent about."[41] In 1985, Bird became well known for *Tracers*, his collaborative work with another Vietnam veteran, John Di Fusco, from Los Angeles, California. Di Fusco created the one-act *Tracers* in 1980 to feature individual stories of six veteran-actors. The 1985 two-act *Tracers* presented in New York City maintained two of the original cast and added six new veterans. The show received enthusiastic reviews. Bird commented, "The first time I killed somebody, it transformed my whole life. *Tracers* deals with that question—'How does it feel to kill somebody?' I wanted to produce that question, so to speak."[42] These veterans refused to be forgotten or misunderstood. They spoke of an unpleasant reality of war that only those who lived and died on the battlefield would understand. To borrow Di Fusco's word, the play was "therapeutic" for its creators, actors, and veterans in the audience. It was also an attempt to bridge the gap between veterans and nonveterans, a call for understanding and reconciliation. It was a pursuit of peace.

VETCo extended its activity beyond national borders, organizing cultural exchange programs with Vietnam a decade before diplomatic normalization. In 1986, for example, the company sent its representatives to Vietnam to learn about the country's culture and later invited a group of Vietnamese artists to the United States to explore opportunities for collaborative work. With special interests in Hanoi's water puppetry, Bird worked hard to bring the two countries' puppeteers together.[43] His efforts to promote cultural understanding reflected a desire for peace and friendship. He also proved that international relations were not exclusively governmental tasks and that ordinary citizens could make a difference.

Bird continued to flourish in his peace endeavors. In 1987, he coproduced *Dear America: Letters Home from Vietnam*, an HBO documentary that won several awards, including the 1988 Primetime Emmy and 1989 CableACE awards. In 2011, Bird established the California-based Walking Point Foundation to help Iraq and Afghanistan veterans adjust to civilian life. The nonprofit organization offered one-on-one mentoring programs in such artistic disciplines as film, theater, photography, comedy, painting, drawing, writing, and dancing. In addition to providing veterans an opportunity to use art as a healing tool and to explore their hidden talents, Walking Point Foundation also connected generations of soldiers. Iraq and Afghanistan veterans found comfort in the guidance and care of Vietnam veterans.[44] Bird's lifelong peace efforts were telling. His combat experience in Vietnam in 1965 had a significant impact on his life. While he was "walking point" to reconcile with his own past, Bird led his fellow veterans with great care and nourishment.

Another member of VVA who worked vigorously for world peace was its cofounder and first president Bobby Muller. Unlike many soldiers of the Vietnam War, Muller earned a bachelor's degree before he enlisted in the US Marine Corps and was deployed to Vietnam as an infantry officer in 1968. Like thousands of patriotic Americans growing up after World War II, Muller took the opportunity to serve his country with great enthusiasm and pride. He remembers, "I felt it was my duty as a citizen of the greatest country in the world to join the service. . . . I never questioned the war or studied the history of Vietnam. I only knew that my government wanted me there to repel a massive northern communist invasion threatening the freedom-loving people of South Vietnam."[45] However, the reality of encountering an elusive enemy and having an unreliable ally transformed him into a bitter soldier. He explains, "I was bitter because I put my allegiance in my government. I did so with the best, most honest intentions, believing I was doing the right thing. I gave my country a hundred percent, and they used me as a pawn in a game. . . . The real tragedy is that I was totally naïve. . . . As a college graduate, I was supposed to be educated. I was an idiot. I never asked 'Why?'"[46] After eight months in the country, he was hit by a bullet, which destroyed his lungs and severed his spinal cord, leaving him paralyzed from the chest down.

Physical disability, however, did not hinder Muller from living up to his beliefs. After cofounding VVA in 1978, Muller established the Vietnam Veterans of America Foundation (VVAF) in 1980. Separate and autonomous from the VVA, VVAF is an international organization focused on assisting war victims.[47] Under Muller's leadership, VVAF sponsored a rehabilitation clinic for amputees in Cambodia, where he brought in Indian specialists to teach local people to make aluminum and rubber prostheses at a lower cost. In an effort to raise funds for its activities, VVAF invited international artists to contribute their talents and introduce their cultures to the world. This transnational initiative not only improved the living conditions of people in war-torn countries but also enhanced the Western public's cultural knowledge of the countries they knew little about such as Vietnam, Laos, Cambodia, Nicaragua, and Palestine.[48]

Muller's most distinguishing contribution to world peace was probably his leadership in the creation and operation of the International Campaign to Ban Landmines. It all started in 1992, after his first visit to Cambodia, where more than five hundred people per month, mostly women and children, suffered landmine casualties. Muller started by asking for help from Senator Patrick Leahy of Vermont. In the same year, Senator Leahy and Representative Lane Evans of Illinois introduced a bill, the approval of which made the United States the first country in the world to ban trafficking in antipersonnel landmines. Enthusiastically, Senator Leahy urged President Bill Clinton to recommend the initiative to the United Nations, calling for an international moratorium in the production of the weapon. The president did in 1994, and three years later, the Mine Ban Treaty came into existence, with 142 nations voting in its favor. Ironically, the United States abstained. Nevertheless, the International Campaign to Ban Landmines coshared the 1997 Nobel Peace Prize with its coordinator Jody Williams.[49] Although Muller was not specifically named for the prestigious award, his contribution was obvious. The empathy that he had for the Cambodians and his vision for a landmine-free world inspired many people. That inspiration transpired across boundaries, bringing people to work together for a safer world.

Another Vietnam veterans' early initiative for postwar healing and reconciliation was the William Joiner Center for the Study of War and Social Consequences at the University of Massachusetts, Boston. Established in 1982 and named after the university's first director of veterans affairs who died of Agent Orange-induced liver cancer in 1981, the center set out to serve veterans and all victims of war in dynamic ways. In 1987, the center held a conference that discussed the effects of Agent Orange. For the next two decades, it sent many groups of veterans to Vietnam with various tasks, accompanied by shipments of medical supplies and equipment. It also provided medical training to personnel in hospitals and clinics throughout Vietnam. Among its many incentives was the Full Circle Project, which studies the effects of experiencing Vietnam in peacetime on veterans with post-traumatic stress disorder (PTSD).[50]

The Joiner Center's initiatives were expanded to include varied educational and cultural missions as well. Its first and longtime director, Dr. Kevin Bowen, was a Vietnam veteran who served in the 1st Air Cavalry Division in Vietnam from 1968 to 1969. Since 1987, Bowen crossed the Pacific Ocean many times. In 1989, for example, he joined a small group of veterans to document the ongoing impacts of the war and the effects of the US embargo on the Vietnamese. The following year, 1990, the Joiner Center and the Vietnam Writers Association co-organized the first conference of US and Vietnamese veteran authors in Hanoi. Because of the success of the conference, combined with the belief that "literature heals the consequences of war," the two organizations continued their writers' exchange program, which had started earlier. By exchanging writers and translating literary works into English and Vietnamese, the program enriched its participants' experiences and enhanced the understanding of each other's ways of life in both countries, which, in turn, formed a strong foundation for long-lasting friendship. In 2011, the Vietnamese government honored Bowen with the Phan Chau Trinh Award, an award named after an early twentieth-century Vietnamese poet, writer, and nationalist. The award recognized Bowen's leadership and devotion to the promotion of mutual understanding for peace.[51]

The road that Bowen, the Joiner Center, and their partners had taken, however, was not always smooth. In 1988, the Joiner Center invited two Vietnamese communist writers to attend a literary conference in Boston. One of them was Le Luu, who had published a novel that had stirred debates both inside and outside the borders of Vietnam two years earlier.[52] Extremist, conservative authorities condemned Le for an unpatriotic, counter-revolutionary description of postwar society. The year 1986, however, also signaled a major social transformation for Vietnam with the Communist Party's open-door policy. Subsequently, liberal readers praised Le for his courageous denunciation of both opportunistic quasicommunists and the fractured membership of the ruling party. When his invitation to visit the United States arrived in Vietnam, it caused widespread controversy and deep suspicion. After multiple meetings among Vietnamese authorities, and with the intervention of Le Duc Tho, former prime minister of North Vietnam, Le finally gained approval to visit the United States. Nevertheless, that was only the beginning of the veteran's arduous journey. Without a US embassy in Vietnam, Le and another writer had to go to Thailand to obtain tourist visas to the United States. After three weeks of numerous phone calls among Thailand, the United States, and Vietnam, including those of Vietnam's Foreign Minister Nguyen Co Thach, Le finally obtained a visa; the other writer had to return to Vietnam. When Le arrived in Boston, the twelve-day conference had concluded its eighth day.[53]

The visit of the first Vietnamese communist writer since 1975 caused much curiosity in Boston. Le spent most of his time answering questions from both veterans and nonveterans. Recalling the experience twenty-two years later, the old veteran sobbed as he repeated the sarcastic questions of some hostile Americans: "Would you like to renew your relations with the United States?" "What do you come here for?" "How many more tons of rice do you think you could get?" "The remains of forty-one American soldiers are still in Vietnam. Where are they? Once you return them all to us, we will give you some rice." In 1988, however, Le shed no tears in front of the questioners. In his simple and straightforward manner, he replied, "How could you be that disrespectful to Vietnamese people? How could you show such cruelty to your fellow soldiers? Trading rice for their bodies seems malicious to me." Le recalled that these questioners seemed to soften after the conversation and that he understood their bitterness.[54]

Le's overall impression, however, was that great commonalities existed between US and Vietnamese veterans. They shared similar concerns about postwar adjustments, government policies toward veterans, and the relations between the two countries. The friendliness and sincerity of many warmed his heart. In one meeting, Le was telling of a battle that he had witnessed as a war correspondent; a US veteran spoke up to say that he was there on the same battlefield, and that he was glad that they had not killed each other. In a still moment, the former warriors hugged each other, realizing they had more in common than they had thought.[55]

The ordeals undergone by Kevin Bowen, Luu, and other members of the Joiner Center's programs proved that they were true warriors for peace. In the fog of hostility that obscured the vision of many, these veterans held strong beliefs in their peace efforts. They projected a historical perspective of conflict, believed that they could affect transformation, and assumed their responsibility. Obviously, they endured uneasy, awkward moments but they were willing to set aside their differences and focused only on mutual understanding based on their shared unpleasant pasts. It seems ironic that former combatants of the war built the bridge of reconciliation on the foundation of horrific memories of wartime. Nonetheless, these veterans proved that the paradox was logical, for only those who had survived war could truly understand the value of peace.

The Joiner Center's literary exchange and collaborative programs significantly contributed to the enhancement of mutual understanding among US and Vietnamese veterans. Through scholarly visits and translated works, veteran writers had great opportunities to share their experiences and learn more about their colleagues on the other side of the former frontline. Renowned novels such as *Paco's Story* by Larry Heinemann and *Nỗi Buồn Chiến Tranh* (*The Sorrow of War*) by Bao Ninh were translated into Vietnamese and English, respectively. *Paco's Story* won the 1987 National Book Award for Fiction and the 1988 Carl Sandburg Literary Arts Award. *The Sorrow of War*, arguably the most popular book about the Vietnam War written by a Vietnamese author, won the 1991 Vietnam Writers Association Award and the 2011 Nikkei Asia Prize for Culture.

Both novels reflected personal wartime experiences of the authors, who later became close friends. Heinemann returned to Vietnam in 1990 for the first time since 1968, thanks to the Joiner Center. Later he made several trips to collect Vietnamese folklore and mythologies.[56] According to Heinemann, he and Bao Ninh "shared a great deal."[57] Heinemann remembers a conversation with his Vietnamese friend: "I asked Bao Ninh, 'What was the most difficult task that you were asked to do during wartime?' He stayed quiet for a moment, looking into the distance, and then said, 'Burying my brothers—my fellow soldiers.' From then on, I stopped complaining about the heat, humidity, monsoon, and other trouble of my service in Vietnam."[58] Being one of the three survivors from an original battalion of five hundred soldiers after six years of combat, Bao Ninh was not dramatizing his experience. As Heinemann observes, "Bao Ninh just looks like he never had an easy day in his life."[59] Via the Joiner Center, Bao Ninh visited the United States in 2000. In a public reading of his book at Harvard University, the English version read by Heinemann was greeted with "stunned silence followed by thunderous applause."[60] Bao Ninh's story was not one of the victor but one of a combat soldier narrowly escaping death and one of a veteran struggling to adjust to civilian life. His story highlighted the human price of a political victory and emphasized the far-reaching effects of combat experiences. He spoke not only for the North Vietnamese soldiers but for all combat veterans. Revealing the horror of war, Bao Ninh was in search of peace.

Sharing a vision similar to that of the Joiner Center, Fredy Champagne worked with other veterans from Garberville, California, to establish the Veterans Vietnam Restoration Project (VVRP) in 1988. Inspired by Oliver Stone's movie *Platoon* and a team of veterans "doing citizen reparations work" in Nicaragua, Champagne decided that he and other veterans should do what his government had failed to do. He asserted, "I wanted to break down the embargo, to work on healing PTSD, and, in general, to do people-to-people diplomacy. I wanted to discover the Vietnamese people as a people, not just an enemy."[61] Champagne's initial thoughts evolved into VVRP's two-fold mission: first, "to promote friendship" between the two peoples, "leading to the normalization of relations between the two countries," and second, "to assist the U.S. veterans and other Americans in healing from the psychic ravages of the war by allowing them to return to Vietnam to help rebuild a country which they once sought to destroy."[62] In April 1989, the organization sent its first team of twelve to Vung Tau, a coastal city sixty miles east of Saigon, for eight weeks to help build the Friendship Clinic. Until this operation ended in 2014, VVRP had sent twenty-nine teams, including approximately one hundred and sixty veterans, to work side by side with the Vietnamese in construction projects. For twenty-five years, the organization's volunteers built hundreds of elementary schools, medical clinics, vocational centers, and houses for disabled veterans.[63]

When Champagne founded the VVRP, he emphasized the essential "meaningful interactions" between US veterans and the Vietnamese. It was through these interactions that they got to understand each other and embrace their connections. Larry Hlavaty told a powerful story of his last work day in a commune of an ethnic minority in central Vietnam. A ninety-year-old lady signaled that she wanted to talk to him. She touched his gray hair then removed her traditional hat and took Hlavaty's hand to feel a large scar on her head and another on her cheek. Through the translator, she told Hlavaty that she got those scars from US bombs and that she was the sole survivor of her entire family. Hlavaty recalled, "My heart sank. As my tears began to flow, I told her how sorry I felt. A few seconds later, she began to smile and said, 'Thank you for coming to see us. Thank you for building us a school. Thank you, thank you . . . thank you,' and she reached out and hugged me."[64] The elderly lady's "ability to forgive" was unbelievable to Hlavaty, but he did not realize that his and his team's efforts were equally incredible to her, and probably in a similar way, she finally felt at peace.

Tony Shaw, who served in the Twenty-Fifth Division in 1969, shared a detailed blog on the organization's website. One of his special moments was when he gave his bike to a little boy in a remote area by the Laotian border. Shaw wrote, "I will never adequately be able to describe the look on this little boy's face when our interpreter Tuyen told him I was giving him the bike. He bowed deeply and said in halting English with extreme politeness, 'Thank you.' . . . It is moments like this that have made this trip so worthwhile." Shaw echoed Hlavaty's remarks on his experience, "These people, our former bitter enemies, responded to us in the warmest possible manner."[65] Another veteran, Charles W. Bruton, volunteered for a project in Quang Tri, where he had served in the 1st Aviation Brigade in 1968 to 1969. After thirty-four years struggling with nightmares and obsessions of "that traumatic year," he returned to the old demilitarized zone (DMZ), which he "knew like the back of [his] hand, but only from the air." His team's mission in 2002 was to build ten homes for disabled veterans and a computer room for an orphanage in the same area where he had directed artillery and air strikes almost every day in 1968. At first, the journey was nerve-racking for the former warrior, but it ended with his profound transformation. Bruton wrote, "The gift of forgiveness I received from the Vietnamese people has healed me from the scars of the past. It has allowed me to rest at night knowing that it is over and all is well with the people on the DMZ. That gift is priceless!"[66] VVRP's achievements consisted not only of the much-needed facilities that it built but also stories like those of Bruton, Shaw, and Hlavaty. The transnational projects allowed the possibility of reconciliation—with oneself, one another, and the hostility of the past. Perhaps it was not coincidental that VVRP chose what to build, for the construction categories were perfectly symbolic: the veterans' homes were for them to adjust and move on, the medical clinics were to heal, and the schools were to nurture.

Another significant organization founded before the normalization of diplomatic relations between the two countries was Vets With A Mission (VWAM). Bill Kimball, the founder of VWAM, had served as a mortarman of the US Army's First Cavalry Division during the Tet Offensive. Kimball returned to Vietnam as a pastor in 1988, twenty years after he had seen the country for the first time. To his dismay, not much had changed; the scars of the conflict were ubiquitous and seemed beyond the ability of the locals. He decided that his fellow Americans could and should do something to help the Vietnamese. Upon his return to the United States, he gathered a small group of Vietnam veterans and founded VWAM in the same year.[67]

VWAM's goal was to bring former US soldiers back to Vietnam to help the country recover from the wounds of war. As one member posted on the organization's website, "It is our heart's desire to see the people of this country know that former enemies can come together in forgiveness and reconciliation to each other."[68] The organization's mission focused on medical care and training. Its volunteers included both veterans and nonveterans. Soon after its establishment, VWAM began its commitment with the first group of volunteers helping Polio Orphanage #5 in Saigon in 1989. By 2014, the organization had built more than thirty medical clinics and health stations as well as a few orphanages and other facilities, mostly in remote, rural areas. It also sponsored heart surgery for impoverished children. Furthermore, it offered medical training and provided medical supplies and equipment to the clinics that it helped build as well as to other existing clinics.[69] In addition to humanitarian programs, VWAM got permission from the Vietnamese government to distribute Bibles and Christian literature in areas where its teams worked. That VWAM could include a Christian mission in its humanitarian agenda reveals the Vietnamese government's special respect, trust, and appreciation of the teams' efforts. Proselytization is outlawed in Vietnam, and the government rarely grants similar favors to foreign religious groups.

What surprised the members of VWAM was that their assistance to the Vietnamese turned out to help them in unexpected ways. Chuck Ward, who had served in the Navy in Da Nang from 1969 to 1972 commented after his second trip to Vietnam in 1994:

[It] really helped to meet ex-VC and ex-NVA soldiers when I was there. They had already moved on from the war. I spent a lot of time with them, and it didn't take long to see that they were just like us—they had been soldiers doing what they had to do, what our governments wanted us to do, but they were really just normal people. And they were very happy we were there.[70]

Ward, who continued to work with VWAM, eventually became its executive director.

Roger Helle, vice chair of the VWAM board, had an experience similar to that of Ward. Helle served three tours in Vietnam as a marine and was wounded three times. He made his first trip to Vietnam with VWAM in 1989 and continued to do so on sixteen further occasions. One of the reasons that compelled Helle to keep returning to Vietnam was an unexpected reunion with the former North Vietnamese regiment commander whose unit almost wiped out Helle's company in a heated battle. Helle recalled, "He starts asking me, 'Why are you doing all this to help us?' I told him, 'God has taken away all my pain of Vietnam. He loves me. He loves you. I love you. And that's why.' The translator couldn't translate everything for a minute because she was crying. When she finished, the guy got up and walked around the table and gave me a hug."[71] The story is a powerful example of reconciliation. A quick read of the veterans' profiles shows only differences: they were citizens of enemy nation-states, speaking different languages, and they would have killed each other if they could when they were younger. Nevertheless, they overcame their personal pain and spoke to each other in the language of friendship and love.

Despite its long-term commitment and prestige in Vietnam, VWAM occasionally had to endure bureaucratic harassment. After twenty years of service, the organization faced an unprecedented ordeal in 2014. Three weeks before its medical team left for Vietnam, local police visited VWAM's office in Da Nang and told the staff to remove the organization's sign. The following week, Hue Friendship Organization (HueFO), the team's sponsor in the province of Thua Thien Hue, announced that team members had to get tourist visas at an extra cost of $2,400 instead of the visas it normally obtained for them. Next, the entry airport customs officials confiscated most of the medicine and eyeglasses they brought for humanitarian purposes despite VWAM's customs clearance letter, which had always worked before. However, the items were mysteriously returned after forty-eight hours. When the team arrived in Hue two days later, HueFO still could not obtain permission for its activities, and nobody knew when or if permission would be granted. Unable to obtain an explanation to these unprecedented obstacles, VWAM's team refused to be harassed further. Its members met and unanimously agreed to shift their humanitarian efforts to Cambodia instead. They canceled all plans for Vietnam and booked tickets for a flight to Cambodia the next day. Then the tide turned. Learning about VWAM's changed plans, Vietnamese officials in Hue and Hanoi vehemently worked after hours, and all permissions were granted within five hours. On top of that was a "serious meeting" between Vietnamese authorities and VWAM's team on the same evening. With apologies made and accepted, the team stayed.[72] While the hassle was unusual, it showed VWAM's capability to deal with the inappropriate exercise of power. Ward once wrote, "Sometimes reconciliation, forgiveness and charity are not the easiest things to do."[73] Although that statement referred to a different challenge, it applied perfectly to VWAM's experience in 2014. Despite the provocation, the team stayed true to its core missions: reconciliation, forgiveness, and charity.

Another demonstration of transnational love and friendship was the testimony of George Mizo, founder of the Vietnam Friendship Village in Hanoi. Inspired by President John F. Kennedy, the young, patriotic Mizo had enlisted in the army and landed in Vietnam shortly before the Tet Offensive. Soon he realized that what his parents, teachers, and government had taught him was not exactly true. They told him, "It is wrong to kill, except in war." The Search and Destroy mission taught him that "it is wrong to kill. Period!"[74] After he was wounded the third time and learned that he was the sole survivor of his platoon, Mizo decided to devote the remaining years of his life to peace. In 1986, he returned to Vietnam, sharing his intention of building a pagoda of peace. However, when he discussed the idea again in 1989 with Georges Doussin, the French president of the Association Républicaine d'Anciens Combattants et Victimes de Guerre (Republican Association of Retired Veterans and Victims of War), and Phan Binh, the Vietnamese ambassador to France, in Paris, the men chose a more practical project. They began to discuss the construction of a residential facility for Vietnamese disabled veterans and orphaned children. Mizo worked tirelessly and got support from veterans not only in the United States but also in Germany, France, Japan, Britain, and later on Canada and South Korea. Together with the Veterans Association of Vietnam, these international veterans saw the beginning of their dream materialize in 1993 with the groundbreaking ceremony of the Vietnam Friendship Village on the outskirts of Hanoi.[75]

Built on Mizo's endeavor for peace and reconciliation, the Friendship Village signified the strength of friendship and the possibilities it presented. While the governments remained contentious, these individuals came together with a shared belief: former foes could become friends. Mike Cooper, president of the Santa Cruz Veterans Affairs Office, stated, "What we're seeing now is the end of a war and the making of a long friendship between peoples and individuals. Our soldiers are ending that war. We're not going to wait for the government."[76] When construction was completed in 1998, it became a "home" to hundreds of children and veterans with Agent Orange–related health problems.[77] For Mizo, a victim of dioxin himself, the villagers were his extended family.

Mizo passed away in 2002, but his inspiration lived on, and his German wife Rosemarie continued to devote herself to the cause of peace, giving substance to Mizo's words: "Hope is an illusion. If you want to create something, you have to actively work it and not hope that somebody else . . . somehow . . . some miracle is going to happen."[78] Today, the facility is capable of providing medical care to one hundred and fifty individuals at any one time; children can stay there for up to two years or to fourteen years of age, and veterans can stay for up to one year. The village strives for self-sufficiency, with residents growing their own rice and vegetables as well as raising livestock. The children not only learn basic life skills but also receive vocational training. Referring to transnational efforts to overcome the aftermath of war, a French veteran humbly remarked: "The village is a tiny little light, a tiny little light in this tunnel we are in. But with a little light, sometimes we can find the sun."[79] The "little light" that these veterans brought to the victims of war is a magnificent demonstration of reconciliation and love across boundaries.

Diverging from common themes of US veterans' projects in Vietnam, which emphasized practical humanitarian endeavors, David Thomas sought to build a cultural bridge across the Pacific Ocean with a different medium: the arts. Drafted right after his graduation from the Portland School of Art in Maine, Thomas set foot in Vietnam for the first time in 1968 as a member of the Twentieth Combat Engineer Battalion of the Eighteenth Brigade. He furthered his education after coming home from the war and became an arts professor at Emmanuel College in Boston. Thomas "buried Vietnam until 1987." Then, US popular culture revived memories of the distant conflict that many wanted to forget through movies like *Platoon*, *Full Metal Jacket*, and *Born on the Fourth of July*. Deciding to return to Vietnam, he was impressed that the locals "had no anger, no hostility, no sense of revenge."[80] Thomas visited the National Museum of Fine Arts in Hanoi, bringing along a dozen of his Vietnam paintings, mostly portraits of children. As Nguyen Van Chung, the museum's deputy director, showed interest and appreciation, Thomas said, "They're yours." Touched by this gesture of friendship, the deputy director tried to think of a way to return the favor. The two men agreed on mounting a small exhibition featuring two US artists and two Vietnamese artists, two paintings each, at Emmanuel College.[81] That spontaneous decision was a prelude to significant cultural transnationalism.

In early 1988, Thomas exhibited his old and new Vietnam paintings in Boston, Massachusetts, including depictions of the children he encountered during his summer 1987 trip and a portrait of Ho Chi Minh, the iconic wartime leader of Vietnam. Then he returned to Vietnam again in 1988, 1989, and 1990 to collect artwork for the Indochina Arts Project, which he established with the assistance of the Joiner Center of the University of Massachusetts. In those trips, he continued to bring along gifts from US artists and art books, which were invaluable to his Vietnamese colleagues. In January 1991, with some small grants and $20,000 from his own savings from three years of hard work, Thomas introduced to the US public the exhibition *As Seen by Both Sides*. Journalist Christine Temin described Thomas's show as "unique" among all the exhibits about Vietnam because it was the first to feature twenty Vietnamese colleagues alongside twenty US artists, among them former fighters of opposing sides. In addition to the eighty art works, the show also included an invaluable 128-page catalog consisting of interviews with all the artists and their photographs. A Boston family donated nearly $100,000 for the creation of the catalog.[82]

As Seen by Both Sides traveled to seventeen museums in the United States and three in Vietnam. Designed as a cultural bridge that promoted mutual understanding for peace, the project achieved its objective and received positive responses. Thomas claimed, "Literally, hundreds of people have come to me after seeing this exhibit and said, 'I never thought of the Vietnamese as real people.' We thought of Vietnam as a war, not as a nation of mothers, children, artists, plumbers or whatever."[83] A Vietnamese journalist commented, "The war chapter has closed. It may take decades to heal its wounds. But 'As Seen by Both Sides' is a sign of lasting peace that arts can contribute."[84] An article in the *Battle Creek Enquirer* of Michigan remarked, "'As Seen by Both Sides' has helped to launch that healing process in Battle Creek. For that, we are grateful. But this is only a beginning. More sides to this story need to be seen, touched, and heard, so the horrors of the past can help to prevent new ones."[85] As John Olbrantz, director of the Whatcom Museum of History and Art in Bellingham, Washington, stated, "I think this exhibit will continue to drive home the point that war is ugly. . . . War, regardless of where it is, is hell." The exhibit's journey, however, was bumpy at times.

Without diplomatic relations between the two governments, everything had to go through the US embassy in Thailand. According to journalist Christine Temin, telephone communication via Bangkok cost ten dollars per minute, and one of Thomas's calls actually cost him $600.[86] Even at that cost, Thomas failed in his attempt to obtain visas for two of the Vietnamese artists to attend the show's grand opening. The exhibition also faced protests and cancellations because numerous Americans and Vietnamese immigrants considered it "communist propaganda." One member of the Vietnam Veterans of America Chapter 313, for example, viewed the show as "an inherent—and upsetting— apology to the Vietnamese."[87]

By and large, *As Seen by Both Sides* succeeded and paved the way for more exciting ideas to follow. The Smithsonian approached David Thomas, and he suggested an exhibit that would bring together Vietnamese artists from both sides of the Pacific, whose work would solely depict Vietnamese culture, with nothing about war. That was the birth of *An Ocean Apart: Contemporary Vietnamese Art from the United States and Vietnam*, a show launched by the Smithsonian Institution Traveling Exhibition Service in 1995, in time to celebrate the diplomatic normalization between the two countries. Thomas's initial Indochina Arts Project had evolved into the Indochina Arts Partnership (IAP), continuing its mission to connect artists across borders and enrich transnational communities.[88] While still focusing on Vietnam, IAP expanded its partnership with other Southeast Asian countries. Hundreds of artists, arts faculty, and students have crossed the Pacific in both directions to learn and to contribute. In Vietnam, Thomas was nicknamed "the ambassador who heals the wounds of war." In 2000, he became the first foreigner to receive the Vietnam Medal of Culture, and in 2010, he was awarded the Vietnam Medal of Fine Arts, tokens of appreciation for his contributions to Vietnamese arts.[89]

In the context of restricted communication between the United States and Vietnamese governments, Thomas's initiative was daring. On the one hand, Vietnam's leadership was still suspicious about the influence of the Western world. The import of "American culture" was a sensitive issue in Vietnam in the 1980s. On the other hand, the US public was not quite ready to see visual images that might remind it of a foreign conflict that had dramatically divided the nation. Vietnamese immigrants' memories of the war and their desperate escapes were still fresh; reconciliation seemed premature for them. To an extent, Thomas "forced" people from all sides to face the images that troubled them and to realize that the war was actually over. By introducing Vietnamese people in their daily life and their worldviews, he humanized the Vietnamese people, compelling Americans to connect to them in new ways. His transnational cultural endeavors reminded people from all sides that, as human beings, they had much in common and yet they had much more to learn from one another. It is unlikely that those who understood each other would go to war.

Peace Tours on Bumpy Roads

On November 3, 1985, an article on the *New York Times* stirred attention with the title "Vietnam Is Giving American Tourism a Trial Run." The article claimed that "Vietnam is ready to experiment with American tourism," suggesting it would accept the first group of ten tourists by the end of the year. Vietnam's business partner was Greg Kane and his company, the Indochina Consulting Group of Westbury, Long Island, New York. The company specialized in Vietnam veterans' issues. Kane, who had traveled to Vietnam several times, said that he had "a backlog of people asking how they could get to go" but that for the first trip, he would give priority to Vietnam veterans. The article clarified, "Although the two nations do not have diplomatic relations, Americans are not prohibited by the United States from visiting Vietnam. But in the past, Vietnam, which wants an American embassy in Hanoi, has denied Americans tourist visas."[90] A hope for a normal relationship between the two countries was glimmering "at the end of the tunnel." However, the road to normalization was to remain bumpy for years.

In March 1988, the US Department of the Treasury issued a new rule prohibiting US travel agents and nonprofit organizations from "arranging, promoting, or facilitating" tours to places that it listed as "enemy countries," among them Cuba, North Korea, Cambodia, and Vietnam. The regulation sought to prevent the flow of the US dollar and products into these nations. Under this ban, US tourists to "enemy countries" could only buy air tickets from American travel agents but had to make all other travel arrangements in the country of destination or a third country such as Canada, Mexico, or Thailand. In late 1988, the Connecticut-based Lindblad Travel, which started organizing tours to Vietnam and Cambodia in 1987, was raided by "armed Treasury Department agents" who "seized documents and a major bank account at the company." The ban fueled outrage among Vietnam veterans. Don Mills, a former army infantryman, commented, "Twenty years ago, the government was going to arrest me because I didn't want to go to Vietnam. Now they are going to arrest me because I want to go."[91] Mills was chairman of the Return Trip Committee of the VVA Akron chapter in Ohio, which had organized tours to Vietnam for 205 veterans between 1985 and 1990. Like other travel agents, he was ordered to "immediately terminate performing any activities involving travel tours to Vietnam"; otherwise he was facing punishment ranging from fines of up to $50,000 or up to ten years' imprisonment, or both, under the new law.[92]

The new regulations of the Treasury Department reflected the US government's inability to move on from the past conflict. It maintained hostility toward Vietnam while criticizing the latter for not being cooperative. High politics once again proved punitive, not only to the US government's former enemy but also to its own citizens. Concerned about the material flow into Vietnam, government bureaucrats ignored the need of numerous Americans to reconcile with past memories of war. Christopher G. Hankin, deputy assistant secretary of state, claimed, "The purpose of travel restrictions is simple: to deny the target country the hard currency revenues that travel would produce."[93] It was simple indeed! Hankin and proponents of the ban simply saw the money potentially flow into Vietnam, but they did not bother to wonder why the warriors wanted to revisit the landscapes that had taken away part of their youth. Failing to put the Vietnam veterans in perspective, US bureaucrats allowed politics to obscure the legitimate needs and rights to travel of American citizens.

Return trips, especially group tours, proved beneficial to veterans. Many expressed their gratitude to the tour organizers and shared the healing effects that they experienced because of the trips. Joseph M. Lafatch wrote to the Return Trip Committee, "Prior to my return in '88 I often experienced vivid nightmares and even reenacted these combat experiences mentally during my waking hours. Having returned, I am now sometimes often able to replace these thoughts with memories of the now peaceful, seemingly timeless little country we saw together. The respect the Vietnamese people showed us for being warriors was something I'd yearned for but frankly never received it at home."[94] Similarly, Gary Parker considered the trip "the most therapeutic thing a Viet vet could do" because "it allows one to write their own final chapter on the war." He poetically said that his trip to Vietnam in 1969 was a "lifetime of experiences," while his return in 1988 was "an experience of a lifetime."[95] Maribeth Theisen, a mental health professional who joined one of the tours, observed that "those who began the trip with apprehensions and painful memories undergo a steady transformation as the trip progressed." In her description, the veterans opened themselves to embrace the local people, to learn about their culture, and to build new memories of Vietnam.[96] According to Dr. Matthew J. Friedman, executive director of the US Department of Veterans Affairs' National Center for Post-Traumatic Stress Disorders, image replacement is crucial to the treatment of PTSD. Image replacement is the concept of visiting the changed landscape of the scene of the trauma in order to perceive the changes that have taken place and to integrate one's new interactions with that environment so as to diminish old images of the trauma.[97]

Greg Kleven, who served in Vietnam in 1967, decided to revisit Vietnam twenty years later. He had tried to move on with his life and thought he had "learned to live with the flashbacks and nightmares," but then his flashbacks and nightmares became worse and "more frightening than ever."[98] After more than six months of struggling and getting frustrated with bureaucratic procedures to obtain necessary travel documents, he found out about the VVA Return Trip Committee. In January 1988, he joined the committee's tour, thinking he "was returning to a war zone." The trip, however, helped him discover that "not only the war was over, but there wasn't any resentment on the part of the Vietnamese," and that "finding an enemy to fight was impossible." For Kleven, the return allowed him to put his war memories in perspective and add new memories that were not combat related, which helped balance his thoughts and dreams about Vietnam. He appreciated the organized group and thought of it as "a hand to hold or a shoulder to lean on, "especially for those who took their first trip back.[99] Kleven voiced his opposition to the travel law in an eloquent letter to John Myers, treasurer of the Return Trip Committee:

> When I hear of the trouble that you and Don [Mills] are having with our Treasury Department it makes me mad. The trips should be encouraged, not restricted. It should be made as easy as possible for those vets who choose to return. There are enough obstacles in the way to getting over the war. We don't need the Treasury Department making it more difficult. . . . Every year thousands of WW2 veterans return to the place of their battles, driven by a thousand different reasons. And never are their motives questioned. Why do Vietnam vets have to explain or justify their wanting to return? I'm being told that Vietnam is our enemy, and that travel over there is trading with the enemy. But what am I trading? Some of my own hard earned dollars in exchange for peace of mind.[100]

Similarly, another participant on such a return trip wrote to John Myers and Don Mills about its positive effects and his disappointment with the tour ban. It is worth quoting him in full:

Your term of "image replacement" is, at least in my experience, completely accurate. For me, the return trip was a true cathartic experience. The old terrifying and evil images of Vietnam were purged, being replaced by new and more placid and less sinister images. . . . I think if most folks were aware of the amount of work it entails to help others return to face what was once a nightmare, and for many still returns as a nightmare all too often, they would give you the highest possible award for good citizenship.

For the Treasury to threaten you with fines and imprisonment for these very same acts of benevolence is incomprehensible; or at the very least a travesty of the system of justice in this country. . . . No person, agency or government should have the right to prevent us from returning to a place which had such a great impact on us as individuals and as a society. It is way past time to begin to repair that which was so painfully injured so long ago. As it says in the Old Testament "there is a time for everything" and this is a "time to heal."[101]

In opposition to the ban, some veterans employed legal procedures to re-move the restrictions imposed by the Treasury Department. Myers and Mills sought help from US Representative Tom Sawyer from Ohio. Greg Kleven of California followed suit, writing to US Representative George Miller of California. Kleven highlighted the devotion of Myers and Mills and the sig-nificance of their continued assistance to veterans or anyone interested in vis-iting Vietnam. He pleaded, "I am asking you, as my elected representative, to help in any way that you can to help change the law."[102] Others testified for Representative Howard Berman's "Free Trade in Ideas" bill. During the congressional hearing, Joseph Lafatch spoke of his personal transformation after returning to Vietnam: "I opened up and talked about things I'd tried to bury and listened to others do the same. I started to let the wall down and made new friends." He concluded, "If America wants to send Don Mills and John Myers to prison for organizing these trips then shame on her for she is wrong."[103] John Terzano, VVAF president and one of the first four combat veterans who returned to Vietnam in 1981, argued in the same hearing that the right to travel, which was recognized as a fundamental human right by the United Nations in 1948, "is important to the democratic ideals upon which the United States was established."[104] He analyzed that although the existing law did not prohibit Americans from traveling to the "enemy" countries as individuals, it hindered individuals' ability to travel because many could not handle what journalist David C. Unger called the "double paper curtain"—the bureaucratic hassles in both countries.[105] Terzano also pointed out that the US embargo on Vietnam, which was effective under the Trading with the Enemy Act of 1917, "defies logic that Vietnam is still being punished under a law designed to prevent Americans from assisting an enemy during a time of war when the United States signed Peace Accords with Vietnam 17 years ago."[106] Tom Condon, a Vietnam veteran and journalist, cited other reasons why people should be free to travel to Vietnam, whether as individuals or in groups:

> Veterans who'd like to go back should be able to do so. Vietnamese-Americans should be able to come and go without hassle. American businessmen should be there. Our allies are certainly jumping with both feet. . . . American scientists should be there in strength, working on mutual problems such as Agent Orange damage. At the Brandie Schieb Children's Fund, we have heard from the parents of 64,000 children with maladies that may be related to Agent Orange. The Vietnamese people have more than a million people so afflicted. It's a crime we're not working together.[107]

From different arenas, veterans voiced their concerns about the travel restrictions in particular and the grim effects of the US embargo on Vietnam in general. Larry Pressler, the first Vietnam veteran elected to the US Senate and a member of the Senate Foreign Relations Committee, stated that upon his return from a visit to Vietnam in 1988, many veterans contacted him expressing their "eager[ness] to renew their ties to that country." Pressler cited several reasons for their eagerness, including searching for children and Vietnamese friends, working on MIA issues, and simply revisiting the places where they had served. He stated that while Vietnam was ready to normalize its relations with the United States, the latter's policy gave Vietnam no choice but to ally with the Soviet Union, which in turn would potentially do more harm than good to the United States. For Pressler, if the United States wanted Vietnam to cooperate more in resolving MIA questions, Americans should consider establishing regular official contacts with the Vietnamese and responding to urgent humanitarian needs. Similarly, he argued, the United States could not simply "preach about withdrawal to the Vietnamese" regarding the issue of Cambodia; rather, it needed to "shoulder some share of responsibility" by working with China and the Association of South East Asian Nations (ASEAN) to ensure peace and freedom from the Khmer Rouge in Cambodia.

Viewing the embargo from a strategic perspective, he remarked, "Our policy of isolation has reached the point of diminishing returns."[108]

In opposition to roadblocks, some veterans chose to circumvent the law—a strategy often employed by the powerless in their struggle against established authority. This time, however, the powerless made international headlines. On August 29, 1991, an unusual scene took place in Vietnam: a group of more than thirty American men and women, ranging from nineteen to seventy-five years of age, walked the streets of Hanoi holding US and Vietnamese flags. Mixing among the professionals and retirees were four Vietnam veterans, a World War II veteran being the oldest and a Vietnamese-born American being the youngest. Singing "We Shall Overcome," the activists were conducting their "peace walk" to oppose the US embargo on Vietnam and to call for normalization of relations between the two countries. The "peace walkers" planned to do symbolic walks in major cities of Vietnam, including Hanoi, Vinh, Hue, Da Nang, and Saigon. Before the walk, the group gave twenty boxes of medical supplies to flood victims of a remote mountainous province. Originally, the California-based International Peace Works (IPW) organized and sponsored the peace walk. However, when the Treasury Department denied the group a license to travel and warned that its members may face fines and imprisonment under the existing law, IPW dropped out and the participants made their own travel arrangements. Technically, they traveled to Vietnam as law-abiding individuals—IPW President Allan Affeldt was among them—but the group's spirit and activities remained unchanged. World War II veteran Kermit Dorius asserted, "The main purpose [of the walk] is to call attention to the U.S.-imposed trade embargo and the difficulties it has created for the Vietnamese and their economy."[109] Affeldt pointed out that the US public was not aware of the crippling effects of economic isolation and, for him, "there are at least as many casualties from the embargo as from the war."[110]

The peace walk is an excellent illustration of the strength of people's agency against institutional power. Prohibition of organized travel caused trouble for participants, but it could not stop them. In fact, the peace activists made extra efforts to overcome roadblocks. To some extent, the power relationship shifted. The peace walkers claimed the victory of winning the hearts and minds of international communities. There is no quantifiable evidence of how directly the veterans' activities affected policy change; other social groups' contributions were undeniable, and changing international politics also played a significant role. Nonetheless, restrictions on organized travel to Vietnam became ineffective in December 1991, opening opportunities for the transnational flow of people, goods, and ideas. Immediately following the lifting of the travel ban, Lindblad Cruising Company, whose Vietnam tours were jeopardized in 1988 because of the law, organized its first cruise to Vietnam's major ports in January 1992.[111]

An Aura of Peace Initiatives on Varied Fronts

In addition to US veterans, other citizens also ardently advocated for normalized relations between the two countries. Among the most influential of the organizations that promoted US-Vietnam friendship was the US Committee for Scientific Cooperation with Vietnam (USCSCV). Founded in 1978 by Edward Lee Cooperman, a physics professor at California State University, Fullerton, the committee dedicated its efforts to "alleviating the academic isolation and continuing underdevelopment suffered by the people of Vietnam and Laos." USCSCV promoted the principles that scholarly inquiry should expand beyond national boundaries and that transnational interactions would enhance mutual understanding and respect. It started with small academic exchange programs, but it soon evolved into a major organization that sponsored scientific, humanitarian, and academic projects.[112] By 1989, the nonprofit organization, which had five hundred and fifty academic members, had sponsored some forty projects in Vietnam.[113] USCSCV's vision not only brought US and Vietnamese scientists together through exchange and collaborative research but also saved many Vietnamese lives through extensive medical aid programs.

USCSCV underwent perhaps the worst tragedy in the history of NGOs when Cooperman was murdered in 1984 by a Vietnamese refugee who was also Cooperman's student. The murderer, Lam Van Minh, was convicted of involuntary manslaughter, in what many called a "mistrial," and sentenced to three years in prison. However, he was released after twenty months due to his "good behavior." Although Lam claimed that Cooperman's death had resulted from a gun accident when Cooperman was showing him how to aim a gun, and although his attorney, Alan May, successfully defended Lam's innocence, the trial remained controversial. Cooperman's family, friends, and colleagues argued that it had been a political assassination ordered by radical right-wing Vietnamese refugees. A few months before his murder, Cooperman had received several death threats hinting at his advocacy for reconciliation and cooperation with Vietnam. Two inmates, at different periods of time, informed authorities of Lam's admission that the murder was a political plot and that he had been ordered, even threatened, to kill Cooperman. May, however, discredited the inmates' information and eventually blocked them from testifying. He also successfully prevented the testimony of a handwriting expert, who affirmed the falsification of a signature on a check allegedly signed by Cooperman to Lam.[114] The murder of Cooperman was devastating to his family, the academic community, and USCSCV, but his peace endeavors lived on and continued to thrive.

Judith Ladinsky, one of USCSCV's leaders after Cooperman, relentlessly devoted her life to the fulfillment of the organization's missions. Visiting Vietnam for the first time in 1978, Ladinsky made more than one hundred trips to the country before her passing in 2012. An expert in rural health care, she became the head of USCSCV's Health Committee in 1980 and succeeded Cooperman in 1984. The main reason Ladinsky returned to Vietnam so many times was because the Vietnamese were "warm" and "hospitable" and because the health-care situation was "extremely sad." She described Vietnam's health-care system in 1980 as "the bones without the meat," indicating the existence of organization, staff, and buildings and the lack of medical supplies, equipment, and medicine. That image compelled her to contribute in various ways, from providing the "meat" to strengthening the "bones" of the system. She traveled throughout the country, organizing medical training, raising public awareness of preventive care, conducting research, and promoting exchange programs. She brought tons of medical supplies, equipment, medicine, books, and journals to Vietnam, and she sent hundreds of Vietnamese medical students to the United States for internships or further studies. She also saved many lives by sending people to the United States for medical treatment that was not available in Vietnam or for helping family members with serious health issues.[115] In 1985, for instance, Ladinsky managed to bring Vo Hoang Van from a remote village in the Mekong Delta to Chicago in an effort to save his brother's life. Vo Tien Duc, Van's older brother, was suffering from aplastic anemia and needed a bone marrow transplant. Considering the bureaucratic procedure to obtain exit and entry visas for Van and travel ordeals in rural Vietnam in 1985, the event was a "massive international effort" (to borrow journalist Larry Green's words) that reflected the interconnectedness of ordinary citizens across the Pacific Ocean.[116]

Pete Peterson, a former POW and the first American ambassador to Vietnam upon the two countries' diplomatic normalization in 1995, rightfully labeled Ladinsky "the real first American Ambassador to Vietnam." In fact, Vietnamese people lovingly call her "Madame Vietnam," and most people would agree she was the best-known American in Vietnam in the 1980s and 1990s. Ladinsky received several awards from Vietnam's government—among them the Friendship Medal, as a token of the country's deep appreciation for her far-reaching contributions to its health care and educational systems. In 2011, she was named Peacemaker of the Year by the Wisconsin Network for Peace and Justice. To honor her extraordinary service, the Center for Southeast Asian Studies of the University of Wisconsin-Madison established the Judith L. Ladinsky Memorial Fund and the annual Judith L. Ladinsky Lecture, starting in 2015.[117] Ladinsky's bonds with Vietnam lasted beyond her lifetime: She wished to be buried in Vietnam. On July 22, 2013, Ladinsky's family transferred her ashes to Vietnam's Ministry of Science and Technology in order to be buried at Vinh Hang Cemetery, Hanoi.[118] Ladinsky's final wish represented an ultimate gesture of peace and friendship. For the Vietnamese people, she was coming home.

Another organization that dedicated its efforts to improving US-Vietnam relations through academic and cultural exchange was the US-Indochina Reconciliation Project (USIRP), which was founded in 1985 by John McAuliff, an ardent antiwar activist of the 1960s and 1970s. As its name indicated, USIRP had well-defined objectives to work as a catalyst "to end US embargoes and to restore diplomatic, economic, and cultural relations with Cambodia, Laos, and Vietnam." After Vietnam and the United States normalized relations in 1995, USIRP shifted its focus to Cuba and changed its name to the Fund for Reconciliation and Development (FFRD).[119]

McAuliff relentlessly advocated for reconciliation and diplomatic normalization between former enemies. He voiced his concerns and opinions via the media and testified before Congress. Like veterans' organizations that facilitated trips to Vietnam, USIRP was warned to "cease entering into such transactions" because the Treasury Department categorized USIRP as a "travel service provider." In his congressional testimony, McAuliff pointed out that the Treasury Department issued its first travel advisory two weeks after General John Vessey's trip to Vietnam in 1987, a landmark in postwar relations between the two countries on the basis of humanitarian concerns. He then eloquently questioned "whether this was the case of what the right hand giveth the left hand taketh away; or perhaps the Treasury Department . . . had its own policy." Pointing out the educational benefits of opportunities for first-hand experiences through cultural and academic exchanges, McAuliff requested a different policy that would not hinder people from seeing and learning about the world.[120]

Considering the US laws, bureaucratic procedures in both countries, and transpacific communication at the time, USIRP's first landmark activity was impressive: in 1987, nine US college faculty and two high school educators visited Vietnam for one month, meeting with high-ranking officials and colleagues in numerous cities to discuss exchange opportunities. Subsequently, USIRP organized twice-annual trips to Vietnam for US faculty, staff, and students from colleges throughout the country. Its diverse agenda, ranging from seminars and conferences, to intensive academic courses and field trips, effectively promoted mutual understanding.[121]

USIRP also dedicated its efforts to hosting Indochinese scholars, professionals, artists, and students visiting the United States. In 1988, the organization managed to bring Vietnamese economist Nguyen Xuan Oanh to the United States for a visit. A Harvard graduate, Nguyen once taught economics at Trinity College, Connecticut, and worked for the International Monetary Fund before becoming deputy prime minister of South Vietnam. When the war ended in 1975, he was detained for a year before the new government of Vietnam realized his value and invited him to work as an economic adviser. By the mid-1980s, he became a key economic reformer and was elected to the national assembly. Nguyen was the highest-ranking Vietnamese official to visit the United States since 1975, but not as an official guest. As a matter of fact, his trip was delayed six months because the US Department of State rejected his visa application. USIRP had to appeal on his behalf and incorporate assistance from the American Civil Liberties Union Foundation (ACLUF) to obtain his visa.[122] An ACLU letter to Abraham D. Sofaer, legal adviser of the US Department of State, indicated that some State Department officials objected to Nguyen's visit because he favored foreign investment in Vietnam. The letter argued that the department "has no authority to exclude Dr. Oanh because his views on foreign investment may be contrary to the policies underlying the US trade embargo with Vietnam or because it does not think that American citizens should not hear such views."[123]

Nguyen's life was symbolic of reconciliation. Trained to be an economist, he dedicated his efforts to his profession wherever he was—in the United States, in South Vietnam, and in a unified Vietnam—regardless of politics. Ironically, because of his background and economic views, he faced obstacles in both countries. Despite his bonds to both countries, the Vietnamese government did not permit him to travel to the United States until 1987, but when it did, the United States denied him an entry visa. Transcending these ordeals, Nguyen maintained his principles while showing his willingness to cooperate for the betterment of society.

USIRP played a crucial role in promoting reconciliation through cultural exchange and cooperation. Its projects planted the seeds, spread the idea, and inspired others to expand its network. Those who joined USIRP delegations to Vietnam often sought reconciliation by developing exchange programs tailored to their personal expertise and institutional needs. The organization's quarterly newsletter, the *Indochina Exchange*, was a valuable resource and a link for NGOs or anyone interested in exchange programs with Vietnam, Laos, and Cambodia. It provided essential information beneficial to project starters and news on NGOs' activities. More importantly, it displayed a refreshing picture of people-to-people connections standing in contrast to sluggish governmental relations.

One long-standing organization inspired by USIRP was the Social Science Research Council (SSRC), a sister organization of the American Council of Learned Societies. Founded in 1923 as a nongovernmental and interdisciplinary organization, SSRC's mission was to advance research in the social sciences and humanities, including international area studies. In 1983, SSRC created the Indochina Studies Program, an associate of which, Mary Byrne McDonnell, joined USIRP's delegation to Indochina in January 1987. Upon her return to the United States, McDonnell drafted what she called "a modest program" consisting of grants for research in Vietnam, academic exchanges, workshops, conferences, scholarly meetings, and gifts of books, professional journals, or educational equipment for Vietnamese colleagues. With the belief that "scholars can move ahead of governments in laying the groundwork for normal scholarly relations," the SSRC moved forward with a plan composed of diverse academic fields for cooperation. Starting in 1988, through SSRC's Indochina Studies Program, many colleges and organizations expanded their exchanges to Indochina for the first time. Among the pioneers were Georgetown University, the University of Hawai'i, the University of Iowa, and Arizona State University. Their programs consisted of diverse disciplines, ranging from English as a second language (ESL), linguistics, history, economics, and agronomics to archaeology.[124]

Another extraordinary contributor to postwar peace efforts was the woman behind the well-known East Meets West Foundation (EMWF), Le Ly Hayslip.[125] Hayslip's life story was one of both extreme tragedy and parallel enlightenment. Growing up in a village in Da Nang controlled by South Vietnam by day and the Viet Cong by night, she experienced the cruelty of war from both sides. At thirteen, she was drafted to the local "self-defense" unit, and her job was basically to inform the Viet Cong of the ARVN's presence. Arrested three times by South Vietnamese troops, Hayslip endured barbaric torture. She remembered:

> They gave me electric shock and threatened to cut off my fingers to feed to their guard dogs. I was roped to a post in an area covered with anthills and my feet were painted with honey. . . . When the guard finally came back, he reached into a bucket and brought out a water snake about the length of his arm. When he dropped it into my shirt, it slithered and probed around my armpits, breasts, and neck, trying to get out. It broke any self-control I had left. I screamed and screamed.[126]

For her third arrest, Hayslip endured the harshest imprisonment in a military POW camp from which few would be released. Upon her return, her Viet Cong comrades suspected that she had turned into a spy for the South. After a so-called trial by her communist unit, two members escorted her to her grave in a clearing. They were supposed to kill her but decided to rape the fourteen-year-old girl instead. Following the incident, Hayslip and her mother moved to Saigon, working as domestic help for a wealthy family. In a year or so, she was impregnated by her boss and thrown out by his wife. Returning to Da Nang, Hayslip moved in with her sister who worked as a bar girl. As her sister often brought home US soldiers, Hayslip soon followed, making easy money from "dating" GIs. Eventually, the nineteen-year-old single mother agreed to marry a fifty-three-year-old US civilian contractor and immigrated to the United States in 1970. By the mid-1980s, Hayslip owned three houses and a restaurant near San Diego. She revisited her family in 1986 for the first time and was shocked to see the wounds of war still deeply carved into her homeland. Upon coming back to the United States, she sold some of her properties and founded the EMWF. She returned to Vietnam in 1988, this time with five Americans, four of them veterans, to dedicate the first clinic in her village, which she named *Tình Mẹ* (Mother's Love).[127]

Aiming to become "a bridge and a catalyst of all people and organizations working on global peace,"[128] the East Meets West Foundation invites veterans to participate in its program to enhance mutual understanding and reconciliation between former fighters and victims of war. One of its veteran-members, Jerry Stadtmiller, confirmed that the program gave him "a sense of forgiveness." He said, "It allows me to love a people who are so in need of love and who, in return, are very loving." Stadtmiller was injured in Vietnam in 1968 and had undergone "well over 100 surgical procedures as well as years of individual and group therapy." His wartime experiences had caused him to "irrationally and indiscriminately hate all Vietnamese people," but EMWF transformed him by giving him a chance to understand the other side.[129]

EMWF thrived over the years and grew into one of the most productive nongovernmental organizations working in Vietnam, sponsoring the construction and improvement of hundreds of hospitals, orphanages, and schools. It also provided multiple scholarship programs to make education accessible to students of all ages. From its original foci on health care and education, EMWF developed new programs such as clean water, improved sanitation, hygiene knowledge, housing for the impoverished, and so on. EMWF's annual expenditures reached tens of millions of dollars. In 2008, EMWF changed its name to Thrive Networks to highlight its new vision and expansive programs across the globe. Starting in 2013, Thrive Networks merged with some other NGOs to further its impact. In 1999, Hayslip also founded Global Village to multiply her successful projects around the world.

Hayslip withstood multiple war traumas before transforming herself into an influential peace builder. She had been politically, physically, and emotionally abused by all sides. Trapped between violent political forces, she did not have an option when joining the self-defense unit. Tortured and suspected by both sides, she could not choose to stay in her hometown either. During the short time she lived in Saigon, Hayslip did not have the power to reject her boss's sexual aggression or to defend herself. Back in her hometown, she continued to endure the chaos of war, which presented few opportunities to improve her life. Yet she transcended them all. She moved across boundaries during wartime to survive, and she did it again after the war to serve. It was memories of her past tragedies that motivated her to improve quality of life for others. From a powerless little girl, Hayslip became a compassionate philanthropist who worked relentlessly to empower the underprivileged.

Throughout the 1980s and early 1990s, the dynamic interactions between US and Vietnamese people against the backdrop of governmental restrictions highlighted a desire for peace among many ordinary citizens. Lingering memories of a devastating war in Southeast Asia, as well as ongoing US military interventions in the Middle East and Central and South Americas, provoked Americans to take action. By bringing to attention the aftermath of war, the humanitarians and activists raised their voices for peace. Transcending roadblocks caused by politics, they creatively initiated programs that paved the way for improved relations between former foes. Although their peace endeavors did not immediately change the two countries' foreign policies, their activities had significant impact on both societies. Many Americans who went to Vietnam to help reconstruct a war-torn country realized they were helping themselves in reconciling their pasts. Their experiences in postwar Vietnam changed their perspectives on the country and its people and compelled many to continue their peace efforts for the rest of their lives. On the other side, Vietnamese people became less isolated, finding a helping hand in a time of need. More importantly, these ordinary citizens moved their national governments, putting them back in conversation during times of tension and making politicians reconsider their policies.

On many occasions, citizens played a catalytic role between the governments. In 1992, after years of rejecting governmental aid to Vietnam, the United States committed $3 million to humanitarian purposes. On April 24 of that year, the State Department informed the Veterans Vietnam Restoration Project and other NGOs that with their financial commitment, funds would be available to organizations that had been working on humanitarian projects in Vietnam.[130] NGO initiatives and experience became handy for the US government's new commitment to the improvement of its relations with Vietnam. Brick by brick, US individuals and NGOs' pioneering efforts laid the groundwork for US-Vietnam diplomatic normalization.

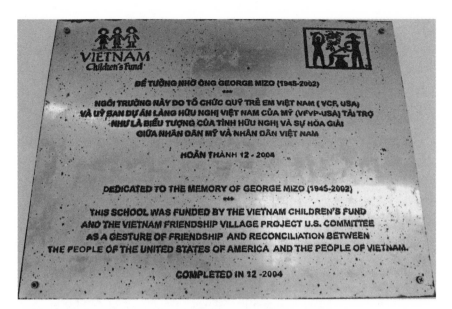

Dedication plaque, Friendship Village, Hanoi

Children affected by Agent Orange learning embroidery

Children affected by Agent Orange learning embroidery

Children affected by Agent Orange learning embroidery

Children affected by Agent Orange learning embroidery

Teacher and students

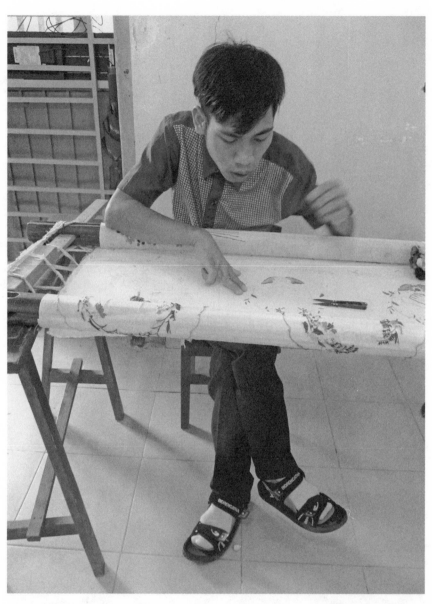

Determination

Coloring

Physical therapy

Physical therapy

Vegetables grown by Friendship Village residents

Quang Tri Citadel (located in the demilitarized zone), the battlefield of the eighty-one-day fight in 1972, now a memorial to fallen soldiers

Quang Tri Citadel (located in the demilitarized zone), the battlefield of the eighty-one-day fight in 1972, now a memorial to fallen soldiers

Flowers blooming on the soil once covered with blood

Thach Han River. The lotuses symbolize the noble sacrifice of fallen soldiers who fought to defend the citadel

A project by PeaceTrees Vietnam

An anonymous poem:
    Please be gentle when paddling on the Thach Han
    Resting on the riverbed are my friends
    Their youth blended into the waves
    Gently lapping the shores over and over again
        (translated by author)

From bombshells flowers grew

From bombshells flowers grew

CHAPTER FOUR

Postnormalization
Quest for Peace

I went back to Vietnam not because I had to. I went back because I wanted to.
I saw the Vietnamese at their very worst, and they saw me at my very worst as
well. I can't do anything about what happened yesterday, but I can help move
forward positively and constructively on what happens tomorrow. And that's
why I'm in Vietnam.

— Douglas "Pete" Peterson, *Pete Peterson: Assignment Hanoi*

Douglas "Pete" Peterson's first encounter with the North Vietnamese in 1966
was tragic. His bomber was shot down, and he spent the next six-and-a half
years in Hanoi as a prisoner of war (POW). Thirty-one years later, in May
1997, he returned to the capital of the Socialist Republic of Vietnam (SRV) as
an ambassador. Peterson never forgot the harrowing experiences of his cap-
tivity. At the moment of his capture, when he heard the Vietnamese soldiers
coming, Peterson had thought of "getting off the planet" and pulled out his .38
revolver. For him, that would have been "easier and a less painful process."
But he made a more difficult choice and survived the tortures. To beat what he
considered "the greatest torture"—isolation—Peterson and other US POWs
employed tap code to communicate through the wall, a skill they had learned
from the US Air Force's survival school.[1] Those memories did not fade away,
but he refused to let them impede his vision. Bearing the scars of war, he
was determined to work for peace. Peterson became a symbolic figure of US-
Vietnam reconciliation not simply because he was the first American to serve

in this position since 1975 but mainly because he demonstrated astounding commitment to reconciliatory efforts.

As the first ambassador to Vietnam, Peterson had much work to do. Even though President Bill Clinton had lifted the US trade embargo against Vietnam on February 3, 1994, and announced "normalization of relations" with Vietnam on July 11, 1995, both countries faced many obstacles in their new relations. On the one hand, Vietnam's economic and legal systems were not ready to integrate into the US market. Bureaucracy and corruption also hindered its reformers from effecting change. On the other hand, for the United States, Vietnam was not a high priority in its foreign policy, and the primary interest of the United States in Vietnam thus far was still accounting for POWs/MIAs. In fact, "[on] July 23, 1998, the US Senate vote[d] 66–34 to continue funding for the US Embassy in Vietnam based on ongoing cooperation on the POW/MIA issue."[2] In addition, US laws still maintained restrictions in trading with a communist country. To promote stronger economic and cultural relations with Vietnam, Ambassador Peterson had to make regular visits to Capitol Hill to persuade his former colleagues to put the war behind them.[3]

For ordinary citizens, diplomatic normalization between the two countries meant easier transnational interactions, especially with the freedom to travel and improvements in paperwork. The establishment of the US embassy in Hanoi and the Vietnam embassy in Washington, DC, enabled direct visa application (instead of getting entry visas in Bangkok, Thailand), saving time and money for travelers. These travel improvements significantly boosted the transpacific flow of people, material goods, and ideas. Endeavors to heal the wounds of war developed at a more "sensitive" level. First, Vietnam's government became increasingly open to foreign tourists, allowing access to former battlefields, especially those in the demilitarized zone (DMZ) in Quang Tri. Access to the DMZ led to transnational efforts to restore the war-torn area, which turned out to be an arduous task. Second, a new phenomenon emerged: the return of war mementos to veterans and families of fallen soldiers on both sides. For many reasons, the keepers of these artifacts had not been ready to deal with this daunting task before. For example, with limited travel and communication conditions, locating the rightful owners of these keepsakes had been mostly impossible. Since the late 1990s, the media, especially with the development of the internet, had become effective searching tools. In addition, time's passage also helped. People tend to be more forgiving and accepting in older age and after a cushion of decades. Third, Vietnamese nonprofit programs came into existence to help individuals find their families. Employing social networking, these programs enhanced reunion opportunities. The participants' stories brought to center stage the silent endurance and onerous odysseys of individuals separated from their families because of war circumstances. While these people set specific goals for their postwar journeys, they were in search of one common thing: peace. All of these peace endeavors were the work of ordinary citizens. Now and then the United States and Vietnamese governments got involved, but even in those cases, governmental roles remained limited and mostly filled the formality requirement.

Peace for the DMZ

Visitors to varied parts of Vietnam in the mid-1990s saw noticeable economic improvement compared to a decade before. Those who stopped by Quang Tri, however, were appalled by its poverty. Straddling the DMZ of the Vietnam War, Quang Tri endured some of the most brutal battles and remained the most unexploded-ordnance-contaminated area in the country. For soldiers of all sides during wartime, deployment to Quang Tri was almost an assurance of death. For local civilians, it was an inescapable hell. An area of eighteen hundred square miles, the province suffered a greater tonnage of bombs dropped than Europe did during World War II, according to historian Tony Edmonds. Approximately 10 to 15 percent of the bombs dropped did not explode as intended.[4] When the war ended, 84 percent of Quang Tri's land area was contaminated with explosive remnants of war (ERW) and landmines.[5] Between April 30, 1975, and December 31, 2010, more than twenty-six hundred people were killed and more than forty-four hundred injured by ERW/landmines. Children accounted for 31 percent of casualties.[6] These factors multiplied the locals' hardship in stabilizing their lives after the war, making Quang Tri one of the poorest provinces in Vietnam for decades. Journalist Elaine Elinson observes, "Though the hot war ended almost four decades ago, the American war of aggression continues to take its deadly toll. Most Americans, including myself and others on our delegation, were not aware of the way the Vietnamese people continue to live with this lethal legacy."[7] Once the Vietnamese government opened the region to foreign visitors, the province's destitution begged attention. Henceforth, transnational initiatives to improve its environment and socioeconomic conditions were established. Some of the projects had been nurtured years before US-Vietnam diplomatic normalization in 1995; others picked up the momentum and flourished in the years to come.

On April 24, 1995, six days before the twentieth anniversary of the end of the Vietnam War, the people of the town of Dong Ha, Quang Tri Province, inaugurated Lewis B. Puller Elementary School. Lewis Burwell Puller Jr. was a US Marine who lost both legs and parts of both hands to a landmine only a few months after his arrival in Vietnam in 1968. He was also a Pulitzer Prize winner for his autobiography *Fortunate Son*, and he was the son of the legendary Lewis B. "Chesty" Puller, the most decorated marine in US history. Puller's brainchild, the elementary school served as a living memorial to fallen Vietnamese people during the war and a stepping stone for the children of Vietnam to build their future.[8]

The concept of a monument to the Vietnamese arose in 1992, when Terry Anderson spoke of reconciliation at an event at the Vietnam Veterans Memorial in Washington, DC. Anderson had served as a marine in Vietnam and as chief of the Associated Press in Beirut, Lebanon, in the 1980s. He was also the longest-held captive of seven years in the Lebanese hostage crisis.[9] Also present at the wall was actress Kieu Chinh, who grew up in Hanoi but established her reputation in Saigon during the Vietnam War. She immigrated to the United States in 1975 and continued her acting career in Hollywood. The Vietnamese actress commented on Anderson's reconciliation speech: "What you said is fine, but what about my people?" Later, Anderson and Puller discussed Kieu Chinh's comment and nurtured the idea of a monument for the Vietnamese.[10] Soon, the Vietnamese Memorial Association came into existence with Puller and John "Jack" Wheeler Jr. as cofounders. Wheeler served as an army officer in Vietnam in 1969; he also served as chairman of the Vietnam Veterans Memorial Fund from 1979 to 1989. He was the driving force behind "the wall" and a most vocal advocate for Maya Lin's controversial design for the monument.[11] In 1993, Puller visited Vietnam. The country's poverty compelled him to change the original initiative of building a conventional monument to constructing a living memorial that would benefit Vietnamese children. Unfortunately, he ended his life in May 1994, presumably because of relapse into alcoholism, an addiction to painkillers, and a failing marriage. His friends insisted that Puller's idea live on. They raised $75,000 to build a sixteen-classroom school in his honor. The completion of the Lewis Puller School, however, was but a beginning.[12] The Vietnamese Memorial Association changed its name to the Vietnam Children's Fund (VCF), and the nonprofit organization continued to grow over the years with generous contributions from individual and corporate donors. By 2015, the VCF had built forty-nine schools across Vietnam, mostly in remote areas. According to its chairman, Terry Anderson, the fund was committed to building "as many seats in new modern schools as there are names on the Vietnam Veterans Memorial."[13]

The schools built by the VCF had profound impacts on many levels. First, in commemorating Vietnamese victims of the war and upholding Puller's reconciliation efforts, the VCF's projects brought together not only former fighters on opposing sides of the conflict but also different generations of Americans and Vietnamese. Transcending their differences and unpleasant memories, these people worked together for a better future. Second, while aiming to provide educational opportunities for Vietnamese children, the projects turned into educational opportunities for adults as well. The cultural and historical lessons that the VCF participants picked up at their working sites might not be found in textbooks. Third, the schools presented a historical transition of US-Vietnam relations. Underpinning that transition were ordinary citizens' endeavors for peace.

Another transnational effort to help restore Quang Tri was PeaceTrees Vietnam, a Seattle-based nongovernmental organization (NGO). PeaceTrees originated from a wartime grief when Lt. Daniel Cheney of the US Army was killed in action on January 6, 1969, the day his engagement was announced in the *Bellingham Herald* in Bellingham, Washington, and three weeks short of his twenty-second birthday. Cheney was providing covering fire for a downed pilot who survived the incident.[14] The tragic news reached his family only four weeks after he left for Vietnam. That horrendous loss compelled Cheney's sister, Jerilyn Cheney Brusseau, to think deeply about the suffering that her parents, other American parents, and Vietnamese parents endured. She began to nurture a dream of building bridges to promote transnational friendship. In 1988, Jerilyn and her husband Danaan Parry created PeaceTrees under the Earthstewards Network, a nonprofit organization that Parry had founded in 1980. PeaceTrees worked with teenagers who had grown up in war zones across the globe to promote mutual understanding among former enemies in a service for peace: planting trees.[15]

A significant change happened on July 11, 1995, when Cheney Brusseau picked up a newspaper on her Berlin–Seattle flight and realized in amazement that the day she had been awaiting for a quarter century had just come: the United States had normalized relations with Vietnam. By the time they landed in Seattle, Cheney Brusseau and her husband had decided to bring Peace-

Trees to Vietnam.[16] On November 12, 1995, Parry flew to Washington, DC, to meet with the first Vietnamese ambassador, Le Van Bang. Parry arrived at the ambassador's reception without an invitation but with "the idea to build the bridges of trust and understanding."[17] The ambassador enthusiastically welcomed Parry, and PeaceTrees Vietnam soon came into existence. Cheney Brusseau and Parry landed in Vietnam on January 6, 1996, coinciding with the twenty-seventh anniversary of Daniel Cheney's ultimate sacrifice. The couple discussed the project with the Vietnamese, and a few months later, Parry returned with three voluntary demining experts to clear a field for the first team of "citizen diplomats" to come and plant trees. Unfortunately, Parry unexpectedly passed away only days before the delegation's departure in November 1996. Cheney Brusseau, however, decided not to postpone the trip, which consisted of forty-two volunteers from seven countries. The group's task was to plant two thousand trees on the newly cleared area.[18]

A quiet yet powerful driving force behind PeaceTrees was Rae Cheney, Lt. Daniel Cheney's Gold Star mother. Rae transcended her grief in order to reach out to the Vietnamese people. In an interview on the Vietnamese channel VTV1's *Talk Vietnam* in 2010, Rae described her enduring commitment: "I've gone to this land every single day since 1969 . . . in memory."[19] The day Cheney Brusseau and the first team embarked for Vietnam, Rae gave Daniel's Purple Heart to her daughter and asked her to "plant" it together with the first tree. Rae admitted that she had been bitter and resentful toward Vietnam, but when Cheney Brusseau told her that PeaceTrees needed a person to write thank-you letters to donors, Rae volunteered for the job. Every time she wrote those letters, Rae thought about the Vietnamese mothers who also lost their sons and daughters to the war. Her desire to know them and to help them grew stronger and stronger. However, fifteen years had passed before she summoned herself to set foot on the land that had been synonymous with her pain. By the time she decided to visit Vietnam in 2010, she had written more than eight thousand letters for PeaceTrees. Her reluctance to visit Vietnam stemmed from the question of whether she would be accepted by the Vietnamese and vice versa. But once she was willing to try the test, she realized that the answer was obvious: the Vietnamese embraced her. Rae came to Vietnam to dedicate the Dan Cheney Kindergarten and the Mothers' Peace Library in honor of all mothers who lost their sons and daughters in the war. At the dedication ceremony of the library in village of Khe Da, a remote community near Khe Sanh, the ninety-year-old American mother met with ninety-two-year-old Vietnamese mother Ho Thi Moan, who lost two sons in a battle in that same village. The mothers embraced. Hearts melted, and wounds closed—at long last. So far as is known, Rae was the first American mother of a fallen soldier to visit Vietnam for humanitarian efforts. As a token of appreciation for Rae's contributions to reconciliation and peace-building, Vietnam's government bestowed on her the Medal for Peace and Friendship among Nations, the highest award for a foreigner. Her daughter also received the honor.[20]

With the slogan "Healing the land; Building community; Planting future," PeaceTrees' specific tasks included demining, educating people about mine risks, assisting ERW survivors, and planting trees to help restore the environment. Between 1995 and 2015, PeaceTrees removed more than eighty-five thousand nine hundred weapons such as landmines, bombs, mortar shells, and grenades from more than eight hundred acres of land. The organization brought to Quang Tri about seven hundred voluntary "citizen diplomats" who planted more than forty-three thousand trees. In addition to clearing ERW and planting trees, PeaceTrees' educational programs significantly helped prevent explosive accidents as more than eighty-six thousand adults and children learned to recognize potentially dangerous objects in their surroundings and to act responsibly. PeaceTrees reached out to approximately nine hundred and fifty ERW victims, offering financial help for medical treatment and devices that enabled independent mobility such as prosthetics, wheelchairs, and ramps. The organization also gave scholarships to children of victims' families, without which furthering their education would likely have remained an unobtainable dream.[21]

Within twenty years, PeaceTrees built ten kindergartens, twelve libraries, and two community centers in Quang Tri and Quang Binh Provinces. One of the community centers included Vietnam Friendship Village Project USA with a hundred homes. The initiative of building the Friendship Village came from an incident occurring during PeaceTrees' second trip in 1997. As Cheney Brusseau recalls, the volunteers were staying in a military guesthouse about a mile from the newly demined field, where they were going to plant trees. On their way to work was a village with primitive living conditions—tiny houses with no electricity or running water. Late one morning, the volunteers were having lunch in the guesthouse after their half day's work when they heard a "horrible explosion." The source of the deafening noise was an M-79 shell, and not far from the kitchen, right by the lane they walked on every day, lay two young boys, seriously injured. As they later learned, one of the boys had seen the shell, picked it up, and threw it away. Cheney Brusseau remembers, "What was most shocking was to see and experience not only the pain of the villagers—the Vietnamese people standing around this—but the sadness in their eyes . . . the heartbreak in their eyes . . . another child . . . another child"[22] The team spent the next few days discussing the tragedy, and Cheney Brusseau asked Nguyen Duc Quang, an official of Quang Tri's Foreign Relations Department, what PeaceTrees could do to help reduce such accidents. The answer was it could help clear the ERW in the village. PeaceTrees raised funds, temporarily relocated the villagers, cleared the forty-acre area, and built a new village. Completed in September 2002, the project consisted of a community hall, a school, a library, and a hundred homes with running water and electricity.[23]

Among the first "citizen diplomats" of PeaceTrees was Sarah Blum, an army nurse during the war. Blum remembered her "worst experience of [her] Vietnam year" after facing war casualties twelve to sixteen hours a day for about six months: "Something inside of me snapped. I ran out the door. There were helicopters right above at the time, all in formation. I raised my fist, and I just yelled at the top of my lungs: 'Kill, kill, kill!' I was totally out of my mind." Since then, she started "building up a brick wall around [her] heart" to get through the remainder of her service, and the wall persisted until her trip with PeaceTrees. Before her departure, a Vietnam veteran gave her a letter, a "good-bye letter to all of his pain," and asked her to read it once she arrived in Vietnam, and then "plant" it under a tree for him. The symbolic act of "planting" the letter together with a peace tree and the experience of working side by side with the Vietnamese were "very meaningful" to Blum.[24]

One long-term contributor for PeaceTrees was Le Quang, a Vietnamese American from California. Born in Hanoi but raised in Saigon, Le witnessed family losses to both sides of the conflict. Choosing to focus on the future instead of the past, Le observed, "In a conflict of any type, there must be a winner and a loser. Politics does not matter much to me. Bitterness is a waste of time. I've seen enough and learned to be sympathetic. All I want to do is to help improve the society, and my work speaks for itself." Le had always wanted to return to Vietnam, but that dream seemed impossible in 1975. An opportunity came in 1991 when a company asked him to work as its representative in Saigon. Le took the chance and returned to his homeland. PeaceTrees approached him in 1995 when he was working for another representative office in Hanoi; he agreed to assist with the construction of the Danaan Parry Landmine Education Center, starting with visiting Quang Tri once a month. Amazed by individual efforts to reach out to the less fortunate, he became increasingly interested in NGOs. Witnessing bureaucratic roadblocks and corruption, Le was trying to figure out how to effectively help the disadvantaged in Vietnam. PeaceTrees answered his question, and he officially became its in-country director in 2000. With family support and sacrifice, Le moved to Quang Tri, devoting himself to PeaceTrees' missions. It was the children of Quang Tri and the ERW victims that made him stay. As a Vietnamese American, his cultural and linguistic flexibility allowed Le to serve as a bridge between Vietnamese and US people.[25] In truth, his work speaks volumes about his peace endeavors. While many Vietnamese sought opportunities to immigrate to the United States, Le chose to live in one of the poorest provinces of Vietnam. While refusing to discuss the past, he chose to deal with its aftermath in order to lay a foundation for the future. In recognition of his dedication and indispensable role in PeaceTrees' success, Vietnam's government bestowed him with the Medal for Peace and Friendship among Nations in 2010.

Besides its direct assistance to local people, PeaceTrees also brought Quang Tri to the world, calling attention to the lingering, dismal aftermath of war. Following PeaceTrees, other international NGOs arrived to shoulder the ERW problem. To efficiently coordinate efforts for the daunting task of clearing ERW, Quang Tri's officials initiated the establishment of Project RENEW (Restoring the Environment and Neutralizing the Effects of War). Founded in 2001 and staffed by more than ninety local youths, RENEW was a "cooperative partnership" between Quang Tri's governmental units and NGOs. While its funding came mainly from the Norwegian People's Aid and Japan, it also received aid from the US Department of State and other organizations. The project consisted of four components: ERW survey and clearance, mine/ERW risk education, mine/ERW victims assistance, and the Mine Action Visitor Center.[26]

Similar to Le Quang of PeaceTrees, RENEW's international advisor, Chuck Searcy, chose to reside in Vietnam for two decades. Searcy returned to Vietnam in 1992, twenty-four years after his service with the 519th Military Intelligence Battalion in Saigon. Joining him in his return trip was another Vietnam veteran. Searcy recalls, "As we landed, both of us had a panic attack. For God's sake, what are we thinking? We are ex-GIs; the country is devastated. But I couldn't believe the welcome we got, the curiosity. 'Were you in the war? My father was in the war. Where were you?' But without any animosity or anger. It was astonishing." During his visit to Khe Sanh, he asked two little boys if there were any bombs around; the boys walked him to the trees nearby and pointed to an unexploded artillery shell on the ground and said they were everywhere. The younger boy, eight or nine years old, "tentatively sticks his toe out, just to nudge it a bit out of curiosity," and

Searcy said, "Stop! Stop!" That moment, Searcy realized the real danger these children and their families were facing. In 1995, he moved to Hanoi to represent the Vietnam Veterans of America Foundation, administering a United States Agency for International Development (USAID)–funded humanitarian project that provided orthopedic braces for children. Starting in 2001, he worked as a representative of the Vietnam Veterans Memorial Fund and was RENEW's international advisor.[27]

Working side by side with Searcy was retired Col. Bui Trong Hong, who had served in the People's Army of Vietnam for thirty years. An expert in ERW, Bui was RENEW's national technical officer. Growing up during wartime and witnessing the bombing of his village, Bui had felt hatred toward Americans. He recalls, "We saw the enemy only coming from the sky, the enemy without a face." According to journalist George Black, however, the retired colonel that he met "seemed to regard life as an inexhaustible source of humor." Dealing with deadly ERW on a daily basis did not diminish Bui's optimism. Several times a day he would join response teams, going to places where unexploded munitions had been reported, to conduct survey and clearance. He would also come to accident sites to assist the victims and clean up the remnants.[28] Together with Searcy, Bui inspired and led younger generations by example. The image of the aged adversaries, Searcy and Bui, working together to restore the environment and save the innocent children of Quang Tri from hidden dangers decades after the end of the conflict exemplified both the harrowing effects of war and heartwarming aspirations for peace.

Mementos of War, Presents of Peace

Although war almost always brings back unpleasant, even cruel, memories, remembering it is significant to those who experienced its effects. For many veterans, one way to remember a war is to return to the place where that war was fought, the place that had attached to their youth and became part of their identity. With bureaucratic blocks gradually lifted thanks to the improved diplomatic relations between the United States and Vietnam, the number of US veterans visiting Vietnam remarkably increased in the late 1990s. As historian Julia Bleakney asserts, the way the Vietnam War is remembered "has shifted from national soul searching toward personal identity and recovery."[29] The stories discussed will attest to this. Bleakney also argues that memorializing has "become increasingly material and commodified."[30] It is true that these veterans' trips involved travel services, including sales and marketing. On the other hand, some veterans also brought home with them war mementos, either real objects or replicas. Nevertheless, the commodification of memorializing should not overshadow the human emotions that underpinned these transnational pursuits of peace.

Viewing the phenomenon of US veterans returning to Vietnam from a different perspective, sociocultural anthropologist Christina Schwenkel maintains that many of those "healing journeys" are "concurrently moral journeys often imbued with paternalistic meaning, convictions, and desires to rescue Vietnam from the privations of communism with capitalist models of development, progress, and aid as their tools."[31] It is uncertain how many of the veterans presented in this research would agree that they were making "moral journeys" and/or were carrying that paternalistic sentiment with them when they returned to Vietnam. Their testimonies seemed to indicate common desires to heal the wounds of war for themselves and for the Vietnamese, whether those wounds were visible or not. It might be unfair to label their genuine peace efforts as "paternalistic" or "capitalistic." Their endeavors to put to rest unpleasant memories of war were not necessarily moral negotiations or "remasculinization projects" conducted by "First World actors" (to borrow Schwenkel's words).[32] In fact, many US veterans emphasized Vietnamese historical agency and the mutual benefit of these transnational interactions.

One crucial organization that helped veterans and their families as well as loved ones of those killed in action (KIA) to reconcile with their pasts was Tours of Peace Vietnam Veterans (TOP). Founded by ex–US Marine Jess DeVaney in 1998, the Arizona-based nonprofit organization "integrates emotional and humanitarian components" to enable transformation for individuals affected by the Vietnam War. Operating with the motto "By helping others, we help ourselves," TOP structured its activities around five programs: veterans, family, humanitarian, education, and personal effects. With an average cost of approximately $3,500 per person, TOP's typical two-week trip allowed participants to visit a place of personal significance, usually an old battlefield, and to engage in a humanitarian project near the site. The tour also included visits to Vietnam's historical, cultural, and natural sites to enhance the image of Vietnam as a country to replace the memory of Vietnam as a war. Understanding the possibility of intense emotions that participants may face, TOP organizers provided counseling before, during, and after the trips and emphasized group support throughout the journey.[33]

As indicated in the organization's name, TOP's major goal was to offer veterans "the opportunity to bring closure to their Vietnam War experience."[34] Seeing the positive effects of image replacement in the treatment of post-traumatic stress disorder (PTSD), TOP tailored its trips to offer its participants a chance to see the changed landscape of places that were familiar to them during wartime. The transformation of an old battlefield or a war-battered zone into a green field or a bustling residential area revealed a reality: the war was long gone, and the land had healed. That realization had a powerful effect on those who held vivid, unpleasant memories of the place. As a former marine put it, "Since my trip to Vietnam, the old images of the war are still with me, but have somewhat faded and are put into the past. Now when I think of Vietnam, I have new images: smiling children, happy faces, a beautiful country, the people are at peace. It makes my heart feel good."[35] Another veteran wrote,

In and out of therapy for 15 years, I finally accepted the fact that PTSD was destroying my life. I needed help; I needed to go back to that place where it all began . . . Vietnam. The help I needed came in the form of TOP Vietnam Veterans. This Veterans organization made it possible for me to return to Vietnam, and in doing so, I was empowered to turn the page, and get on with my life. I have come full circle. I am once again a whole person.[36]

The positive effects of return trips were obvious; expressions such as "close the Vietnam chapter," "turn the page," and "come full circle" almost became clichés among the returnees. The humanitarian component of the tours also had a significant impact. Not only did it enhance American people's interactions with the Vietnamese, it also gave the travelers a sense of fulfillment when they helped alleviate others' misery.

A highlight in TOP's programs was the endeavors to engage veterans' and KIAs' (killed in action) families in the healing process. DeVaney believed that "for veterans to heal, their families need to be involved."[37] In truth, the trip was a valuable opportunity for family members to learn more about the Vietnam experiences of their beloved former soldiers and to understand the emotions that had been inexplicable to them. Even if a veteran was willing to tell his wife about his wartime undertaking, it would not be easy for her to fathom his visceral feelings. Perhaps not until they literally journeyed together and were *there* together — on top of a hill or by a bomb crater in a field — could the spouse comprehend the veteran's memories. Furthermore, TOP's group discussions added dimensions to the educational opportunity. Participants, both veterans and nonveterans, learned more about the war, the soldiers, and the Vietnamese.

Jim Bambenek and his wife, Nancy, found themselves profoundly transformed after their trip with TOP in 2003. According to journalist Cynthya Porter, Jim returned to Vietnam to "exorcis[e] the demons shoved far below the surface of his calm life," and for Nancy, it was "a trip of sharing, of understanding the year of her husband's life that she only knew of through his thrashing nightmares that crept into their bed at night."[38] Returning from Vietnam's Central Highlands after his one-year service with the army, first as a movements control specialist and later as a photographer, Jim put away his jungle memories and moved on with life. He considered himself "fine" until his visit to the Vietnam Veterans Memorial in Washington, DC, which "started the demons to rumbling and Jim to thinking."[39] He and Nancy decided to join TOP, aware that the trip was "not a vacation."[40] As journalist Porter describes, each participant carried three bags on the trip to Vietnam: "One filled with personal items . . . one filled with humanitarian items to give away," and the last one "filled with private pain decades old, a bag that would hopefully be emptied and refilled with good memories."[41] Within two weeks, the group visited several orphanages, a nursing home, a leper village, memorials, My Lai, and battle sites in Khe Sanh. At My Lai, the US visitors met a woman who survived the massacre. She had been mistaken for dead and thrown into a pile of corpses, which included those of her family. In Khe Sanh, the team located the hill where a veteran-member, John, had endured an ambush; they also saw the infamous battlefield of Khe Sanh where a member's father survived the seventy-seven-day siege in a foxhole.[42]

Jim's highlight of the trip was finding the orphanage that he and other GIs helped build, which he considered "one of the few pieces of good that he could recall." He also learned that one of his favorite children, a boy nicknamed "General George," was still in the area and doing well. As Jim observed, "Most vets have a 'moment' where they feel the load is lifted off them."[43] Journalist Porter calls it the "baggage-dumping moment." Jim's "baggage-dumping moment" came unexpectedly at Hue's airport. "That day when we took off, I saw all my garbage laying [*sic*] on the tarmac. That was my moment when I left it all behind, all that weight that I didn't even know I had," said Jim. Inside the airport, he and Nancy had noticed "an air conditioning unit made in La Crosse, Wisconsin, thirty miles from [their] home."[44] Jim's "moment" may have seemed odd compared to those who "dumped" their "baggage" at a historical site or in a meeting with a former foe, but what he and his wife saw was not a meaningless object. They saw a sign of peace, of reconciliation, and of interconnectedness.

While TOP was especially helpful to those who visited Vietnam for the first time since the end of the war, its participants included not only first timers but also some Americans who had earlier come to postwar Vietnam. Daniel Martin and his wife, Pamela, decided to "visit old haunts" (to borrow Daniel's words) in 1999. Daniel had served in a marine fighter-bomber squadron in Da Nang from September 1968 to October 1969. Even though "fear was something [he] lived with every day," Daniel considered himself "luckier" than other marines who had to fight in the jungle or other terrains. However, what bothered him was the fact the US bombs hit not only the enemies but also civilians. He stated, "My shame boils down to the killing of innocent women and children." Daniel carried that fear and shame with him in his 1999 return, which he called "a white-knuckle experience." Even the flight attendant noticed his fear and saw him "cringe" before they landed in Hanoi, and after landing, Pamela and others had to convince him that the war had been over and that he was visiting a country, not a war zone. The Martins soon realized that the Vietnamese had moved on and held no animosity toward them.[45]

The heartwarming experiences that they had in their first trip encouraged the Martins to return to Vietnam "to start the process of healing." They joined TOP's program in 2001, visiting six orphanages among other destinations. Working with disadvantaged children compelled the couple to adopt a child. Upon returning to the United States, they started paperwork through an international adoption agency in Oregon. On Father's Day 2002, Daniel and Pamela were in Vietnam again to meet their five-month-old adopted daughter. Two months later, they returned to the orphanage, accompanied by Pamela's parents, to bring Jessie An Jolie Martin home. With Jessie becoming part of their lives, the Martins developed a new connection with Vietnam: they stayed in touch with Jessie's birth mother and tried to reach out to other disadvantaged children. In 2005, Daniel made his fifth trip to Vietnam to contribute more to humanitarian work.[46]

In some cases, family members needed to heal too. Living with a shock that came when she was a college freshman in 1967, Geneva Duarte finally visited Vietnam in 2003 to say goodbye to her cousin Raymond Barela Palma. Palma died in combat only eight days into his tour. Duarte simply could not let go of her cousin. In 1991, she visited the Vietnam Veterans Memorial in Washington, DC, to see Palma's name on the wall for herself, but the tragedy remained unfathomable for her. However, a magical moment arrived when she and TOP's participants stood by a pagoda on Marble Mountain in Da Nang, central Vietnam. She wrote, "As I stand in the space where he last walked, I feel his spirit calling me. . . . It is time for us to heal, to forgive and to bring our cultures together in mutual understanding and love."[47]

One distinct feature of TOP was its Personal Effects Program, which recovered and returned wartime personal belongings such as dog tags and clothing items to US veterans or families of KIAs. Driven by the belief that these artifacts are "both a remembrance and a way to honor the veteran's service," TOP devoted remarkable efforts to the daunting task. They carefully authenticated each retrieved item to make sure it was not a replica, then verified data and identified its legitimate owner.[48] Once a personal effect was matched with a recipient, its return was accompanied by a letter of appreciation and recognition. A dog tag was enclosed in a dark-blue velvet box. Occasionally, a TOP representative would present the item to its rightful owner in person. All of this was done at no cost. TOP also listed on its website the names on the dog tags in its possession in hopes of finding their owners through word of mouth.[49]

One of TOP's most special memories occurred in 1999 when its delegation was visiting Hoi An, an ancient coastal town in central Vietnam. Le Sinh, a former South Vietnamese soldier and an interpreter for the US Marines during wartime, approached the group and presented an old patched-up sandbag. Inside the burlap sandbag was a green vinyl rain poncho that belonged to his "best friend," Captain Willard Dale Marshall. Choking back his tears, Le recalled, "He died in my arms. There's not a day that goes by that I do not think about my friend." Captain Marshall was wearing the poncho when he got hit by an explosion on June 11, 1968, and died of severe bleeding. Le had kept the poncho for thirty-one years, awaiting an opportunity to return the sacred effect to Captain Marshall's family. TOP conducted a "long, exhaustive search" and located Rod Marshall, the captain's oldest son, who was four years old when Captain Marshall passed away. The poncho finally "came home" in January 2001. In a thank-you letter to TOP, Rod wrote, "I cannot imagine how it must have felt for [Mr. Sinh] to hold on to this item for so many years . . . the attachment he must have felt to my father . . . and then to be able to give it up, just for the chance that it could be returned to the family." Rod also emphasized that Le's actions "answered the question of 'what kind of man was my father' better than anything else could"; apparently, his father was a man who was loved and respected. For Rod, the

Vietnamese soldier had given meaning to "what would have otherwise been a worthless piece of vinyl."[50] The lifetime friendship that Le had for Captain Marshall is illuminating. It speaks volumes about the human aspect of war and the sacred bonds among those who dealt with life and death on a daily basis. Although Le did not literally travel, his postwar journey in search of peace was by no means less arduous. Peace, for Le, was the fulfillment of an unspoken promise to his best friend.

For many veterans, receiving a long-lost dog tag could effect a profound change in their lives. Billy Wiatt wrote,

> When TOP Vets returned my dog tag to me, I cried for three hours. I never shed a tear before. I was very depressed, and I never talked about the war with my family. I started working on my issues, and I am now taking one day at a time. This past Christmas I gave my dog tag to my son, and for the first time talked to him about the war.[51]

For another veteran, Thomas G. Reddecliff, who served in Vietnam from 1969 to 1970, the returned tag "[put] to a close a long troubled 35 years of wondering how this will all end."[52] The unexpected "homecoming" of the tag did not come easily though. Reddecliff described his emotional struggle: "My hair stood up when I got the package. I was afraid to open it. I held it for a few hours wondering if I should just leave that chapter closed." Eventually, he opened the package and "went into a zone [he] thought was over." The tag reminded him of the horrendous days in a combat zone. He could "actually smell the fire," "smell the napalm," "hear the cries, feel the fear, and remember [his] ears ringing after incoming." The experience, however, transformed once he overcame the flashbacks. The veteran realized that his military service was finally recognized. TOP's respectful gesture brought him peace and allowed him to move on. Reddecliff claimed, "From this day on I will wear this tag until one day I can give it to my son. I will always wear it proud, and most of all I will wear it in honor and the utmost respect for the brothers and sisters who never returned, and for the MIA's still there . . . and for all the other vets of other wars and conflicts."[53] The extra care that TOP showed to the veterans and their families brought extraordinary results, and the personal effects were both materially and symbolically the missing pieces of the puzzle these people were trying to figure out.

Some US veterans made their journey to Vietnam with a daunting task of finding surviving families of their former enemies, often to return a personal belonging of a Vietnamese KIA. These veterans' intentions were of the utmost gestures of peace, not only because of the respect they had for fallen soldiers of the other side but also because of the emotional tensions they endured in order to bring peace of mind to people they had never met before. One of the most heartrending stories was Richard Luttrell's thirty-three-year epic. Enlisting in 1967, Luttrell arrived in Vietnam as a member of the 101st Airborne. Soon, he realized that he "was never prepared for" the adversity he was to face—hot and humid weather, life on the frontline, and constant fear. Then came the day he faced a North Vietnamese soldier; they were so close that they could see the fear in each other's eyes. Time froze. The two soldiers "stared at each other for a long time" before Luttrell pulled the trigger. When the firefight was over, still exhausted and shocked at the fact that he had just taken a life, Luttrell saw a tiny photo fall out of the Vietnamese soldier's wallet. It was a portrait of a soldier in uniform and a little girl, approximately six or seven years of age. Perhaps that was the fallen soldier and his daughter, Lutrell thought. He said in an interview on NBC: "I can remember holding the photo and actually squatting and getting close to the soldier and actually looking in his face and looking at the photo, and looking at his face." Luttrell decided to keep the photo in his wallet, unaware that it would become an obsession for decades to come.[54]

Despite the numerous times he changed his wallet since he came home in 1968, Luttrell always kept the photo. He explained, "I really formed a bond, especially with the little girl in the photograph. Here's a young daughter doesn't have a father thanks to me." While he did not regret going to Vietnam as a combat soldier, Luttrell felt "unending guilt" and "uncontrollable sorrow" for having turned a child into an orphan. In 1989, when he and his wife visited the Vietnam Veterans Memorial in Washington, DC, Luttrell decided to end his emotional turmoil by leaving the photo at the wall.[55] He wrote a note, an imagined conversation with the Vietnamese soldier:

Dear Sir,

For twenty-two years, I've carried your picture in my wallet.
    I was only eighteen years old that day we faced one another on that trail in Chu Lai, Vietnam.
    Why you didn't take my life I'll never know.
    You stared at me for so long, armed with your AK-47, and yet you did not fire.

Forgive me for taking your life. I was reacting just the way I was trained, to kill VC. . . .

So many times over the years I've stared at your picture and your daughter, I suspect.

Each time, my heart and guts would burn with the pain of guilt. I have two daughters myself now. . . .

I perceive you as a brave soldier defending his homeland.

Above all else, I can now respect the importance that life held for you.

I suppose that is why I am able to be here today. . . .

It is time for me to continue the life process and release my pain and guilt.

Forgive me, Sir.[56]

The photo caught the attention of Duery Felton, a curator of the Vietnam Veterans Memorial collection. A combat veteran, Felton felt connected with Luttrell's words and became "haunted for years" by the little girl in the picture. When he was asked to assist with the publication of *Offerings at the Wall*, Felton selected the photo and the note. Six years had passed, and Luttrell, now working for the Illinois Department of Veterans Affairs, received a copy of the book. Flipping through the pages, Luttrell felt a shock as he reached pages 52–53. There they were—the familiar faces and his note; the little girl seemed to be staring at him. For Luttrell, the "nightmare" had returned. He stared at the photo with questions running through his mind: "Little girl, what do you want from me? You know, what do you want from me?"[57] Luttrell contacted Felton and said that he wanted the photo back. Felton flew from Washington, DC, to Rochester, Illinois, to hand deliver the photo that had become so special to him. According to NBC journalist Keith Morrison, it seemed unfathomable that "two middle aged men, who didn't know each other, had never met, would hold on and weep real tears for a small girl neither knew."[58] Then Luttrell decided to find the little girl to return the photo to her. He contacted a journalist in St. Louis, and the story appeared on the newpaper *Post Dispatch on Sunday*. Luttrell sent the news story and a letter to Vietnam's ambassador to the United States, asking for help with his quest. Subsequently, a newspaper in Hanoi published the story and the photograph. Luttrell's epic almost sank in the sea of information until a young man in Hanoi accidentally used the newspaper to wrap a care package for his mother, who lived in a small village north of Hanoi. With inexplicable luck, the mother recognized the people in the photo and brought the newspaper to "the little girl," now a forty-year-old woman.[59]

In 2000, Luttrell returned to Vietnam, venturing to the remote village to meet Lan, the child who had haunted him for more than three decades. Lan and her family and neighbors were expecting Luttrell in a small yard when he arrived. Luttrell greeted her in Vietnamese and presented her a bouquet. She gently said, "Thank you, uncle," the way Vietnamese people address one another. The "intimate strangers" (to borrow Morrison's words) seemed awkward for a moment, not knowing what to say to each other. Then Luttrell pulled out a little note containing the Vietnamese version of what he wanted to tell her and read it, "Today I return the photo of you and your father, which I have kept for thirty-three years. Please forgive me." Lan was speechless, fighting to hold back her tears, but when Luttrell reached out and held her hands, she clutched him and let go of her grief in rivers of tears. When Lan finally recomposed herself, Luttrell produced the photo that he had respectfully mounted, asking the interpreter to tell Lan: "This is the photo I took from her father's wallet the day I shot and killed him and that I'm returning it. I'm so sorry." Lan gripped the photo, the only image of her and her father together in her possession, and buried her face in Luttrell's chest, weeping uncontrollably. For Lan and the villagers, the returning of the photograph was tantamount to the homecoming of her father. For Luttrell, as Morrison puts it, "his wounded soul had been stitched up and made new again."[60]

Luttrell's quest for peace strongly illustrates the postwar undertaking of combat veterans. Few could forget their act of killing and move on with life. The unpleasant thought of a human taking another human's life often overpowers politics and other rationales. Luttrell distinguished "guilt" from "regret." He was as proud a veteran as he had been proud a soldier. He never regretted enlisting for Vietnam, but he endured for decades the guilt of ending somebody's life. According to West Point Professor Peter Kilner, "The single greatest factor into whether a Vietnam War veteran experienced symptoms of post-traumatic stress disorder was whether they had killed someone." Kilner also points out that while parents are proud of their sons' and daughters' military service, they do not want to know of their children's act of killing.[61] Thus, combat veterans often bear that torment alone. Unlike physical injuries, which tend to be visible and easily evoke empathy, damages of the soul are invisible and silently erosive.

One of the artifacts returned to Vietnamese people by US veterans became world-renowned: the homecoming of communist medical doctor Dang Thuy Tram's diary in April 2005. It seemed coincidental that only a few days before his departure to Vietnam, photojournalist and Vietnam veteran Ted Engelmann met Frederick and Robert Whitehurst at a conference organized by the Vietnam Center at Texas Tech University in Lubbock, Texas, in March 2005. The Whitehurst brothers made a presentation about the Vietnamese communist's diary, which they intended to publish in hope of finding her family. Engelmann volunteered to take a CD scan of the diary to Vietnam to start the search. He contacted the Quaker's office in Hanoi, and by late April, Quaker staff had located Dang Thuy Tram's family. The Whitehurst brothers and Dang Thuy Tram's younger sister, Dang Kim Tram, started an e-mail exchange. By the time the American brothers visited the Vietnamese family in August, the story had spread across Vietnam, as excerpts from the diary appeared in *Tuoi Tre*, the most prestigious newspaper in the country. When Dang Thuy Tram's diary was published in full length a few months later, it became an unprecedented phenomenon in Vietnam's publishing history: within less than two years, approximately four hundred and thirty thousand copies were sold while the average print run in the country was two thousand.[62] The journal has also been translated into English, French, Japanese, and Korean.

The journey of Dang Thuy Tram's diary started in December 1969. Frederick Whitehurst, an officer of the 635th Military Intelligence Detachment in Quang Ngai, was performing his regular task of burning captured materials that had no intelligence value to the United States when his interpreter, Nguyen Trung Hieu, called out, "Fred, don't burn this one. It has fire in it already."[63] Nguyen's translation of a few excerpts convinced Whitehurst to keep the little notebook. The two soldiers spent the following nights reading the communist's diary, deeply touched by the words of her loving heart. Six months later, Nguyen found another volume of Dang Thuy Tram's diary after she was killed by an American platoon. The final entry in her journal was dated June 20, 1970, two days before the incident. When Whitehurst completed his third tour of duty in 1972, he brought the two-volume diary home with him, regardless of rules and regulations. His brother Robert, who was married to a Vietnamese woman, translated the diary into English, and the brothers occasionally shared the diary with others. They wanted to return the diary to Dang Thuy Tram's family, but because Frederick was working as a forensic scientist for the FBI, he could not contact Vietnamese authorities for help. Their search remained on hold until they met Engelmann in 2005.[64]

Dang Thuy Tram's diary is valuable not only because it presented an honest personal account of life and death on the frontline but also because it revealed the heart and soul of a person so loving and so idealistic amid a destructive conflict. Serving as a medical doctor in a North Vietnamese military mobile clinic, she directly witnessed and dealt with the human cost of war. Her diary detailed both the casualties of her patients and the pain of her heart. As Pulitzer Prize–winning journalist Frances FitzGerald asserts, "Regardless of how the diaries are read or perceived, there are three undeniable truths about the author. First, her heart was noble. Second, her life was guided by ideals. Third, her sacrifice was as tragic as it was heroic."[65] Perhaps writing was Dang Thuy Tram's solution to the pain and tensions that she endured. She filled her diary with various emotions, raw and uncensored. Fear, hope, frustration, love, hate, suspicion, worry, helplessness, loneliness were all powerfully displayed under her poetic pen. In an entry dated June 4, 1968, Dang Thuy Tram wrote, "Last night, I dreamed that Peace was established. . . . For Peace and Independence, we have sacrificed everything. So many people have volunteered to sacrifice their lives for those two words: Independence and Liberty. I too—I have sacrificed my life for that grandiose fulfillment."[66] Nguyen was right when he said Dang Thuy Tram's diary had fire in it—a fire that continued to burn in readers' hearts thirty-five years later. Amid the fire and smoke of war formed a seemingly strange connection among the trio—a North Vietnamese doctor, a South Vietnamese soldier, and an American officer—an astounding connection that illuminated the power of the human heart.

Sometimes the keepsake returned to its owner was beyond imagination. In 2012, Dr. Sam Axelrad from Texas embarked for Vietnam with an unusual piece of luggage: the arm bones of a former North Vietnamese soldier. The story traces its origin back to a rainy day in October 1966, when Nguyen Quang Hung's reconnaissance unit was crossing a stream to gather information about American forces in Phu Cat, Binh Dinh. Ambushed midstream, Nguyen Quang Hung got hit on the right arm in the first round of fire. His group split in two directions to distract enemy fire. Nguyen Quang Hung and another soldier escaped to a nearby village only to realize that it had been raided and most people had evacuated. Some sympathizers gave them food and a small bag of medicine but made it clear that it was too risky for villagers to shelter them in their houses. The two soldiers took cover in a rice warehouse. After three days, they heard gunfire. United States troops were back. The other soldier ran for his life; Nguyen Quang Hung was too weak to escape. Upon discovering Nguyen Quang Hung with his arm rotten from infection, the Americans immediately transferred him to a military hospital by helicopter. In Nguyen Quang Hung's mind, he was "like a fish on the chopping board"—his fate was in the hand of the Americans. To his surprise, however, they took care of him while chaining his leg to the hospital bed.

Through an interpreter, Nguyen Quang Hung claimed that he was a military nurse; the small bag of medicine served as supporting evidence. That he was not carrying any weapons significantly added weight to his claim. The only bad news was that it was too late to save his arm. Axelrad became Nguyen Quang Hung's savior for performing the amputation. After surgery, Axelrad's colleagues boiled off the flesh, restructured the arm bones, and gave them to him as a memento of a good deed he had done for a soldier on the other side.[67]

It turned out that Nguyen Quang Hung ended up living the lie he had told the Americans. He spent several months recovering in the hospital, and out of boredom, he started helping the nurses with little things. His amiable personality developed positive relationships with the hospital staff. Then one day, Axelrad received an order to dismiss the "enemy soldier" within twenty-four hours. Axelrad arranged for Nguyen Quang Hung to work in a civilian clinic in Quy Nhon. A few months later, Nguyen Quang Hung decided to return to An Khe and worked as an assistant for a private nurse who had retired from the military hospital where Axelrad saved Nguyen Quang Hung's life. Nguyen Quang Hung eventually married the nurse's daughter and called An Khe his second hometown. Meanwhile, Axelrad returned to the United States, leaving his "Vietnam bag" in the closet and moved on to become a urologist. Not until 2011 did he open the bag, and as he said in an interview, "It just blew me away what was in there." In addition to the skeleton arm were old photos, among which was a shot of him and Nguyen Quang Hung standing together with broad smiles and Axelrad holding Nguyen Quang Hung's arm bones in his hand. Axelrad returned to Vietnam in November 2012 but did not know how to start the search. He visited An Khe but did not look for Nguyen Quang Hung, assuming the soldier had returned to his hometown in the north. With luck, his tour guide in Hanoi was also a journalist who had a keen interest in war stories. The journalist sent Axelrad's quest to the newspaper *Thanh Nien* and the story circulated in other media, which eventually caught the attention of Nguyen Quang Hung's brother-in-law in Saigon. With the journalist's help, a unique reunion between the two men, now in their seventies, became a reality in July 2013. For Axelrad, "it [was] just time for closure." For Nguyen Quang Hung, it was beyond his imagination to be reunited with the person who had saved his life. It was also beyond his expectation to have his bones back so that when he died, he would "be buried as a whole person."[68] In a most wonderful irony of war, Nguyen Quang Hung owed his life, and a peaceful death, to a person on the other side of the frontline.

June 4, 2012, became a historic day in US-Vietnam relations. On that day,

US Defense Secretary Leon Panetta and Vietnamese Defense Minister Phung Quang Thanh exchanged fallen soldiers' mementos that had been captured during wartime. The three American letters that Secretary Panetta brought to Vietnam belonged to US Army Sgt. Steve Flaherty, who fell in March 1969. A North Vietnamese soldier, now retired Col. Nguyen Phu Dat, had felt deeply connected with Flaherty's depiction of the cruelty of war and kept the letters as special "souvenirs" from his opponents. Nguyen Phu Dat even quoted the letters in his wartime broadcast for propaganda purposes. When he came home after the war, Nguyen Phu Dat's mother told him in tears how she had desperately awaited his letters from the frontline. Touched by his mother's words, Nguyen Phu Dat began to treasure Flaherty's letters at a deeper level, nurturing the thought of returning them to his family. He asked the media for help, but the search remained fruitless for decades. Finally, he found a website about war artifacts, which brought miraculous results. In a similar manner, the Vietnamese diary belonged to North Vietnamese soldier Vu Dinh Doan, who died in Quang Ngai in 1966 after serving in the military for six years. Robert Frazue found the diary by Vu's body in the aftermath of Operation Indiana. Like Nguyen Phu Dat, Frazure had always wanted to return the keepsake to the Vietnamese soldier's family. Through a friend, he sent the diary to the PBS series *History Detectives*, whose research team successfully located Vu's family.[69] The returning of the materials had dual healing effects. For the veterans, they obtained peace of mind for fulfilling an unspoken promise to a soldier, regardless of politics. For the KIAs' families, the artifacts not only helped them further understand their heroes but the homecoming of the objects was also a reunion with the souls of their beloved soldiers.

According to an announcement by the Pentagon, the event was the first of its kind since 1975.[70] A closer look at the "landmark," however, reveals that only the presence and formality of the two top military leaders was historic. On the one hand, it was ordinary citizens who made efforts to preserve wartime artifacts and locate their rightful owners. Governmental involvement was no more than a final touch at the exchange ceremony. On the other hand, as documented in this research, US and Vietnamese veterans had been doing this for decades. The exchange was a continuation of citizens' work, not a landmark of governmental achievement.

With the passage of time, more and more reconciliatory endeavors surfaced, adding dimension to the picture of postwar relations between US and Vietnamese citizens. Retired Brigadier General Dan Cherry's story stood out as another fascinating illustration of the power of forgiveness. Cherry joined the US Air Force in 1959 and stayed for twenty-nine years. During the Vietnam War, he flew 295 combat missions; one of those flights scored him a victory for shooting down a North Vietnamese MiG-21. In 2004, Cherry accidentally rediscovered the plane that he was piloting for his victorious mission on April 16, 1972—the F-4D #66-7550, Phantom 550—in Ohio. Cherry and his friends started a project to restore the plane and to bring it to his hometown in Bowling Green, Kentucky. As the Phantom 550 was rolling into Aviation Heritage Park in Bowling Green in December 2005, Cherry's decades-long question resurfaced: What happened to the Vietnamese pilot of the MiG-21?[71]

Cherry started his search, which appeared to be fruitless, until a friend introduced him to "As If They Had Never Been Separated," a Vietnamese television show that helped families and friends reunite.[72] The program staff successfully located the MiG-21 pilot, Nguyen Hong My, and invited Cherry to come to Vietnam for a televised reunion. Thirty-six years after their dogfight, Cherry and Nguyen Hong My met for the first time on April 5, 2008. The firm handshake they exchanged on stage added a new chapter to the story of these warriors. After the public event in Saigon, Nguyen Hong My invited Cherry to his home in Hanoi; Cherry agreed. The next day, the two former combat pilots on opposing sides of the war sat side by side on a Vietnam Airlines plane, flying the length of the country they both knew so well from an aerial view. Cherry admitted that "it felt strange."[73] It must have felt strange—the victory of one had translated into broken arms and severe back injuries of the other, but it was that fatal incident that brought them together as friends.

The two veterans had much more to share with each other than they had imagined. They caught up with each other's life like old friends. Together they visited historical places, including Hoa Lo Prison, known to US soldiers as "Hanoi Hilton." Cherry recognized a friend's face among the pictures of US POWs in the eerie place. In a moment of unspeakable sorrow, the veterans seemed to understand each other at a deeper level: words were unnecessary, and a pat on the shoulder said it all. As Cherry put it, "In April, [sic] 1972, Hong My and I had met as enemies in the skies over North Vietnam. Thirty-six years later to the month, we had come full circle. That day, on the streets of Hanoi, my enemy had truly become my friend."[74] When they bid farewell a few days later, Nguyen Hong My asked Cherry, "When you get back to the United States, will you do research for me?" The Vietnamese veteran wanted to know about the fate of the pilot of an American RF-4 that he had shot down on January 19, 1972. Cherry kept his promise to look for the pilot and found out that both the pilot, Major Bob Mock, and the navigator, John Stiles, of the

RF-4 had been rescued from the crash. Unfortunately, Mock died in an automobile accident two months before Cherry located him.[75]

April 2009 witnessed what Cherry called the "double full circle" as Nguyen Hong My and his son visited Cherry in Kentucky and Stiles in North Carolina. Cherry's role as a "go-between" had not been easy. Stiles's first response to Cherry was frank: "Dan, I stored those traumatic memories away long ago, and now you come along and bring them all back up again."[76] While the time and place of Stiles's crash were confirmed, the military records attributed the incident to ground fire, not a shot from a MiG. Therefore, Stiles had another reason to hesitate to meet with Nguyen Hong My. However, after his long conversation with Nguyen Hong My, Stiles said to Cherry: "Dan, I've been waiting for thirty-seven years for this moment. It's as if a huge weight has been lifted off my shoulders. Now I know for sure exactly what happened that day. Hong My told me things only the two of us could know."[77]

For Cherry, the reunion with Nguyen Hong My was a reconciliation that transformed animosity to friendship, a perspective with which most others would agree. Nguyen Hong My, however, surprised Cherry with a different view. Upon his arrival in Kentucky, Nguyen Hong My received a copy of Cherry's book *My Enemy, My Friend: A Story of Reconciliation from the Vietnam War*. When asked for his opinion before they parted ways a couple of weeks later, Nguyen Hong My said, "I do like your book. I just don't like the title. . . . I don't think you and I were ever enemies. We were just soldiers doing the best we could for our countries during a very difficult time."[78] Nguyen Hong My was right. As individuals, they never had animosity toward each other. They were but patriots serving their countries.

The Arduous Roads Home

Although Vietnam as a country had accelerated its recovery from the war, thousands of individuals still lived in the frozen time and space of their pasts, quietly and desperately searching for inner peace. Every day, they relived memories that were decades old, trying to rearrange the fragments of their lives in the hope of finding some clues to the burning questions in their minds. Many were in search of family members, with strong beliefs that reunions would eventually come; others held only a modest hope of finding the remains of their loved ones. Their quests were personal and private and, more often than not, fruitless. For a few decades, inquiries and success stories occasionally appeared on print media, but not until the mid-2000s were information networks and support systems available to assist.

By and large, public discourse on postwar homecoming mainly focuses on returning warriors' experiences. Vietnam War literature in particular is enriched with large numbers of research, memoirs, and other forms of storytelling such as poetry and visual and performing arts. Civilians' homecoming experiences at best appear as news stories that attract little attention. While common knowledge indicates that warfare almost always results in displacements, we know little about missing civilians' and their families' ongoing struggles. For these people, the war did not end when ceasefire and peace agreements were announced. Until the day they were reunited with their loved ones, they would spend their days, or even decades, reliving wartime memories and juggling intense desperation and faint hope. Their "homecoming" was arduous, and many never arrived home. The stories of Vietnamese civilians' endeavors to help others or help themselves reconnect torn families would deepen our understanding of the Vietnam War. Similar to other Vietnamese, Americans, and Amerasians discussed earlier in this project, these people also struggled to bring closure to the war. Their peace efforts deserve a place in the historical research on war and related issues.

The monthly television live show *Như Chưa Hề Có Cuộc Chia Ly* (As if they had never been separated), accompanied by its website http://www .haylentieng.vn (Raise your voice), played a major role in helping families and friends reunite. Inspired by the Russian program *Zdi Menhia!* (Wait for me!), which helped approximately twenty thousand people find their families and friends in its decade-long existence, journalist Nguyen Pham Thu Uyen created *Như Chưa Hề Có Cuộc Chia Ly* (NCHCCCL) in 2007. The name of the program was the last line of a 1964's poem "Cuộc Chia Ly Màu Đỏ" (A red separation), which described a young couple bidding farewell as the husband leaves for the battlefront. In the poem, the wife was wearing a red blouse, which "looks like a flame burning at the separation." As the poet believed, that red color would follow the husband to the battlefield to warm his heart "as if they had never been separated."[79] Nguyen Pham Thu Uyen's NCHCCCL started with the idea of mobilizing governmental agencies, nongovernmental organizations, businesses, and individuals in order to work together to help people find their lost families, regardless of reasons. The audience became active participants by providing information to the program as well as to individuals looking for their loved ones. Working side by side with professional investigators and information analysts were hundreds of volunteers all over the world. Its websites encouraged people to "raise [their] voice," either to find missing families or to help others. By 2020, the program had solved nine hundred and seventeen cases; many of them had lost families since the Vietnam War.[80]

Nguyen Trung Phuong's earliest memories included a small village road with tall coconut trees on both sides and "a very long bed" that he shared with many children. Not until he came of age did Nguyen Trung Phuong know that the place was Nguyen Ba Ngoc Orphanage in Hung Yen, where he lived for several months in 1969 before a local family adopted him. Because the five-year-old boy did not know his full name, he carried his adoptive father's last name in his new birth certificate. From his adoptive parents, Nguyen Trung Phuong learned that he and his sister came from Vinh Linh, a small town on the north side of the DMZ in Quang Tri. His parents had died during a bombing campaign. He had no further information about his sister. In his middle age, Nguyen Trung Phuong wanted to establish an altar for his biological parents, a Vietnamese tradition seen in most homes. Because he had no pictures of his parents, Nguyen Trung Phuong commissioned a calligraphy artist to write the words "father" and "mother" and put the framed words on the altar in place of their photos. Unsure about the date of his parents' deaths, he chose 2:30 p.m. on the seventh day of the lunar calendar as their death anniversary. That was the time and date when his hometown began its endurance of US bombs in 1965.[81]

To help Nguyen Trung Phuong find his sister, NCHCCCL staff had to understand the history of Vinh Linh. During wartime, this five-hundred-square-mile district received approximately half a million tons of bombs, which resulted in fifteen thousand deaths and three thousand orphans. To survive, the locals created a twenty-five-mile-long tunnel system and thousands of bunkers. The majority of those who survived did so thanks to three great migration campaigns coded K8, K10, and K15. K8 was the evacuation of thirty thousand students aged seven to fifteen, who eventually would be transported to northern provinces between June 1966 and December 1967. It was an organized evacuation divided into stages, with provincial assistance and guidance to safety. With the US bomb campaigns ongoing, the escape involved long walks and night-time activity. Seventy people, including fifty-nine children, died during the long march to safety. K10—the second evacuation of children, the elderly, women with two or more children, and the disabled—started in October 1967 and lasted until 1973. The majority of these refugees temporarily settled down in Nghe An, two hundred miles from Quang Tri. K15 occurred during the Easter Offensive of 1972 launched by North Vietnam, which was nicknamed "the Fiery Red Summer" because of the intense firepower used and its subsequent carnage. This time, the refugees consisted of civilians from the districts on the other side of Ben Hai River, the Geneva Accords' dividing line. The search team looked for those who had been sent to Nguyen Ba Ngoc Orphanage, and the story started to unfold. It turned out that besides his older sister, Nguyen Trung Phuong had a younger brother. All three of them were evacuated in the K10 campaign. They had lived in the same orphanage but were separated by age and later adopted by different families. After more than four decades, Nguyen Trung Phuong's quest finally concluded with a happy ending: He was reunited with his siblings and found his roots in Vinh Linh, where his aunts and uncles still remained.[82]

Few refugees of those migration campaigns were as fortunate as Nguyen Trung Phuong. Nguyen Thi Dong left Vinh Linh during K8 in 1967. Her family joined K10 later the same year. It was Christmas, and the holiday was observed with a ceasefire for twenty-four hours. At 5 p.m. on December 25, the bombing resumed. A B-52 killed Nguyen Thi Dong's parents and injured one of her two older sisters. In the chaos, her four-year-old sister went missing. In 1978, Nguyen Thi Dong went to the pass where her parents died to look for their burial places and her youngest sister but had no luck. Nguyen Thi Dong continued her journey with the pain only she could understand.[83]

Among the first victims of US bombing in North Vietnam was Pham Thi Van's family in Do Son, a town eighty miles east of Hanoi. As Pham remembered, it was 1965; she and her three younger siblings were home with her grandmother. When they heard the bombers coming, her grandmother carried her seven-month-old brother, leading their way down the little bunker under their bed; seven-year-old Pham helped her sisters follow their grandmother. After a few bombings, a neighbor ran over, whispering something to her grandmother. Her grandmother immediately passed the baby brother to Pham, telling her to carry him down to the bunker before helping her sisters if the siren went off again. Then their grandmother vanished with the neighbor. The bombers returned; Pham did what her grandmother had told her and helped her siblings down into the bunker and up to the bed. She could not remember how many times they had to run that day, but it seemed like a long time before somebody took all of them to a site. As they got closer, Pham saw her mother lying on the ground, face down, and there was a big hole in her back. Pham knew a disaster had struck her family. Her father had just returned from the battlefield with a diagnosis of 50 percent disability, and he was on some duty out of town. Unable to feed all their mouths with his condition, the father gave his only son, Pham Phu Toan, to a friend. When Pham Phu Toan was a little older, she asked her father for the names of Pham Phu Toan's adoptive parents. But her father said Pham Phu Toan was living in better conditions than they were, and that if they brought him back, the situation would worsen for everybody. When her father was on his deathbed decades later, he told Van the adopters' names. Van started the search with the only photo of the family—a newspaper cutout of her mother's funeral with her grandmother holding Pham Phu Toan next to her and her two sisters. Her love and determination resulted in a reunion in 2009.[84]

Sometimes the happiness of a reunion blended with the bitterness and irony of wartime circumstances. Luong Thi Chanh and Luong Thi Chuc were twenty and sixteen, respectively, when they parted ways in 1961. Luong Thi Chanh, Luong Thi Chuc, and their two brothers had lived together in the commune of Binh Ba, Ba Ria-Vung Tau Province, for a few years before Luong Thi Chanh got married and moved to another town. Luong Thi Chanh did not know she would never see her brothers again and would have to wait for more than a half century before she was reunited with her sister. Like many other towns during the war, Binh Ba was under control of South Vietnam by day and of North Vietnam's ally, the National Liberation Front, by night. Subsequently, Luong Thi Chanh's three siblings felt the effects of both sides of the conflict. Her oldest brother was drafted by the ARVN while the other brother joined the local guerrillas. Within a few years, both were killed in action. Meanwhile, Luong Thi Chuc got married in the mid-1960s and, together with her husband, joined the National Liberation Front. In 1968, her husband, Phan Thanh Cam, was arrested and transferred to Phu Quoc Prison, a notorious "hell on earth" for political prisoners who fought against South Vietnam and its allies. Concerned that her identity might be disclosed, Luong Thi Chuc escaped to another town. In 1973, her husband became part of a historical event: the POW exchange by Thach Han River before the withdrawal of US troops in accordance with the Paris Peace Accords. Upon his release, Phan was sent to Hanoi to recover, and not until 1977 was he reunited with his wife. Luong Thi Chanh and Luong Thi Chuc still could not find each other despite their efforts. Luong Thi Chanh finally resorted to NCHCCCL, and a miracle happened in 2014. Ironically, the day Luong Thi Chanh found her sister was also the day she learned that both of her bothers had died for the country, on opposing sides.[85]

The Tet Offensive of 1968 is often known as a turning point of the Vietnam

War, with high casualties on both sides, but little is known about its effects on children at the time. Vo Thi Kim Lan was seven years old in 1968, and as she remembered in 2015, she got lost from her family while they were evacuating from Thu Duc, a suburb of Saigon, amid a firefight. A policeman found her on the street and brought her to an orphanage. She stayed in the orphanage until she turned fifteen when she joined others moving to a "new economic zone." When she arrived at the orphanage, seven-year-old Vo carried with her a small bag of clothes, in which she found her birth certificate. She did not know why the document was there or what it meant, but she kept it as a treasure. In 2014, Vo submitted that treasure to NCHCCCL and asked for help in search of her family. Other than that, she also remembered the names of her three brothers and two sisters, but nothing more.[86]

After several months, the search team found Vo's family and learned of the chained tragedies that happened to her family after she went missing. As it turned out, Vo remembered everything correctly except for one detail: her family was not living in Thu Duc in 1968. However, they did live in the area for a few years when her father was stationed in a nearby ARVN camp. Then they moved to Tam Hiep, Bien Hoa, which was only fifteen miles away. Vo used to babysit for a neighbor, who later moved to Thu Duc. For unknown reasons, Vo's parents let her go with the neighbor. In the chaos of the Tet Offensive a few months later, Vo got lost while she was with her former neighbor in Thu Duc. Saddened by the tragic news of Vo going missing, her father drank heavily, which resulted in a fatal traffic accident. Soon after Vo's father died, her brothers started working to help support the family. Within a year or so, her eldest brother died when he fell off a house frame while doing construction work. He was fifteen years of age. A few years later, her second brother, who had become a policeman, was shot to death. After 1975, her family moved to another town, a new economic zone, where her third brother stepped on a landmine that destroyed one of his eyes and left him with many scars. Vo's reunion with her family finally took place after forty-seven years of separation, but the happy ending came with bitterness, as her mother had developed amnesia. The elderly lady barely recognized the daughter she had always yearned to see again.[87]

Wartime circumstances dislocated people in unimaginable ways. Phan Thi Huong lived only a hundred miles from her family, but it took her forty-nine years to cover that distance. In 1965, Phan's family was living in Bu Dop, a remote village by the Vietnam-Cambodia border. This area was under tight military control by both South Vietnam and the Viet Cong. One morning, the twelve-year-old girl was on her way to the market to get some grocery items for her mother. All of a sudden, she was arrested by South Vietnam's military police, who suspected that she was an informant of the Viet Cong. They took her to a town twenty-four miles away and imprisoned her for six months. When she was released, Phan did not know her way home. She ended up working for other people in exchange for food and started her independent life. Following odds jobs, Phan drifted away from her hometown. Within a few years, she found herself in Saigon and decided to settle in the city. She had made efforts to find her family several times but had no luck because she had too little information. NCHCCCL was her last resort, and this time she had great luck. As the host Nguyen Phan Thu Uyen commented, "Despite the short distance [of one hundred miles] between Saigon and her hometown, it was the longest journey in her life."[88]

In the irony of fate, Nguyen Van Huy became a soldier of both sides of the conflict. At fourteen, he joined the Viet Minh in 1954, and his family did not hear from him until sixty years later. Two years after leaving his hometown in Quang Tri, Nguyen became a soldier in a People's Army of Vietnam (NVA) platoon. Then in a battle in 1960, he was captured and was not released until four years later. Before he figured out what to do with his life, Nguyen was drafted by the South Vietnam government and sent to the Mekong Delta. Injured by a landmine in 1968, Nguyen was finally released from the military and started his civilian life. Meanwhile, his family and other villagers moved to another province to escape the heavy bombing and firefights in Quang Tri in 1971. When NCHCCCL found his family in 2014, Nguyen's parents and his eldest brother had passed away; Nguyen himself was hospitalized on reunion day.[89]

Images of thousands of refugees shoving their way aboard a ship at Da Nang Port or an airplane at Tan Son Nhat Airport in Saigon in March and April 1975 became symbolic pictures of the end of the Vietnam War, but little is known about the fates of those people who tried to survive the chaos. Hoang Thi Hoa was eleven months old in March 1975. Her mother was carrying Hoang and her sister, one on each arm. Another daughter was holding on to the mother's neck. As the young mother was pushing and being pushed through the panicked crowd trying to board a ship, Hoang fell off her arm onto the floor of a barge next to the ship. Unable to go back for her daughter, the mother helplessly moved on with the force of the crowd. The family believed the baby would not survive. They often talked about her at family gatherings but did not know how to start their search. Another family on the barge picked up Hoang and adopted her, naming her Nguyen Thi Tien. All they knew was that she was under one year old and had two teeth, a red birthmark on her cheek, and another birthmark on her leg. Those clues did not help Nguyen Thi Tien in her quest, for she was not the only baby girl who was lost on that day. A few families came to see her, but DNA tests did not match. Nguyen Thi Tien had given up her quest when NCHCCCL staff approached her because of another case. Again, she was not the person they were looking for. Nevertheless, NCHCCCL announced Nguyen Thi Tien's case on her behalf. Two mothers in the audience registered for DNA tests. This time, Nguyen Thi Tien's dream came true. Thirty-nine years after the nightmare had overshadowed her life, Nguyen Thi Tien found her family and her real name.[90]

Several more children went missing amid that evacuation at Da Nang Port. Nguyen Thi Bich Van was eight when her family boarded a ship for Saigon against the advice of her uncle. Her parents, grandmother, and four siblings were with her. The next thing she knew was that she woke up on a beach, holding a small bag of chopped sugarcane in her hand. After a few minutes of crying for her mother, Nguyen Thi Bich Van realized she was lost and headed for the road. She grabbed the back of a bicycle, pleading with the woman to take her home. Nguyen Thi Bich Van did not know she was in Nha Trang, more than three hundred miles from Da Nang. Subsequently, Nguyen Thi Bich Van followed the young woman to her home, beginning her new life with a new mother and a new grandmother. Despite her vague memories and little information—even uncertainty about her parents' and siblings' names—Nguyen Thi Bich Van made an effort, and NCHCCCL was her hope. Nguyen Thi Bich Van did not know that her family had also been looking for her all these years. They even appealed to the Red Cross to look for her in the United States. As her siblings remembered, their mother fell in the water when the loaded ship stopped in Nha Trang. Her older sister and brother were crying for help, and amid the chaos, they saw Nguyen Thi Bich Van getting off the ship. The panicked crowd made it impossible to get their sister back. Memories of Nguyen Thi Bich Van and that tragic day lived on in the family for decades to come. On his deathbed, Nguyen Thi Bich Van's father insisted that the rest of the family not give up looking for her. Six years after he died, and forty years after that horrific day, the family was reunited.[91]

The words *Route 7* (present-day Highway 25) still haunted many people decades after the war ended. It was early 1975 when Hanoi launched the Ho Chi Minh Campaign (known to Americans as the Spring Offensive), which was its final, decisive operation against South Vietnam. As the NVA marched southward and took control of more and more provinces that used to be governed by South Vietnam, those who supported or had families fighting for the South abandoned their homes, seeking refuge in bigger cities. The main road connecting the Central Highlands and the coastal city of Nha Trang, Route 7, was jammed with thousands of civilians and soldiers of both sides. Many ARVN soldiers threw away their weapons and took off their uniforms, blending in the flow of refugees. Vo Than, a father of six, was taking his family to safety from Pleiku in a truck. He remembered struggling through the chaos, hearing gunfire in all directions. He made it through for about sixty miles and got off the highway, journeying through villages of ethnic minorities. By late afternoon, the family had to abandon the truck and head into a wooded area. Vo hydrated his children by letting them lick dew on leaves, but that did not lessen their thirst. Desperate, the father let them drink his urine. Then he heard people talking about a nearby waterhole in the rocks. He immediately carried his youngest son, five-year-old Vo Quan, and took a shortcut to the water source. After drinking water, his son felt weak, but knowing his other children were also thirsty, Vo Than left Vo Quan on the ground and went back to get the rest of his family. When they all got to the waterhole two hours later, Vo Quan disappeared. The father noticed broken twigs in the surroundings, which gave him a hope that some NVA soldiers had passed by, picked up his little boy, and brought him to safety. His family spent the next four decades searching for Vo Quan in vain. For them, the horror of March 1975 has yet to close.[92]

Sometimes a perilous, hopeless quest of one person led to unexpected happy endings for others. Thirty-four years after losing his son, Nguyen Ngoc Xem still could not hold back his tears every time he looked at his family photo. Nguyen Ngoc Xem said he would not rest in peace if he could not find out what happened to his five-year-old boy on that disastrous day in March 1975. Over the decades, Nguyen Ngoc Xem traveled by bicycle up and down Route 7, visiting every town and village along the road to look for his son. In 1995, Nguyen Ngoc Xem adopted a young man who was also looking for his biological family. Nguyen Ngoc Xem gave the young man his son's name, Nguyen Bao Chinh, and loved him indiscriminately. Yet Nguyen Ngoc Xem did not give up his search. When he could afford a scooter, Nguyen Ngoc Xem widened his search area to other provinces. He documented the names and circumstances of other orphans that he met in his trips. Thanks to his notes, NCHCCCL unexpectedly located the lost son of another family. The weathered, brokenhearted father asserted that his search would go on as long as he lived. The empty space in his heart may never be filled again, and hope was all he had on those lonely roads.[93]

NCHCCCL unfolded the stories of personal odysseys of thousands of families in Vietnam. For these people, the war did not truly end until they could find peace in their hearts. When they could not travel physically, they did so mentally. As long as they were still separated from their families, they would often travel back in time, reliving the few fragmented memories they had with their loved ones. The circumstances in which they lost their families varied, but they all shared an overarching historical tragedy. Their stories illuminated our understanding of the enduring and pervasive effects of war. They revealed a lesser-known picture of how a war "ended," or did not end in these cases.

NCHCCCL's creator and show host, Nguyen Pham Thu Uyen, also created another TV program: *Trở Về Từ Ký Ức* (Returning from memory). This program was devoted to another kind of postwar journey: the search for the remains of fallen soldiers. *Trở Về Từ Ký Ức* (TVTKU) was born out of the hope of NCHCCCL's viewers. Witnessing the success of NCHCCCL in helping families reunite, many people sent assistance requests to find the remains of their beloved soldiers. Touched by the personal stories and having experience with social networking, journalist Nguyen Pham Thu Uyen decided to launch TVTKU in 2011. After four years, TVTKU helped identify 307 sets of remains and returned them to their surviving families. According to 2015's statistics, more than three hundred thousand soldiers' graves in military cemeteries remained unidentified. In addition, approximately two hundred thousand fallen soldiers buried during wartime had not been reinterred in military cemeteries; hundreds of them were still in Laos and Cambodia.[94]

One unexpected outcome of TVTKU in 2015 was its investigation of fraudulent psychics, who claimed to have found the remains of dozens of soldiers. Desperate in their search, many families resorted to psychics. These psychics asserted that they could communicate with the dead, or with some superpower, that they could see "the other world," and had a picture of the burial places their clients were looking for. TVTKU's investigative journalists, coordinating with military and police units, discovered that the psychics had their relatives bury animal bones and fake clothing items or mementos in predetermined places before showing their clients directions. DNA tests of the bones revealed the crime.[95] Nguyen Pham Thu Uyen and her team not only contributed to the national service of honoring fallen soldiers but they also helped assuage the pain of individuals in their personal journey.

Another significant helper of those looking for the burial places of soldiers was Nguyen Sy Ho. It all started when his family received a notice from the NVA informing him that his older brother, Nguyen Dang Khoa, had died "on the Southern front in 1973." In 1977, with that little piece of information, Nguyen Sy Ho began his journey throughout the south, visiting all of the cemeteries that he knew. Thirty-one years passed before Nguyen Sy Ho located his brother's grave in a cemetery in Long An Province. His overwhelming joy on that day prompted him to help those in similar situations. He reflected on the problems he had faced and started to systemize his notes. The result was a website with detailed information about the cemeteries that he had visited. After he retired from his teaching career, Ho and his wife returned to those cemeteries and visited new ones to take pictures of all the tombstones, and then he listed on his website the names and other identification information of the soldiers. That work was important, because few cemeteries in Vietnam had a website, and not everybody could travel. People looking for family members could also submit a persons' identification information and Ho would look them up. By 2015, Nguyen Sy Ho had systemized information of more than 161,000 interred soldiers in 268 military cemeteries throughout Vietnam.[96]

National narratives did not necessarily resonate with individuals' experiences. The ending of the war was a long, arduous process for people of all allegiances. Decades after the war "ended," numerous ordinary citizens on both sides of the Pacific Ocean still strove for peace in personal ways. Diplomatic normalization enhanced transnational interactions, especially because of improved bureaucratic procedure. However, whether it was to restore the landscape, to "dump" their "garbage," or to search for a loved one, these US and Vietnamese individuals took on painstaking tasks. As diverse as their stories can be, the historical actors presented in this chapter shared a commonality: while trying to heal their own wounds, they reached out to others. Be it an American or Vietnamese mother, the pain of losing a son was probably the same. Be it an American or a Vietnamese family of a fallen soldier, it was equally significant to know what happened to their loved one. It was universal human emotions that connected them. Regardless of their national and political boundaries, their shared memories of war strengthened their desire for peace and directed their actions to the benefit of other people. The paths they took were challenging, but they did not give up. From the ashes of war bloomed flowers of compassion and love.

Conclusion

A part of us died here in Vietnam, for American veterans. There was a part of us that died, so we need to come back here to reclaim that, and we can do that by helping. We can alleviate some of the guilt we felt in helping other people that really need help. So coming back for me is about that. It's about not only helping people but helping myself because there is no difference between giving and receiving. And that's the thing about war. We are so wounded, and it changed what we've seen and what we've done that we don't want anybody to know. We don't even want you to know that we've been there, and no one really understands that.

—Manus Campbell, quoted from Pankaja Brooke, dir., *You're the Enemy—Welcome Back!*

Manus Campbell was one of many Americans who made Vietnam their home in the past two decades. Drafted in 1966, nineteen-year-old Campbell arrived in the demilitarized zone of Quang Tri, Vietnam, in June 1967, serving in the US Marines. Upon finishing his one-year tour of duty, Campbell returned to the United States "wounded in the soul," as he described, with much survival guilt and nightmarish memories of life on the front line. Forty years later, he returned to Vietnam, feeling nervous about how the Vietnamese would treat him. His worries soon faded as he realized that Vietnamese people "embraced [him] warmly."[1] During his visit to Hue, a city south of Quang Tri and Vietnam's former capital, Campbell stopped by a Buddhist pagoda that sheltered disabled and orphaned children. Touched by the nuns' humanitarian work, Campbell started contributing money to the pagoda on a monthly basis. In 2009, he founded Helping Invisible Victims of War (HIVOW), a nonprofit organization dedicated to the education of disabled children and victims of unexploded ordnance (UXO) in central Vietnam. The following year, he moved to Hue to devote his time to the cause. A hotel staff member, whose parents had fought against the Americans, invited Campbell home. Having learned about Campbell's commitment to the pagoda and HIVOW, the man's eighty-year-old mother told her children to consider Campbell a family member. "She told me that I was her son. My mom in the U.S. had just passed away four months before. I was deeply touched and felt like crying then," Campbell remembers. He remained in Hue for a year and then moved to Da Nang, calling the place "home."[2] Like other Americans, Campbell chose to stay because of the commonalities he shared with the Vietnamese. Their universal emotions overpowered differences.

At first glance, the bonds among American and Vietnamese people—the people on opposing sides of one of the most devastating conflicts in the twentieth century—may seem paradoxical and unfathomable. A closer look at the nature of their relationships, however, revealed a logical explanation. The national, and perhaps political, boundaries imposed upon these people were social constructs. Because they were social constructs, these boundaries were created and recreated over time. They were but temporary labels. The one thing that was permanent lay in their shared human emotions. Despite the military uniforms that they had put on, or the flags that they had chosen to carry, they all wanted peace—peace of mind and peace for their living space.

The transnational peace endeavors of US and Vietnamese people were founded upon "universal human aspirations and emotions" (to use historian Akira Iriye's term)[3] and aimed toward a sustainable peace grounded in mutual understanding. Understanding is crucial in relationships. Poet John Balaban explains differences between his view of Vietnam as "a real place" full of loving people and poetry even during wartime and the perspectives of American soldiers who saw Vietnam as a hostile place full of hatred and dangers: "In all fairness, those 500,000, or even 600,000 Americans weren't really given the chance. They were afraid. They were confused. And they hardly ever had any real contact with the Vietnamese. Whereas I lived in a Vietnamese community, rented a home from a Buddhist nun, actually a lay nun, whose son was a law student at the university, and whose life changed with mine when the university was bombed."[4] The experiences that Balaban had with the Vietnamese allowed him to understand them as human beings and see the commonalities that they shared instead of the boundaries that differentiated them.

It is useful to conclude this study with Balaban's story—an epic of transnational culturalism that started on the hottest days of the Vietnam War. Through International Voluntary Services, Balaban, a conscientious objector, served in

Vietnam as a linguistics teacher for Can Tho University in the Mekong Delta. He remembers: "I objected to the war, yet I had the strange notion that it was a kind of obligation to go." His teaching job lasted only a few months "because the whole place was bombed flat during the Tet Offensive,"[5] and because he was wounded. Balaban went home but soon returned to Vietnam, working for the Committee of Responsibility to Save War-Burned and War-Injured Vietnamese Children (COR). Founded in 1966 by US physicians, COR dedicated its efforts to rescuing children in Vietnam and brought those with severe injuries to the United States for medical care; the children would return home after recovery, except for cases in which no surviving relatives were located. Since Balaban could speak Vietnamese, one of his tasks was to visit with the children's families and discuss the option of sending their children to the United States for medical treatment. Ironically, it was in one of those intense, awkward moments that he discovered something special about Vietnam. The defining moment came one late afternoon, when he was awaiting a couple's decision about their injured son. Sitting in their backyard, Balaban heard a sweet voice singing Vietnamese folk poetry. Although he had heard Vietnamese folk poetry before, and although he could not see the singer this time, her song left a remarkable impression in his mind, one that diverted his life in an unexpected direction.[6] Balaban found his new love for Vietnamese culture while dealing with child casualties between firefights.

Balaban's fascination about Vietnamese folk poetry dictated the course of his life. After his two-year service in Vietnam, he came home, but by 1971, he was in Vietnam again. This time, as a National Endowment for the Humanities fellow, he walked the dirt roads in the countryside of Vietnam to collect *ca dao*, oral folk poetry. Although most Vietnamese people knew by heart at least a few folk poems, written collections were not available at the time. What Balaban did was unprecedented on many levels. The American war was still going on, and this American young man, equipped with a tape recorder, roamed the countryside, going from door to door, asking whoever answered the door to sing his or her favorite folk poem. Some people asked him to come back at a different time, but most would do as requested. One could hear gunfire in the backgrounds in some of his recordings.[7]

Balaban's cultural bonds with Vietnam kept evolving. In his conversations with the peasants who sang poems for him, a name repeatedly arose: Ho Xuan Huong. She was the eighteenth-century *Bà Chúa thơ Nôm* (Queen of poetry in the ancient Vietnamese language), known for her rebelliousness, cleverness, and naughtiness because of her humorous and sarcastic poems about taboo subjects such as sex, polygamy, and misogyny. Balaban became interested not only in Ho's poems but also in chữ Nôm, the ancient Vietnamese written language. Chữ Nôm was a Vietnamese creation in approximately 1000 AD and was in use until the 1920s when the French outlawed it by decree. By 2001, according to Balaban, only about thirty people left in the world could read it.[8] Throughout the decades, Balaban dedicated his efforts to translating Vietnamese folk poetry and Ho's poems. In 2009, with assistance from Vietnamese colleagues, Balaban founded the Vietnamese Nôm Preservation Foundation (VNPF). This foundation resulted from efforts to standardize the Nôm script for use in computers. The project involved collaborative work among US and Vietnamese scholars and software engineers as well as contributions from philanthropists. In addition to developing software to digitize Nôm materials and compiling a Nôm dictionary, VNPF also encouraged the study of the ancient language through scholarship programs.[9] VNPF did not simply contribute to the preservation of a language but enabled the rediscovery of a nearly thousand-year-old Vietnamese cultural heritage.

The transnational cultural projects of Balaban were rooted in his emotional connections with Vietnamese people. The peasants' poems touched his heart, convincing him that there was more to remember about Vietnam than just gunfire and burning smells. For Balaban, perhaps poetry was the tie that bound him and the Vietnamese. It was in those Vietnamese poems that he found the souls of the people whom he had barely known. Balaban explains:

> It's simply true that the beauty of the poetry is so entrancing that one would have to be dead in your head not to want to go back to it again and again. And once you've latched onto a poet like Ho Xuan Huong–so clever–just your own sense of being alive as a human being on the planet, never mind what culture you happen to be born into, it just became a much larger affair.[10]

Poetry broke boundaries and inspired lasting peace endeavors.

Although Balaban took a very different kind of journey compared to the aforementioned stories in this study, his undertaking strongly resonated with the peace efforts of those other US and Vietnamese people in varied ways. Like them, he demonstrated a heartfelt desire for peace and transcended boundaries. Like many, he witnessed and endured the consequences of war but chose to transform unpleasant experiences into positive impacts. And like them, he made a profound but quiet journey, which remained little known in the narrative of US-Vietnam relations.

The ordinary citizens presented in this research deserve better attention in our historical understanding of the relationship between the two countries. Whether they were "boat people," Amerasians, former warriors, prisoners of war, family members of those who lost their lives because of war, or simply little-known folks with good hearts, these people's stories provoked our perceptions of national boundaries and diplomatic relations. Common concepts of boundaries emphasize differences, and conventional knowledge of diplomatic relations focuses on high politics, thus highlighting state roles. The people in this study and their transnational peace endeavors underscored an often-forgotten fact that we, human beings, have much more in common than we thought. Once we strip off labels such as nationality, politics, religion, social status, etc., which are invented, added on, and can be changed, our common nature would be revealed. We all want peace and love.

The famous Russian poet Yevgeny Yevtushenko offered a wonderful thought on borders, which can be aptly borrowed to describe the transnational peace efforts of US and Vietnamese citizens in a testing era:

> I suppose
> that at first, it was people who invented borders,
> and then borders
> started to invent people.
> It was borders who invented police,
> armies, and border guards.
>
> . . .
>
> Thank God,
> we have invisible threads and threadlets,
> born of the threads of blood
> from the nails in the palms of Christ.
> These threads struggle through,
> tearing apart the barbed wire
> leading love to join love
> and anguish to unite with anguish.
>
> . . .
>
> While borders still stand
> we are all in prehistory.
> Real history will start
> when all borders are gone.[11]

NOTES

Introduction

1 Robert O. Keohane and Joseph S. Nye, *Transnational Relations and World Politics* (Cambridge, MA: Harvard University Press, 1981), xi.
2 Patricia Clavin, "Defining Transnationalism," *Contemporary European History* 14, no. 4 (2005): 438.
3 Akira Iriye, *Cultural Internationalism and World Order* (Baltimore and London:Johns Hopkins University Press, 1997), x.
4 Iriye, *Cultural Internationalism*, 2.
5 Akira Iriye, *Global and Transnational History: The Past, Present, and Future* (Basingstoke, UK: Palgrave Macmillan, 2013), 48.
6 Iriye, *Global and Transnational History*, 48–49.
7 Iriye, 49.
8 Edwin A. Martini, "Invisible Enemies: The American War on Vietnam, 1975–2000," *Culture, Politics, and the Cold War*, ed. Christian G. Appy (Amherst: University of Massachusetts Press, 2007), 7.
9 John Dumbrell, *Clinton's Foreign Policy: Between the Bushes, 1992–2000* (London and New York: Routledge, 2009), 106.
10 Please see Trin Yarborough, *Surviving Twice: Amerasian Children of the Vietnam War* (Washington, DC: Potomac Books, 2005); Thomas A. Bass, *Vietnamerica: The War Comes Home* (New York: Soho Press, 1996); Steven DeBonis, *Children of the Enemy: Oral Histories of Vietnamese Amerasians and Their Mothers* (Jefferson, NC: McFarland, 1995); Robert S. McKelvey, *The Dust of Life: America's Children Abandoned in Vietnam* (Seattle: University of Washington Press, 1999).

Chapter 1: Turbulent Years of Peace

1 Gerald R. Ford, Address at a Tulane University Convocation, April 23, 1975, The American Presidency Project, accessed September 29, 2020, http://www.presidency.ucsb.edu/ws/index.php?pid=4859.
2 Richard L. Madden, "Ford Still Seeks More Saigon Aid: Wants Military Assistance Despite Declaration on End of Involvement," *New York Times*, April 25, 1975.
3 Gerald R. Ford, Address at the University of Hawaii, December 7, 1975. Gerald R. Ford Presidential Library and Museum, Ann Arbor, Michigan.
4 Harish Chanola, "New Pacific Doctrine," *Economic and Political Weekly*, January 10, 1976.

5 William Safire, "The Chinese Key," *New York Times*, January 12, 1976.

6 Ford, Address at the University of Hawaii. The italicization is mine.

7 Ford.

8 John LeBoutillier, *Vietnam Now: A Case for Normalizing Relations with Hanoi* (New York: Praeger, 1989), 21; Kevin Bowen, "Notes from When the War Was Over: Remembering the Embargo," *Massachusetts Review* 36, no. 4 (Winter 1995): 527–538.

9 Gareth Porter, "The U.S. and Vietnam: Between War and Friendship," *Southeast Asian Affairs* (1977): 325–338.

10 Edwin A. Martini, "Invisible Enemies: The American War on Vietnam, 1975–2000," in *Culture, Politics, and the Cold War*, ed. Christian G. Appy (Amherst: University of Massachusetts Press, 2007), 14.

11 LeBoutillier, *Vietnam Now*, 95–96.

12 Flora Lewis, "North Vietnam Demands U.S. Fulfill Its Promise of Postwar Aid," *New York Times*, March 30, 1976.

13 Lewis, "North Vietnam."

14 "Vietnam Offers Amity to the U.S.: Hanoi Leader Conciliatory at Third-World Meeting," *New York Times*, August 18, 1976.

15 Martini, "Invisible Enemies," 32.

16 Clyde Farnsworth, "Vietnam: To Aid or Not to Aid?" *New York Times*, June 26, 1977.

17 Kathleen Teltsch, "U.N. Panel Votes Priority Economic Aid for Vietnam," *New York Times*, October 7, 1977.

18 Henry Kamm, "Vietnam's Premier Says He Wants U.S. Friendship: Vietnam's 'Duty' to Help," *New York Times*, August 8, 1978.

19 Gary R. Hess, *Vietnam and the United States: Origins and Legacy of War* (New York: Prentice Hall International, 1998), 145–154. This issue is discussed in more detail in chapter 3.

20 Hess, *Vietnam and the United States*. Many argue that the outside world did not know about the Khmer Rouge genocide. Hess, however, points out that the United States simply ignored the information because its priority at the time was to befriend China in opposition to the Soviet Union.

21 "Current Situation in Indochina," June 1, 1979, Folder 06, Box 22, Douglas Pike Collection: Unit 06—Democratic Republic of Vietnam, The Vietnam Center and Archive, Texas Tech University, Lubbock, Texas (hereafter, VCA, TTU, LT). The italicization is mine.

22 Quoted from Martini, "Invisible Enemies," 166.

23 Robert D. Schulzinger, *A Time for Peace: The Legacy of the Vietnam War* (New York: Oxford University Press, 2006), 4–5.

24 Schulzinger, *A Time for Peace*, 33.

25 Martini, "Invisible Enemies," 41.

26 Quoted from Martini, "Invisible Enemies," 22–23.

27 Jay Price, "Having Changed America, the League of POW/MIA Families Fades," National Public Radio, October 19, 2017.

28 Martha Winnacker, "By Aiding the Future, U.S. Could Ease the Burden of the Past: My Lai—Where the Rice Will Grow Again," *Los Angeles Times*, July 25, 1977.

29 Winnacker, "By Aiding the Future."

30 "Replies by the President (Carter) to Questions Asked at a News Conference, Washington, D.C., March 24, 1977," *American Foreign Policy Basic Documents 1977–1980* (Washington, DC: US Department of State, 1983), 1101–1103.

31 Winnacker, "By Aiding the Future."

32 Mary Hershberger, *Traveling to Vietnam: American Peace Activists and the War* (Syracuse, NY: Syracuse University Press, 1998), xxi.

33 Hershberger, *Traveling to Vietnam*, xx.

34 Hershberger, xx–xxi.

35 Eileen Shanahan, "Aid Group Says U.S. Curbs Export of Items to Vietnam," *New York Times*, July 26, 1975.

36 Shanahan, "Aid Group Says."

37 Elinor Ashkenazy, "Is Sending Plows to Vietnam 'Trading with the Enemy?'" *Los Angeles Times*, November 7, 1975.

38 "Quakers Will Defy Curb on Vietnam Aid," *New York Times*, July 29, 1975.

39 Marjorie Hyer, "Quakers to Flout Law on Viet Aid," *Washington Post*, November 11, 1975.

40 Marjorie Hyer, "Quakers Get Approval for Vietnam Aid," *Washington Post*, November 17, 1975.

41 "Quakers, Friends, Set to Hold Prayer Vigil at Home of Jimmy Carter," *Philadelphia Tribune*, December 18, 1976.

42 "Quakers, Friends."

43 "U.S. Groups Seeking Help for Vietnam," *New York Times*, October 3, 1975.

44 Janis Johnson, "U.S. Urged to End Vietnam Ban," *Washington Post*, May 7, 1976.

45 "Religious Leaders Plan Vietnam Tour," *Washington Post*, March 5, 1976.

46 Johnson, "U.S. Urged."

47 Cora Weiss, "Vietnam: To Heal Wounds," letter to the editor, *New York Times*, December 17, 1976.

48 "Vietnam Gets $150,000 for Mylai Hospital," *Washington Post*, March 17, 1977.

49 Church World Service, "History," Church World Service, accessed September 19, 2020, http://www.cwsglobal.org/who-we-are/history.html.

50 Church World Service Vietnam, "Home," Church World Service Vietnam, accessed November 21, 2020, http://cws.org.vn.

51 "Church World Service to Ship $2 Million in Wheat to Vietnam," *Washington Post*, November 23, 1977.

52 "Churches Ship Wheat to Vietnam," *New York Times*, April 4, 1978.

53 Kenneth A. Briggs, "Church Group Reports on Vietnam," *New York Times*, June 2, 1978.

54 "Rice on Way to Vietnam from 4 Relief Agencies," *New York Times*, December 22, 1976.

55 Marian Wright Edelman, "Vietnam's Hungry Children," *New York Times*, August 14, 1977.
56 Edelman, "Vietnam's Hungry Children."
57 "Current Situation in IndoChina."
58 Milton Osborne, "The Indochinese Refugees: Cause and Effects," *International Affairs* 56, no. 1 (January 1980): 38, 42.
59 In Vietnamese, it is called *phong trào vượt biên*, literally translated as "the border-crossing movement." However, the term only applies to the boat people; it does not include those who crossed land borders into China, Laos, or Cambodia.
60 Michael E. Latham, "Redirecting the Revolution? The USA and the Failure of Nation-Building in South Vietnam," *Third World Quarterly* 27, no. 1 (2006): 29–30.
61 Joseph B. Treaster, "Black Market Down, Saigon Hopes Rise," *New York Times*, January 29, 1972.
62 "U.S. Spent $141-Billion in Vietnam in 14 Years," *New York Times*, May 1, 1975.
63 Samuel P. Huntington, "The Bases of Accommodation," *Foreign Affairs* 46, no. 4 (July 1968): 648–649.
64 William S. Turley, "Urban Transformation in South Vietnam," *Pacific Affairs* 49, no. 4 (1976–1977): 607.
65 Quoted from Briggs, "Church Group Reports on Vietnam."
66 "Vietnamese Sell $40,000 Worth Daily: Refugee Camps Become Gold Mines," *Los Angeles Times*, July 27, 1975.
67 Arjun Makhijani, *Manifesto for Global Democracy: Two Essays on Imperialism and the Struggle for Freedom* (New York: Apex Press, 2004), 235.
68 House of Representatives, *Hearings Before the Subcommittee on Asian and Pacific Affairs of the Committee on Foreign Affairs*, 96th Cong., 1st Sess. on 1979: Tragedy in Indochina: War, Refugees, and Famine, 1980, Folder 21, Box 10, Douglas Pike Collection: Unit 11—Monographs, VCA, TTU, LT, 36.
69 Martin Woollacott, "The Boat People," *Guardian*, December 3, 1977.
70 Woollacott, "The Boat People."
71 Woollacott.
72 Jacqueline Desbarats, "Population Redistribution in the Socialist Republic of Vietnam," *Population and Development Review* 13, no. 1 (March 1987): 46, 48. Other sources estimate that Saigon's population in 1975 was "over three million" or 3.5 million.
73 Turley, "Urban Transformation in South Vietnam."
74 For more information on the specific results and impacts of the New Economic Zones policy, please see Desbarats, "Population Redistribution"; and Turley, "Urban Transformation in South Vietnam.")
75 House of Representatives, *Hearings Before the Subcommittee on Asian and Pacific Affairs*, 34.
76 Turley, "Urban Transformation in South Vietnam," 620.
77 Michael H. Lang, "Locational Components of Urban and Regional Public Policy in Postwar Vietnam: The Case of Ho Chi Minh City (Saigon)," *GeoJournal, South East Asia* 4, no. 1 (1980): 14.

78 Elof Axel Carlson, "Commentary: International Symposium on Herbicides in the Vietnam War: An Appraisal," *BioScience* 33, no. 8 (September 1983): 507.

79 Gordon H. Orians and E. W. Pfeiffer, "Ecological Effects of the War in Vietnam," *Science, New Series* 168, no. 3931 (May 1970): 551.

80 E. W. Pfeiffer, "Final Word on Defoliation Effects," *Science, New Series* 171, no. 3972 (February 1971): 625.

81 Orians and Pfeiffer, "Ecological Effects of the War in Vietnam," 552.

82 Joseph P. Hupy, "The Environmental Footprint of War," *Environment and History* 14, no. 3 (August 2008): 415.

83 Turley, "Urban Transformation in South Vietnam," 615.

84 Turley.

85 Turley, 615–616.

86 More details about these border conflicts will be discussed in chapter 3.

87 Douglas E. Kneeland, "Wide Hostility Found as First Exiles Arrive," *New York Times*, May 2, 1975.

88 Kneeland, "Wide Hostility Found."

89 Kneeland.

90 Clyde Taylor, "A Black Teacher's Agonized Message to the Vietnamese Refugees," *Los Angeles Times*, May 26, 1975.

91 Alden Roberts and Paul Starr, *Attitudes Toward Indochinese Refugees: An Empirical Study*, n.d., Folder 01, Box 01, Alden Roberts Collection, VCA, TTU, LT.

92 Taylor, "A Black Teacher's Agonized Message to the Vietnamese Refugees."

93 Frances FitzGerald, "Punch In! Punch Out! Eat Quick!" *New York Times*, December 28, 1975.

94 FitzGerald, "Punch In!"

95 FitzGerald.

96 FitzGerald.

97 FitzGerald.

98 Woollacott, "The Boat People."

99 Keyes Beech, "'Boat People' Easy Prey for Asia's Pirates," *Los Angeles Times*, August 7, 1979.

100 George McArthur, "Viet Refugees Victimized at Sea: Helpless 'Boat People' Known as Easy Pickings," *Los Angeles Times*, June 11, 1978.

101 "Vượt Biên Sau 30/4/1975—Nhân Chứng Sống Nguyễn Ngọc Ngạn Kể Lại" (Ocean crossing after April 30, 1975: Told by living witness Nguyen Ngoc Ngan), YouTube, 5:40, April 25, 2013, https://web.archive.org/web/20140407123342 /https://www.youtube.com/watch?v=7KmZnnp6YwM.

102 Paul Dean, "Coming to the Aid of the Boat People," *Los Angeles Times*, July 23, 1979.

103 Dean, "Coming to the Aid."

104 Peter Arnett, "Refugees from 'Boat with No Smiles' Find New Life in U.S.," *Los Angeles Times*, June 23, 1978.

105 Peter Arnett, "'Worse Off Than I Ever Expected': Monsoons Halt Aid for 'Boat People.'" *Los Angeles Times*, November 16, 1978.

106 Richard H. Growald, "Odyssey of a 'Boat People' Family: Safety at Last," *Los Angeles Times*, August 15, 1979.

107 Growald, "Odyssey of a 'Boat People' Family."

108 McArthur, "Viet Refugees Victimized at Sea."

109 Arnett, "Refugees from 'Boat with No Smiles.'"

110 House of Representatives, *Hearings Before the Subcommittee on Asian and Pacific Affairs*, 24.

111 House of Representatives, 33.

112 Indochina Refugee Action Center, *Special Report: Physical and Emotional Health Care Needs of Indochinese Refugees*, March 20, 1980, Folder 17, Box 01, Douglas Pike Collection: Other Manuscripts—Jackson-Desbarats Study, VCA, TTU, LT, 5–6.

113 *Refugee Crisis in Indochina, 1978: Hearings Before the Subcommittee on Asian and Pacific Affairs*, 1978, Folder 09, Box 09, Douglas Pike Collection: Unit 11—Monographs, VCA, TTU, LT, vi.

114 House of Representatives, *Hearings Before the Subcommittee on Asian and Pacific Affairs*, iii–iv.

115 Quoted from *Refugee Crisis in Indochina, 1978*, 17.

116 Cyrus Vance to President Jimmy Carter, Memorandum, June 23, 1977, Office of Staff Secretary, Presidential Files, Folder 7/15/77[3], Container 31, Jimmy Carter Presidential Library and Museum, Atlanta, Georgia.

117 Zbigniew Brzezinski to President Jimmy Carter, Memorandum, July 15, 1977, Office of Staff Secretary, Presidential Files, Folder 7/15/77[3], Container 31, Jimmy Carter Presidential Library and Museum, Atlanta, Georgia.

118 Zbigniew Brzezinski to President Jimmy Carter, Memorandum, July 1, 1977, Office of Staff Secretary, Presidential Files, Folder 7/15/77[3], Container 31, Jimmy Carter Presidential Library and Museum, Atlanta, Georgia.

119 Cyrus Vance to President Jimmy Carter, Memorandum, December 6, 1977, Office of Staff Secretary, Presidential Files, Folder 12/20/77[1], Container 55, Jimmy Carter Presidential Library and Museum, Atlanta, Georgia.

120 Zbigniew Brzezinski to President Jimmy Carter, Memorandum, December 19, 1977, Office of Staff Secretary, Presidential Files, Folder 12/20/77[1], Container 55, Jimmy Carter Presidential Library and Museum, Atlanta, Georgia.

121 Henry Kamm, "Geneva Meeting Yields Few Pledges of Aid for Indochinese Refugees: Thai Delegation Supports Plan," *New York Times*, December 17, 1978.

122 William Shawcross, "Refugees and Rhetoric," *Foreign Policy* 36 (Autumn 1979): 7.

123 Shawcross, "Refugees and Rhetoric," 5.

124 Kathleen Teltsch, "3 Faiths' Leaders in Refugee Plea: Catholic Groups Involved," *New York Times*, June 29, 1979.

125 Barry Stein, "The Geneva Conferences and the Indochinese Refugee Crisis," *International Migration Review* 13, no. 4 (Winter 1979): 716–723.

126 Stein, "The Geneva Conferences," 718.

Chapter 2: Derelicts of War and Their Metamorphoses

1 Randy Trane, "Sau Cuộc Chiến" (After the war). This song is translated by the researcher. Born Tran Quoc Tuan, he adopted the name Randy Tran upon arriving in the United States. After he was naturalized and became a US citizen, he changed his name to Randy Trane. He appeared in most sources as Randy Tran, but this research uses his official American and stage name Randy Trane.

2 The term *Amerasian* was coined by American writer and human rights activist Pearl Buck to refer to Asian children fathered by Americans. In this research, Amerasians refers to children of American personnel and Vietnamese women during the Vietnam War.

3 Kevin Minh Allen, "Identity at War's End: The Amerasian Legacy," *International Examiner*, May 4, 2011.

4 David J. Elkins, "Globalization, Telecommunication, and Virtual Ethnic Communities," *International Political Science Review* 18, no. 2 (1997): 139–152.

5 Gloria Anzaldúa, *Borderlands*, 2nd ed. (San Francisco: Aunt Lute Books, 1999), 19.

6 Bill Kurtis, "The Plight of the Children Abandoned in Vietnam," New York Times, March 2, 1980.

7 Kurtis, "The Plight of the Children."

8 Kurtis.

9 US Senate, *Hearing Before the Subcommittee on Immigration and Refugee Policy of the Committee on the Judiciary*, 97th Cong., 2nd Sess. on S. 1698, a Bill to Amend the Immigration and Nationality Act to Provide Preferential Treatment in the Admission of Certain Children of the United States Armed Forces Personnel, June 21, 1982, 60–631982 (Opening Statement of Hon. Senator Edward M. Kennedy, US senator from the state of Massachusetts), Library of Congress, Washington, DC.

10 US Senate, *Hearing Before the Subcommittee on Immigration and Refugee Policy of the Committee on the Judiciary*, 97th Cong., 2nd Sess. on S. 1698, a Bill to Amend the Immigration and Nationality Act to Provide Preferential Treatment in the Admission of Certain Children of the United States Armed Forces Personnel, June 21, 1982, 60–631982 (statement of Hon. Senator Carl Levin, US senator from the state of Michigan), Library of Congress, Washington, DC, 21.

11 US Senate, 20

12 US Senate, opening Statement of Hon. Senator Edward M. Kennedy.

13 Sue-Je Lee Gage, "The Amerasian Problem: Blood, Duty, and Race," *International Relations* 21, no. 1 (2007): 93.

14 *Hearing Before the Subcommittee on Immigration, Nationality and International Law* (1982) (Statement of Fr. Alfred Keane), Folder 1, Box 44, Vietnam Veterans of America–Vietnam Project Collection, The Vietnam Center and Archive, Texas Tech University, Lubbock, Texas (hereafter VCA, TTU, LT).

15 Stanley Karnow, "Amerasians—Tragic Legacy of the U.S. Era in Vietnam," *Los Angeles Times*, March 16, 1981.

16 Karnow, "Amerasians."

17 Bob Secter, "Amerasians Will Join Fathers: 11 Vietnam Children Fly to a New World—the U.S," *Los Angeles Times*, October 1, 1982.

18 Kathleen Teltsch, "Many Agencies Joined in Retreiving Vietnam Children," *New York Times*, October 1, 1982.

19 Colin Campbell, "Outcast Vietnam Children Still Hope," *New York Times*, June 5, 1982.

20 Holt International Children's Services, "Amerasian Project: Vietnam. A Proposal for Participation by Holt International Children's Services, Inc.," July 1982, Folder 2, Box 44, Vietnam Veterans of America–Vietnam Project Collection, VCA, TTU, LT.

21 Holt International Children's Services, letter to Congressman Peter W. Rodino, September 1982, Folder 2, Box 44, Vietnam Veterans of America–Vietnam Project Collection, VCA, TTU, LT.

22 Holt International Children's Services, letter.

23 Church World Service, Mennonite Central Committee, and American Friends Service Committee, Letter to Senator Carl M. Levin, August 11, 1982, Folder 2, Box 44, Vietnam Veterans of America–Vietnam Project Collection, VCA, TTU, LT.

24 Church World Service, Mennonite Central Committee, and American Friends Service Committee, Letter to American Council of Voluntary Agencies and other NGOs, September 2, 1982, Folder 2, Box 44, Vietnam Veterans of America–Vietnam Project Collection, VCA, TTU, LT.

25 "Vietnam Official Wants Talks on Amerasians," *New York Times*, July 31, 1984. There are no accurate data of Amerasians born in Vietnam, but the most common estimate is twenty thousand.

26 "Vietnam Asks U.S. to Take More Refugees," *Los Angeles Times*, June 25, 1984.

27 Barbara Crossette, "Hanoi Asks to End Amerasians' Issue," *NewYork Times*, October 20, 1985.

28 Carol McGraw, "Vietnamese Teen Reunited with American Father, Family," *Los Angeles Times*, June 11, 1988.

29 McGraw, "Vietnamese Teen."

30 David Lamb, "Children of the Vietnam War," *Smithsonian Magazine*, June 2009.

31 Irene Virag, "Lawmakers Ask Shultz to Help Amerasian," *Newsday*, March 7, 1987.

32 Irene Virag, "Long Island Diary: Orphan Becomes a Symbol of Diplomacy," *Newsday*, March 23, 1987.

33 Edna Negron, "Le Van Minh's Americanization," *Newsday*, November 16, 1987.

34 Pamela Constable, "For Area's Amerasians, More Struggle: Many Children of GI's Find It Hard to Adjust," *Washington Post*, April 13, 1998.

35 Quoted in Constable, "For Area's Amerasians."

36 "Người Mẹ Việt và Đứa Con Lai Ca Sĩ Nổi Tiếng" (A Vietnamese mother and a famous Amerasian singer), *VnExpress*, August 2, 2012.

37 "Người Mẹ Việt và Đứa Con Lai Ca Sĩ Nổi Tiếng."

38 R. Robin McDonald, "Vietnamese Gangs: War's Bitter Fruit Prosecutors Are Targeting Amerasians in Atlanta Who Prey on Asian Merchants," *Atlanta Journal Constitution*, July 14, 1996.

39 Ahrin Mishrin, "Vietnamese Gangs: Identity and Discourse in 'Little Saigon,'" (grad thesis, University of Southern California, August 1993), quoted in Trin Yarborough, *Surviving Twice: Amerasian Children of the Vietnam War* (Washington, DC: Potomac Books, 2005), 167.

40 McDonald, "Vietnamese Gangs."

41 Dianne Klein, "Vietnam's Lingering Casualties," *Los Angeles Times*, June 30, 1991.

42 John Needham and Thuan Le, "Slaying Mars Youth's Dreams of a New Life," *Los Angeles Times*, April 5, 1992.

43 US Department of State, General Office Files—Office Correspondence—Incoming, n.d., Folder 047, Box 164, Families of Vietnamese Political Prisoners Association Collection, VCA, TTU, LT.

44 Margaret L. Usdansky, "Amerasians: Caught between Cultures," *USA Today*, May 18, 1993.

45 Quoted in Needham and Le, "Slaying Mars Youth's Dreams of a New Life."

46 Jeffrey Brody, "Amerasians Exploited as Ticket to United States," *Orange County Register*, April 7, 1991.

47 Needham and Le, "Slaying Mars Youth's Dreams of a New Life."

48 Erin Marcus, "A Search for Family, Amerasian Odyssey: Few Find the Fathers Who Left Them Behind in Vietnam," *Washington Post*, March 8, 1992.

49 George Esper, "Amerasians: Vietnam's Misbegotten Legacy," *Los Angeles Times*, April 30, 1989.

50 Lamb, "Children of the Vietnam War."

51 Dianne Klein, "He Looks Like Me: Two Amerasians Seek Their Dads—and Their Missing Heritage," *Los Angeles Times*, July 7, 1991.

52 Diane Klein, "Vietnam's Lingering Casualties," *Los Angeles Times* , June 30, 1991.

53 Diane Klein, "Search for Father Is a Search for Self," *Los Angeles Times* , July 4, 1991.

54 Diane Klein, "Child of War Still Searching for Father," *Los Angeles Times*, September 29, 1992.

55 James Dao, "Vietnam Legacy: Finding G.I. Fathers, and Children Left Behind," *New York Times*, September 15, 2013.

56 Irene Virag, "In the Land of Their Fathers," *Newsday*, June 15, 1986.

57 Virag, "In the Land of Their Fathers."

58 Lisa Belkin, "Children of 2 Lands in Search of Home," *New York Times*, May 19, 1988.

59 Gaiutra Bahadur, "Citizenship Bill Holds Promise for Disenfranchised Amerasians," *Philadelphia Inquirer*, October 27, 2003.

60 My-Thuan Tran, "Children of Vietnam War Servicemen Seek U.S. Citizenship," *Los Angeles Times*, October 10, 2008.

61 Benedict Anderson created the term *imagined community* to indicate shared nationhood and nationalism among citizens of a nation-state. See Benedict Anderson, *Imagined Communities: Reflections on the Origin and Spread of Nationalism* (London: Verso, 1991).

62 Jonathan Watts, "GIs Return to End 30 Years of Pain for Vietnam's Children of the Dust," *Guardian*, May 1, 2005.

63 "11 Amerasian Kids Leave Vietnam and Happily Embrace Their U.S. Families," *People*, October 18, 1982; "11 American-Vietnamese Fly to New Home," *Boston Globe*, October 1, 1982.

64 "11 Amerasian Kids Leave Vietnam."

65 Andrew MacLeod, "Amerasian Daughter Adapts to U.S. after Rough Start," United Press International, January 23, 1983.

66 Tom Vesey, "A Project of Love: Driven by Memories of Son in Vietnam, Veteran Seeks Help for Amerasian Youth," *Washington Post*, September 1, 1982.

67 Vesey, "A Project of Love."

68 Vesey.

69 C. S. Manegold, "Born in Vietnam: An American Veteran Returns to Asia to Claim His Son," *Ottawa Citizen*, July 23, 1988.

70 Manegold, "Born in Vietnam."

71 Robert Woodward, "Ex-GI Dedicates Life to Help Amerasians," *Los Angeles Times*, October 15, 1989; Paul Wedel, "Viets Allow U.S. Charity to Aid Amerasians," United Press International, March 22, 1989.

72 Indira A. R. Lakshmanan, "The Children They Left Behind," *Boston Globe*, October 26, 2003.

73 Watts, "GIs Return to End 30 Years of Pain."

74 Lakshmanan, "The Children They Left Behind."

75 Robin Jennings, "Michigan Man Reunites with His Half-Vietnamese Children," Michigan Live, May 16, 2009.

76 Sue Lloyd Roberts, "A U.S. Soldier Searches for His Vietnamese Son," BBC News, April 27, 2014.

77 Roberts, "A U.S. Soldier Searches for His Vietnamese Son."

78 Tara Leaman, "A Memoir of an Amerasian Orphan," Amerasian Voice, newsletter 2, no. 3, November 2009.

79 Giao Chỉ, "Giới Thiệu 'Đường Khuynh Diệp'" (Introduction to "The roads of eucalyptus"), *Việt Báo Online*, October 15, 1915; Jenny Do for City Council, "Home," Jenny Do for City Council, https://web.archive.org/web/20160223033352/http://www.jennydoforcouncil.com/; Ao Dai Festival, "Origin Story," Ao Dai Festival, accessed September 20, 2020, http://www.aodaifestival.com.

80 "Luật sư Jenny Đỗ tâm sự về cuộc đời bên bờ sinh tử" (Attorney Jenny Do discussing life on the edge), interview, *Cali Today*, October 22, 2015.

81 Minh Quynh, "Giao lưu hội ngộ Babylift tại Báo Tuổi Trẻ" (Babylift reunion at Tuoi Tre's newspaper headquaters), announcement, *Tuoi Tre*, April 29, 2011; Trista Goldberg, "The 35th Anniversary," Vietnamese Adoptees, April 28, 2010; Annie Gowen, "Legacies of War," *Washington Post*, April 17, 2015.

82 Cẩm Giang, "Phi Nhung: Con lai bị chối bỏ và nỗi đau đớn khó quên về mẹ ruột" (Phi Nhung: An unwanted biracial child and an unforgettable, painful memory of her mother), *Soha News*, March 3, 2015.

83 Lâm Nguyễn, "Phi Nhung và chuyện đời đầy nước mắt trước khi nổi tiếng" (Phi Nhung and her ordeals before becoming famous), *Đời sống và Pháp luật*, August 10, 2015.

84 Tử Văn, "Phi Nhung và mối lương duyên với trẻ em" (Phi Nhung and her predetermined bonds with children) *Người Đưa Tin*, September 28, 2015.

85 "Phi Nhung: 'Kiếp này tôi chọn sống độc thân'" (Phi Nhung:"I chose to stay single for the rest of this life"), *Cali Today*, February 23, 2015.

86 "Randy và hành trình tìm mẹ" (Randy and the journey to look for his mother; documentary), *Người Việt Bốn Phương*, channel VTV4, July 30, 2012, https://www.youtube.com/watch?v=_6B4XwqD87M; "Randy Tran: An Amerasian and a Singer," Amerasian Voice, November 22, 2012, https://amerasianvoice.wordpress.com/2012/11/22/randy-tran-an-amerasian-and-a-singer/; Trường Kỳ, "Randy—Người ca sĩ mồ côi" (Randy—the orphaned singer), radio interview, *Chương trình Nghệ sĩ và Đời sống*, 2005. https://www.voatiengviet.com/a/a-19-2005-09-06-voa14-81660467/505850.html.

87 Trường à Trường Kỳto, "Randy."

88 Trường à Trường Kỳto; "Orphan Singer Returns in Search of Peace," *Việt Nam News*, December 6, 2010.

89 "Randy và hành trình tìm mẹ."

90 Randy Trane, "Mẹ" (Mother), *Mẹ*, 2000. Lyrics translated by the researcher.

91 My-Thuan, "Children of Vietnam."

92 Other Amerasian singers who established their names in the United States and also became well known in Vietnam included Manh Quynh, Thien Phu, Minh Tri, and Minh Trang.

93 Susan Schindehette, "Against the Odds," *People*, May 1, 2000; "Hành trình 28 năm tìm cha của ca si 'Xe đạp ơi' Phương Thảo," (Singer of the song "Xe Đạp Ơi" found her father after 28 years), *Tri Thức Sống*, May 1, 2000; Edith M. Lederer, "Singer Adapts to U.S.-Vietnam Roots," Associated Press, April 29, 2000.

Chapter 3: Groundwork for Diplomatic Normalization by Ordinary Citizens

1 House of Representatives, Statement by David Lamberston Before the Subcommittee on East Asian and Pacific Affairs, June 30, 1988, Folder 21, Box 42, Vietnam Veterans of America–Vietnam Project Collection, The Vietnam Center and Archive, Texas Tech University, Lubbock, Texas (hereafter VCA, TTU, LT).

2 House of Representatives, Statement by David Lamberston.

3 Notes from Solarz's press briefing on his trip to China, Cambodia, Vietnam, Thai-

land, Singapore, and the Philippines, April 7, 1989, Folder 21, Box 42, Vietnam Veterans of America–Vietnam Project Collection, VCA, TTU, LT.

4 Originally founded as the Federation of Atomic Scientists in 1946, the organization focuses its efforts on disarmament and other international security issues. Among its sponsors are numerous American Nobel Prize laureates; Jeremy J. Stone, "Preventing the Return of Pol Pot: Conventional Wisdom versus New Apraisal" (Washington, DC: Federation of American Scientists, 1989), Folder 1, Box 40, Vietnam Veterans of America–Vietnam Project Collection, VCA, TTU, LT.

5 The most common estimate of the genocide victims is "nearly 2 million," which can be found in numerous articles in the *New York Times*, the *Washington Post*, or the BBC as well as the *Cambodia Tribunal Monitor* at http://www.cambodiatri bunal.org and http://www.globalsecurity.org. The Cambodian Genocide Program of Yale University cited the lowest estimate of 1.7 million. The highest estimate is 2.4 million. See Rudolph J. Rummel, *Statistics of Democide: Genocide and Mass Murder since 1900* (Munster: LIT Verlag, 1998).

6 "Chuyện kinh hoàng chưa biết về tội ác diệt chủng của Pol Pot ở Tây Ninh" (Unknown horror of Pol Pot's genocidal crime in Tay Ninh), VTC News, September 10, 2015. https://vtc.vn/chuyen-kinh-hoang-chua-biet-ve-toi-ac-diet-chung-cua -pol-pot-o-tay-ninh-ar222068.html.

7 Stone, "Preventing the Return of Pol Pot."

8 Jeremy J. Stone, *Every Man Should Try: Adventures of a Public Interest Activist* (New York: Public Affairs, 1999), 269.

9 Abdulgaffar Peang-Meth, "A Study of the Khmer People's National Liberation Front and the Coalition Government of Democratic Kampuchea," *Contemporary Southeast Asia* 12, no. 3 (1990): 172–185, http://www.jstor.org/stable/42707623.

10 Robert G. Sutter, "Vietnam-U.S. Relations: The Missing-In-Action (MIA) and the Impasse over Cambodia," *Congressional Research Service*, May 20, 1988, Folder 21, Box 42, Vietnam Veterans of America–Vietnam Project Collection, VCA, TTU, LT.

11 Notes from Solarz's Press Briefing.

12 David Reuther, interview with Ambassador David Lamberston, Association for Diplomatic Studies and Training, Foreign Affairs Oral History Project, August 31, 2004, 90–92. Manuscript/Mixed Material. https://www.loc.gov/item/mfdip bib001387/.

13 Stone, *Every Man Should Try*, 269–70.

14 Alan Cranston, opening statement, *Subcommittee on East Asian and Pacific Affairs, Committee on Foreign Relations*, September 19, 1990, Folder 28, Box 42, Vietnam Veterans of America–Vietnam Project Collection, VCA, TTU, LT.

15 Quoted from Stone, *Every Man Should Try*, 272.

16 Notes from Solarz's press briefing.

17 David B. Ottaway, "Covert Military Aid for Cambodia Is Debated," *Washington Post*, June 13, 1989.

18 David Rogers, "Senate Panel Votes to End Covert Aid to Non-Communist Forces in Cambodia," *Wall Street Journal*, June 29, 1990.

19 Mark O. Hatfield, "Statement before the Senate Subcommittee on East Asian and Pacific Affairs," August 2, 1988, Folder 22, Box 42, Vietnam Veterans of America–Vietnam Project Collection, VCA, TTU, LT.

20 Edmund S. Muskie, "Testimony of the Honorable Edmund S. Muskie to the U.S. Senate Committee on Foreign Relations, Subcommittee on East Asian and Pacific Affairs," February 28, 1990, Folder 29, Box 40, Vietnam Veterans of America–Vietnam Project Collection, VCA, TTU, LT. The emphasis in the sentence was Muskie's.

21 Jim Mann, "U.S. May Let Groups Travel, Do Business in Vietnam " *Los Angeles Times*, April 11, 1991.

22 Bernard Weinraub, "Vietnam Veterans Take an Emotional Journey to Hanoi: 'Nothing Has Changed,'" *New York Times*, December 19, 1981.

23 "Four Veterans Defend Visit to Vietnam," *New York Times*, December 29, 1981.

24 "Four Veterans Defend Visit to Vietnam."

25 "Four Veterans Defend Visit to Vietnam."

26 Bernard Weinraub, "Four Veterans End Vietnam Trip Nervous About Return to U.S.," *New York Times*, December 25, 1981.

27 Fred Bernstein, "Vet-Turned-Vip Tom Bird Is Stuck on New York's 'Mayflower Madam,'" *People*, June 17, 1985.

28 Weinraub, "Four Veterans End Vietnam Trip."

29 Julia Bleakney, *Revisiting Vietnam: Memoirs, Memorials, Museums* (New York: Routledge, 2006), 8.

30 Wayne Biddle, "The Ragtag and Regimental Legacies of Vietnam," *New York Times*, May 30, 1984.

31 *Vietnam Veterans of America Trip to Vietnam, March 28–April 12, 1984*, report to VVA board of directors, July 1984, Folder 2, Box 50, Vietnam Veterans of America–Vietnam Project Collection, VCA, TTU, LT.

32 *Vietnam Veterans of America Trip to Vietnam.*

33 Robert O. Muller, letter to George P. Shultz, February 8, 1984, Folder 2, Box 50, Vietnam Veterans of America–Vietnam Project Collection, VCA, TTU, LT.

34 Paul F. Gardner, letter to Robert O. Muller, March 1984, Folder 2, Box 50, Vietnam Veterans of America–Vietnam Project Collection, VCA, TTU, LT. The italicized words are the researcher's emphasis.

35 Gregory Kane, letter to Nguyen Can, October 26, 1984, Folder 2, Box 50, Vietnam Veterans of America–Vietnam Project Collection, VCA, TTU, LT.

36 "VFW Tells VVA to Step Aside," VFW news release, March 20, 1984, Folder 8, Box 44, Vietnam Veterans of America–Vietnam Project Collection, VCA, TTU, LT.

37 Clifford G. Olson Jr., letter to U.S. House of Representatives, May 3, 1984, Folder 2, Box 50, Vietnam Veterans of America–Vietnam Project Collection, VCA, TTU, LT.

38 *Vietnam Veterans of America Trip to Vietnam.*

39 Greg Kane, letter to Nguyen Dang Quang, January 23, 1985, Folder 11, Box 40, Vietnam Veterans of America–Vietnam Project Collection, VCA, TTU, LT.

40 Remarks by John F. Terzano, president of Vietnam Veterans of America Foundation before the National Conference on Ending the Cold War at Home, February 1–2, 1991, Folder 11, Box 40, Vietnam Veterans of America–Vietnam Project Collection, VCA, TTU, LT.

41 Leslie Bennetts, "The Vietnam War as Theater and an Act of Exorcism," *New York Times*, January 27, 1985.

42 Bennetts, "The Vietnam War."

43 Thomas Bird, letter to Nguyen Dang Quang, May 15, 1986, Folder 36, Box 39, Vietnam Veterans of America–Vietnam Project Collection, VCA, TTU, LT; Thomas Bird, letter to Ngo Quynh Giao, August 15, 1986, Folder 36, Box 39, Vietnam Veterans of America–Vietnam Project Collection, VCA, TTU, LT.

44 Alex Horvath, "Veterans Heal through Laughter," *Press Democrat*, March 17, 2015.

45 Marc Siegelaub, "A Man Reborn," *Long Island Newsday*, October 16, 2001.

46 Siegelaub, "A Man Reborn."

47 "Peace Profile: Bobby Muller," *Peace Review* 13, no. 1 (2001) 129–133TOP.

48 Barbara Crossette, "Veterans to Help Mine-Field Victims," *New York Times*, April 19, 1992.

49 "Peace Profile"; Robert O. Muller, "The Land Mine Scourge—How Much Longer?" *Christian Science Monitor*, February 8, 1996; The International Campaign to Ban Landmines, "The Treaty," The International Campaign to Ban Landmines, http://www.icbl.org/en-gb/the-treaty.aspx.

50 Interview with Kevin Bowen, Carbon Innovations, 2001, http://carboninnovations.net/node/372 . For information about the Joiner Center, visit http://www.umb.edu/joinercenter/about.

51 Colleen Locke, "William Joiner Center Director Receives Award in Vietnam," University of Massachusetts, Boston, April 17, 2011, https://www.umb.edu/news/detail/william_joiner_center_director_receives_award_in_vietnam#:~:text=For%20more%20than%2025%20years,of%20the%20effects%20of%20exposure.

52 Members of the Joiner Center later translated the novel into English with the title *A Time Far Past*. For more information on the novel, visit http://www.umass.edu/umpress/title/time-far-past. A Vietnamese film director living in Switzerland turned the novel into a movie in 2004, which won several prizes in Vietnam, France, Singapore, and China. See Lan Dung, "Thời Xa vắng Đoạt Giải Thưởng tại LHP Quốc Tế Thượng Hải," (*A Time Far Past* winning award at Shanghai International Film Festival) *Thanh Niên Online*, June 20, 2005; Phạm Xuân Hướng, interview with film director Phạm Quang Minh, *Nhân Dân*, August 14, 2004.

53 Xuân Anh, "Lê Lựu—Nhà Văn Cộng Sản Việt Nam đầu tiên đến Mỹ," (Le Luu—The first Vietnamese communist writer to visit the United States) *Phong Điệp.Net*, May 1, 2008; Huy Thông, "Nhà văn Lê Lựu: Kể chuyện "đi sứ" Văn

học đến Mỹ," (Writer Le Luu remembers his literary "ambassadorial" trip to the United States) *Thể thao Văn Hóa*, May 31, 2010.

54 Thông à Huy Thông, "Nhà văn Lê Lựu"; William Plummer and Richard Woodley, "A Vietnamese Novelist Makes Peace with Some Wartime Foes," *People*, November 14, 1988.

55 Le Luu joined the People's Army of Vietnam in 1959 and stayed in combat for three years before becoming a war correspondent for another nine years. Thông à Huy Thông, "Nhà văn Lê Lựu"

56 Larry Heinemann's other publications included *Close Quarters* (1977), *Cooler by the Lake* (1992), *Black Virgin Mountain* (a memoir, 2005), and numerous short stories and anthologies.

57 Kurt Jacobsen, "Larry Heinemann in Conversation with Kurt Jacobsen" *Logos Online* 2, no. 1 Winter 2003, 141–160, http://www.logosjournal.com/issue_2.1 .pdf.

58 Larry Heinemann, personal conversation with the author, College Station, Texas, March 23, 2013.

59 Jacobsen, "Larry Heinemann in Conversation with Kurt Jacobsen."

60 Marc Levy, "An Interview with Bao Ninh: Part Two," *Veteran*, 30, no. 1 (Spring/ Summer 2000): 16.

61 Fredy Champagne, "The Founding of the VVRP," Veterans Vietnam Restoration Project, https://web.archive.org/web/20150225032712/http://www.vvrp.org /?page_id=133.

62 "U.S. Veterans Build Surgical Ward for Children's Hospital in Northern Vietnam," press release, Veterans Vietnam Restoration Project, October 31, 1989, Folder 13, Box 40, Vietnam Veterans of America–Vietnam Project Collection, VCA, TTU, LT.

63 Veterans Vietnam Restoration Project, "Home," accessed September 25, 2020, http://www.vietvet.org/vetviet.htm.

64 Veterans Vietnam Restoration Project.

65 Veterans Vietnam Restoration Project.

66 Veterans Vietnam Restoration Project.

67 William Triplett, "On a Mission to Win 21st Century Hearts and Minds," *VVA Veteran*, March/April 2012, https://vvaveteran.org/32-2/32-2_vwam.html; Vets With A Mission, "Past Projects," accessed September 25, 2020, http://www .vetswithamission.org/past_projects.html.

68 Vets With A Mission, "Past Projects."

69 "Past Projects."

70 Triplett, "On a Mission to Win."

71 Triplett.

72 Vets With A Mission, "Medical Team Overcomes Major Obstacles to Complete Mission," Vets With A Mission, https://web.archive.org/web/20150426173943 /http://www.vetswithamission.org/2014_March-April_Medical_Team_Report .pdf.

73 Chuck Ward, "Reconciliation, Forgiveness and Charity," Vets With A Mis-

sion, April 27, 2015, https://web.archive.org/web/20150530162543/http://www
.vetswithamission.org/blog/2015/04/reconciliation-forgiveness-and-charity
/#comment-29217.

74 Michelle Mason, dir., "The Friendship Village," 2003; Cypress Park Productions.

75 Vietnam Friendship Village Project USA, "Historical Highlights," Vietnam
Friendship Village Project USA, accessed November 6, 2020, http://www.viet
namfriendship.org/wordpress/project-history.

76 Vietnam Friendship Village Project USA.

77 From 1961 to 1971, the United States sprayed approximately twelve million gal-
lons of Agent Orange over sixty-six thousand square miles in South Vietnam,
aiming to defoliate the country, thus exposing the enemy. An estimated three
million Vietnamese people suffer from illnesses or disabilities caused by Agent
Orange, including about one hundred and fifty thousand children and grandchil-
dren born with dioxin-related birth defects. For more information about Agent
Orange, see Agent Orange Record, "Home," Agent Orange Record Project, accessed September 25, 2020, http://www.agentorangerecord.com.

78 Quoted from Mason, "The Friendship Village."

79 Quoted from Bacon, William, III, dir., *Friendship Village: A Place of Healing*, 2003; produced by Reed Bovee; Vietnam Friendship Village Project USA,
"About Us," Vietnam Friendship Village Project USA, accessed September 25,
2020, http://www.vietnamfriendship.org/wordpress/newsletters.

80 Christine Temin, "An Artist Returns to Faces of Vietnam's Children," *Boston
Globe*, February 28, 1988; Christine Temin, "A Time for War, a Time for Art,"
Boston Globe, January 13, 1991.

81 Lois Tarlow, "The Indochina Arts Partnership Turns Twenty-Five," Art New
England, accessed September 25, 2020, http://artnewengland.com/ed_picks/the
-indochina-arts-partnership-turns-twenty-five.

82 Temin, "A Time for War"; Indochina Arts Partnership, "As Seen by Both Sides,"
Indochina Arts Partnership, accessed September 25, 2020, https://web.archive
.org/web/20160701043214/http://indochinaartspartnership.org/as-seen-by-both
-sides/.

83 Saul Rubin, "Both Sides Now: Artists Depict Vietnam War from 2 Perspectives,"
n.d., Folder 7, Box 44, Vietnam Veterans of America–Vietnam Project Collection,
VCA, TTU, LT. Different sources disagreed on the number of exhibit venues in
the United States for the collection. The data cited in this research (seventeen museums) is based on the organization's website Indochina Arts Partnership, http://
indochinaartspartnership.org.

84 Nguyễn Quốc Chính, "Một dự án nghệ thuật—Một dự án hòa bình" (An art
project—a peace project), *Hà Nội Mới*, April 20, 1991.

85 "Art that Reaches into Our Guts," opinion, *Battle Creek Enquirer*, September 11,
1991.

86 Temin, "A Time for War."

87 "Art that Reaches into Our Guts."

88 Tarlow, "The Indochina Arts Partnership Turns Twenty-Five."

89 Wendy Seadia, "Artist Profile—C. David Thomas," *Wellesley Weston*, February 18, 2010; Trinh Nguyễn, "'Đại sứ' hàn gắn vết thương chiến tranh" (The "ambassador" who heals the wounds of war), *Sức khỏe & Đời sống*, April 29, 2013; "David Thomas: Họa sĩ Mỹ đầu tiên vẽ chân dung Bác Hồ" (David Thomas: The first American artist to portray Uncle Ho), *Thời báo Ngân hàng*, August 30, 2013.

90 Barbara Crossette, "Vietnam Is Giving American Tourism a Trial Run," *New York Times*, November 3, 1985.

91 Laura Bly, "Vietnam Tour Ban Comes under Fire," *Orlando Sentinel*, June 18, 1989.

92 Steven Pinter, letter from Department of Treasury to Don Mills and John Myers, February 10, 1989, Folder 31, Box 42, Vietnam Veterans of America–Vietnam Project Collection, VCA, TTU, LT; Alan C. Miller, "Veterans Testify on Bill Allowing Trips to Vietnam," *Los Angeles Times*, March 14, 1990.

93 Alan C. Miller, "Veterans Find Peace in Vietnam," *Los Angeles Times*, July 5, 1990.

94 Joseph M. Lafatch, letter to the Return Trip Committee, February 28, 1990, Folder 3, Box 53, Vietnam Veterans of America–Vietnam Project Collection, VCA, TTU, LT.

95 Gary Parker, letter to Don Mills and John Myers, March 4, 1990, Folder 3, Box 53, Vietnam Veterans of America–Vietnam Project Collection, VCA, TTU, LT.

96 Maribeth Theisen, letter to John Myers, March 6, 1990, Folder 3, Box 53, Vietnam Veterans of America–Vietnam Project Collection, VCA, TTU, LT.

97 Miller, "Veterans Find Peace in Vietnam."

98 Greg Kleven, letter to John Myers, n.d., Folder 3, Box 53, Vietnam Veterans of America–Vietnam Project Collection, VCA, TTU, LT

99 Kleven, letter to John Myers.

100 Kleven.

101 Mark J. McCausland, letter to John Myers/Don Mills, March 3, 1990, Folder 3, Box 53, Vietnam Veterans of America–Vietnam Project Collection, VCA, TTU, LT.

102 Greg Kleven, letter to Congressman Miller, April 22, 1989, Folder 4, Box 50, Vietnam Veterans of America–Vietnam Project Collection, VCA, TTU, LT.

103 Joseph Lafatch, "Statement of Joe Lafatch, Vietnam Veteran, before the Subcommittee on International Economic Policy and Trade Committee on Foreign Affairs," US House of Representatives, Washington, DC, March 13, 1990, Folder 31, Box 42, Vietnam Veterans of America–Vietnam Project Collection, VCA, TTU, LT.

104 United Nations, "Universal Declaration of Human Rights," United Nations, accessed September 25, 2020, https://www.un.org/en/universal-declaration-human-rights/.

105 David C. Unger, "Editorial Notebook: How to Look for M.I.A.'S; Travel Barriers Invite Scams," *New York Times*, August 4, 1991.

106 John F. Terzano, "Statement of John F. Terzano, President, Vietnam Veteran of America Foundation, before the Subcommittee on International Economic Policy

and Trade Committee on Foreign Affairs," US House of Representatives, Washington, DC, March 13, 1990, Folder 31, Box 42, Vietnam Veterans of America–Vietnam Project Collection, VCA, TTU, LT.

107 Tom Condon, "Statement before the Subcommittee on International Economic Policy and Trade Committee on Foreign Affairs," US House of Representatives, Washington, DC, March 13, 1990, Folder 4, Box 50, Vietnam Veterans of America–Vietnam Project Collection, VCA, TTU, LT.

108 Larry Pressler, "We Can't Isolate Vietnam Forever," *New York Times*, May 23, 1988.

109 "Americans Begin 'Peace Walk' through Vietnam," *United Press International*, August 29, 1991.

110 "Thirty-Three Americans to Start 'Peace Walk' in Vietnam," *Agence France-Presse*, August 28, 1991; Kathleen Callo, "Americans Begin 'Peace Walk' in Vietnam Against U.S. Embargo," Reuters News Agency, August 29, 1991; "Vietnam Peace Walk," Associated Press, August 29, 1991. These sources disagreed on the numbers of the participants, citing from thirty-one to forty people.

111 "Travel Advisory: U.S. Lifts Ban on Travel to Vietnam," *New York Times*, February 5, 1992.

112 *Bulletin of the US Committee for Scientific Cooperation with Vietnam* 6, no. 1 (Summer 1987), Folder 8, Box 44, Vietnam Veterans of America–Vietnam Project Collection, VCA, TTU, LT.

113 Sue Downie, "Wisconsin Teacher Aids Vietnamese," *Sun-Sentinel*, April 16, 1989.

114 Jerry Hicks, "Professor's Killer Freed from Prison," *Los Angeles Times*, July 1, 1986; Jerry Hicks, "Inmate Says Lam Told of Political Plot behind Killing of Cooperman," *Los Angeles Times*, January 8, 1985; "Dismissal Sought in Cooperman Case after Hung Trial," *Morning Call*, February 22, 1985; Jerry Hicks, "2nd Inmate Says Lam Called Killing Deliberate," *Los Angeles Times*, March 26, 1985; Jerry Hicks, "Lam Attorney Asks Court to Bar Handwriting Expert," *Los Angeles Times*, January 15, 1985.

115 Jessica Genova, "A Case of Academic Good Will: How a UW-Madison Professor Kept a Scientific Link Open to Vietnam," *Wisconsin State Journal*, December 3, 1995.

116 Larry Green, "Refugee Gets Transplant of Bone Marrow," *Los Angeles Times*, May 14, 1985.

117 University of Wisconsin-Madison, "Ladinsky Memorial Fund Receives Gift, Launches Lecture," International Division, University of Wisconsin-Madison, August 22, 2015, http://international.wisc.edu/blog/index.php/2015/08/22/ladinsky-fund-lecture.

118 "'Madame Viet Nam' Finds Her Final Resting Place in Ha Noi," *Vietnam News*, July 22, 2013.

119 The Fund for Reconciliation and Development, "Home," The Fund for Reconciliation and Development, accessed September 25, 2020, http://www.ffrd.org.

120 John McAuliff, "Testimony to the Committee on the Judiciary. Subcommittee

on Courts, Intellectual Property, and the Administration of Justice," 1988–1989, Folder 21, Box 38, Vietnam Veterans of America–Vietnam Project Collection, VCA, TTU, LT.

121 McAuliff, "Testimony."

122 Susan Manuel, "Vietnam Top Capitalist Predicts U.S. Ties," *Star Bulletin*, October 29, 1988; McAuliff, testimony and internal correspondence.

123 Kate Martin, letter to Abraham D. Sofaer, May 4, 1988, Folder 18, Box 52, Vietnam Veterans of America–Vietnam Project Collection, VCA, TTU, LT.

124 Mary Byrne McDonnell, "Indochina Activity by Nongovernmental Organizations," May 1988, Folder 3, Box 38, Vietnam Veterans of America–Vietnam Project Collection, VCA, TTU, LT; letter of intent between the Social Science Research Council and the Vietnam Committee for the Social Sciences, May 1988, Folder 3, Box 38, Vietnam Veterans of America–Vietnam Project Collection, VCA, TTU, LT.

125 The subheading in this chapter "When Rifles and Tools Changed Places" is an homage to the title of Le Ly Hayslip's memoir, *When Heaven and Earth Changed Places*.

126 Le Ly Hayslip, "A Vietnam Memoir," *Voices*, n.d. Hayslip published two memoirs. The first one, *When Heaven and Earth Changed Places*, came out in 1989 and was turned into a film entitled *Heaven and Earth* by Oliver Stone in 1993. The second book, *Child of War, Woman of Peace*, was published in 1993.

127 Hayslip, "A Vietnam Memoir."

128 East Meets West flyer, Folder 14, Box 40, Vietnam Veterans of America–Vietnam Project Collection, VCA, TTU, LT.

129 Jerry Stadtmiller, open letter, n.d., Folder 14, Box 40, Vietnam Veterans of America–Vietnam Project Collection, VCA, TTU, LT.

130 "U.S. Commits to 3,000,000 in Humanitarian Aid to Vietnam," Veterans Vietnam Restoration Project newsletter, no 14, June 1992.

Chapter 4: Postnormalization Quest for Peace

1 Sandy Northrop, producer, "Pete Peterson: Assignment Hanoi," PBS, documentary, 1999.

2 US Embassy, "Chronology of U.S.-Vietnam Relations," US Embassy & Consulate in Vietnam. https://vn.usembassy.gov/our-relationship/policy-history/chronology-of-us-vietnam-relations/.

3 Northrop, "Pete Peterson."

4 Zoltan Istvan, "Vietnam Villagers Find Profit, Risk in Bomb Hunting," *National Geographic News*, January 7, 2004.

5 According to the international legal definition, ERW consists of unexploded ordnance (UXO) and abandoned explosive ordnance (AXO) such as artillery shells, grenades, mortars, rockets, air-dropped bombs, and cluster munitions, but not mines. For more information, please see the Landmine and Cluster Munition

Monitor, "Explosive Remnants of War," Landmine and Cluster Munition Monitor, accessed September 27, 2020, http://www.the-monitor.org/en-gb/the-issues/erw.aspx.

6 Project RENEW, "A Study of Explosive Remnants of War Accidents and the Knowledge—Attitudes—Practices–Beliefs of People in Quang Tri Province, Vietnam," Project RENEW, 2011, http://landmines.org.vn/publications/a-study-of-erw-accidents-in-quang-tri-province.

7 Elaine Elinson, "Fellow Traveler's Notebook," *Veteran* 43, no. 2 (Fall 2013), http://www.vvaw.org/veteran/article/?id=2481

8 David Broder, "To Bind up Wounds of Vietnam, Lewis B. Puller, Jr.," *Orlando Sentinel*, May 19, 1994; "Vietnam Inaugurates Puller School," *Associate Press / Daily Press (Newport News, Virginia)*, April 25, 1995; William H. McMichael, "Work Starts on Puller School," *Associate Press / Daily Press (Newport News, Virginia)*, October 1, 1994.

9 Chris Hedges, "The Last U.S. Hostage," *New York Times*, December 5, 1991.

10 Broder, "To Bind up Wounds of Vietnam."

11 Joachim Hagopian, "The Life and Death of Vietnam War Veteran Jack Wheeler: A Good Man in an Evil World," Global Research, April 7, 2015, http://www.globalresearch.ca/the-life-and-death-of-vietnam-war-veteran-jack-wheeler-a-good-man-in-an-evil-world/5441165.

12 McMichael, "Work Starts on Puller School."

13 Vietnam Children's Fund, "About Us," Vietnam Children's Fund, http://www.vietnamchildren.org/about.html

14 The Virtual Wall, "Daniel Bernard Cheney," The Virtual Wall, accessed September 27, 2020, http://www.virtualwall.org/dc/CheneyDB01a.htm; Jerilyn Cheney Brusseau, "Greetings from Family of Dan Cheney," Northwest Vets, January 6, 2013, http://www.northwestvets.com/spurblog/2013/01/06/greetings-from-family-of-dan-cheney.

15 Earthstewards, "Home," Earthstewards, accessed September 27, 2020, http://www.earthstewards.org.

16 TedxSeattle, "Jerilyn Brusseau," TedxRainier, December 2, 2010, http://www.tedxrainier.com/speakers/jerilyn-brusseau.

17 Anne-Marie O'Neill, "Seeds of Hope: American Jerilyn Brusseau Turns Minefields into Peace Arbors," People, May 1, 2000

18 Tran Thuy Duong, "Talk Vietnam: American Mothers Plant Peace Trees in Vietnam," television interview, VTV1, Northwest Vets, n.d.; O'Neill, "Seeds of Hope."; Minh Thu, "Mothers Share Sorrow of War," Viet Nam News, September 16, 2010, https://vietnamnews.vn/society/203707/mothers-share-sorrow-of-war.html.

19 Tran, "Talk Vietnam."

20 Thu à Minh Thu, "Mothers Share Sorrow of War"; TedxSeattle, "Jerilyn Brusseau."

21 PeaceTrees Vietnam, "Home," PeaceTrees Vietnam, accessed September 27, 2020, http://www.peacetreesvietnam.org.

22 PeaceTrees Vietnam, "Home."

23 Tran, "Talk Vietnam."

24 Gay-Wynn Cooper, "Peace Trees, Vietnam," *Yes! Magazine*, June 30, 1999, http://www.yesmagazine.org/issues/cities-of-exuberance/peace-trees-vietnam.

25 Hang Le-Tormala, interview by the author, August 22, 2015, Ho Chi Minh City, Vietnam.

26 Project RENEW, "What We Do," Project RENEW, accessed September 27, 2020, http://www.landmines.org.vn/what-we-do; Chuck Searcy, "A Personal Note from Chuck Searcy about Project RENEW," *"Lemon Juice" Bruce* (blog), January 18, 2013, http://www.lemonjuicebruce.blogspot.com/2013/01/a-personal-note-from -chuck-searcy-about.html.

27 George Black, "The Lethal Legacy of the Vietnam War," The Nation, February 25, 2015, https://www.thenation.com/article/archive/lethal-legacy-vietnam-war/.

28 Black, "The Lethal Legacy."

29 Bleakney, *Revisiting Vietnam*, 3.

30 Bleakney, 7.

31 Christina Schwenkel, *The American War in Contemporary Vietnam: Transnational Remembrance and Representation* (Bloomington: Indiana University Press, 2009), 28.

32 Schwenkel, *The American War.*

33 TOP Vietnam Veterans, "Home," TOP Vietnam Veterans, https://web.archive.org /web/20160316152218/http://topvietnamveterans.org/index.html.

34 TOP Vietnam Veterans, "Home."

35 TOP Vietnam Veterans

36 TOP Vietnam Veterans.

37 TOP Vietnam Veterans.

38 Cynthya Porter, "A Long, Hard Trip to Visit the Past and See the Future," TOP Vietnam Veterans, April 16, 2003, https://web.archive.org/web/20160418123919 /http://topvietnamveterans.org/WinonaPost/April-16-2003.html.

39 Porter, "A Long, Hard Trip."

40 Porter.

41 Porter.

42 Porter.

43 Porter.

44 Porter.

45 Bill Hess, "Sierra Vista Man's Trips Help Make Peace," *Sierra Vista Herald*, September 16, 2005, http://www.topvietnamveterans.org/SVHearald/index.html.

46 Hess, "Sierra Vista Man's Trips."

47 Carmen Duarte, "Cousin Finds Closure after 36 Years," *Arizona Daily Star*, April 5, 2003; Geneva Maria Escobedo, "Remembering Raymond," TOP Vietnam Veterans, February 25, 2003.

48 Tourists often find replicas of US soldiers' dog tags in gift shops at historical places of the Vietnam War, usually with made-up names and military information.

49 TOP Vietnam Veterans, "Personal Effects Program," TOP Vietnam Veterans, ac-

cessed November 9, 2020, https://web.archive.org/web/20160315031201/http://topvietnamveterans.org/p-pe.html.

50 TOP Vietnam Veterans, "TOP Vietnam Veterans Finds Captain Marshall's Family, Reunites Personal Effect," TOP Vietnam Veterans, accessed November 9, 2020, https://web.archive.org/web/20160315031201/http://topvietnamveterans.org/p-pe.html.

51 TOP Vietnam Veterans, "Personal Effects Program."

52 TOP Vietnam Veterans.

53 TOP Vietnam Veterans.

54 Keith Morrison, "Coming Home: One Veteran Heals through a Battlefield Keepsake," *Dateline NBC*, May 25, 2008, http://www.nbcnews.com/id/24818399/ns/dateline_nbc-international/t/coming-home.

55 Morrison, "Coming Home."

56 Thomas B. Allen *Offerings at the Wall: Artifacts from the Vietnam Veterans Memorial Collection* (Atlanta, GA: Turner, 1995), 52.

57 Morrison, "Coming Home."

58 Morrison.

59 Morrison.

60 Morrison.

61 Morrison.

62 Michael Sullivan, "A Wartime Diary Touches Vietnamese," National Public Radio, November 15, 2006; Seth Mydans, "Diary of North Vietnam Doctor Killed in U.S. Attack Makes War Real," *New York Times*, June 6, 2006.

63 Mydans, "Diary of North Vietnam Doctor Killed in U.S. Attack Makes War Real."

64 Mydans.

65 Dang Thuy Tram, *Last Night I Dreamed of Peace: The Diary of Dang Thuy Tram*, trans. Andrew X. Pham (New York: Random House, 2007), xx.

66 Dang, *Last Night I Dreamed of Peace*.

67 Mike Ives, "Dr. Sam Axelrad, Former U.S. Military Physician, Returns to Vietnam to Give Back Arm to Soldier," Huffington Post, July 1, 2013; Nguyễn Trường, "Rung động cựu binh Mỹ trả lại xương cánh tay cho người lính Bắc Việt" (A touching story of an American veteran wishing to return arm bones to a north Vietnamese soldier), *Tiền Phong*, November 11, 2012.

68 Ives, "Dr. Sam Axelrad"; Trần Quỳnh Hoa, "Kỷ vật lạ lùng của một cựu bác sĩ quân y Mỹ" (A strange keepsake of an American military physician), *Thanh Niên*, November 11, 2012.

69 "PBS History Detectives Returns Soldier's Diary to Vietnam through U.S. Department of Defense," PBS Press Release, June 3, 2012, http://www.pbs.org/about/blogs/news/pbs-history-detectives-returns-soldiers-diary-to-vietnam-through-us-department-of-defense; Ngọc Nga, "Món nợ cuộc đời" (A debt to life), *Tuổi Trẻ*, May 20, 2012.

70 Richard Allen Greene, "Decades after War, U.S. and Vietnam Swap Slain Troops' Papers," CNN, June 5, 2012, http://www.cnn.com/2012/06/04/us/us-vietnam-war-letters.

71 Daniel Cherry and Fran Erickson, *My Enemy, My Friend: A Story of Reconciliation from the Vietnam War*, 2nd ed. (Bowling Green, KY: My Enemy, My Friend, 2009).

72 More details about this TV program and its history are discussed on pages 151–159.

73 Cherry, *My Enemy, My Friend*, 56.

74 Cherry, 62.

75 Cherry, 65–71.

76 Cherry, 74.

77 Cherry, 89.

78 Cherry, 93.

79 Hồng Quân, "BTV Thu Uyên với chương trình truyền hình 'Như Chưa Hề Có Cuộc Chia Ly': Lại một cuộc dấn thân" (TV show host Thu Uyen and "as if they had never been separated": Another undertaking"), *Thanh Niên*, November 14, 2007; Nguyễn Mỹ, "Cuộc chia ly màu đỏ" (A red separation), *Cuộc chia ly màu đỏ*. Hanoi Publisher, Hanoi: 1979. Poet Nguyen My fought in both the French War and the American War (as the Vietnamese call them) and was killed in action in 1971.

80 *Như Chưa Hề Có Cuộc Chia Ly*, accessed November 9, 2020, http://www.hay lentieng.vn.

81 Nguyễn Phạm Thu Uyên, "NCHCCCL số 31: Những chiếc mũ rơm" (NCHCCCL no 31: The straw hats, video), Hãy Lên Tiếng, June 6, 2010; Ngày Phát Sóng, "Truyền Hình," Hãy Lên Tiếng, July 6, 2020, http://www.haylentieng.vn.

82 Nguyen, "NCHCCCL số 3."1.

83 Nguyen.

84 Nguyen, "NCHCCCL số 16" (NCHCCCL no. 16: video), Hãy Lên Tiếng, March 14, 2009.

85 Nguyen, "NCHCCCL số 70: Lá rụng về cội" (NCHCCCL no 70: Returning to the roots, video), Hãy Lên Tiếng, January 4, 2014.

86 Nguyen, "NCHCCCL số 81: Luôn hướng về nhau" (NCHCCCL no 81: Always in each other's thoughts, video), Hãy Lên Tiếng, January 3, 2015.

87 Nguyen, "NCHCCCL số 81."

88 Nguyen, "NCHCCCL số 79: Như dòng đời xô dạt" (NCHCCCL no 79: In the drift of life, video), Hãy Lên Tiếng, October 4, 2014.

89 Nguyen, "NCHCCCL số 79."

90 Nguyen, "NCHCCCL Gala 2014: Phút giây này, có ai ngờ, chợt đến" (NCHCCCL gala 2014: The unexpected moment arrived, video), Hãy Lên Tiếng, February 4, 2014.

91 Nguyen, "NCHCCCL số 84: Sự đối nghịch của chiến tranh" (NCHCCCL no 84: Paradoxes of war, video), Hãy Lên Tiếng, April 4, 2015.

92 Nguyen, "NCHCCCL số 18: Những người con nuôi từ đường 7" (NCHCCCL no 18: Adopted children from Route 7, video), Hãy Lên Tiếng, May 16, 2009.

93 Nguyen, "NCHCCCL số 18."

94 Hoàng Phương, "Còn hơn nửa triệu liệt sĩ chưa xác minh được thông tin" (More than a half million of fallen soldiers unidentified), *VnExpress*, July 25, 2015,

http://vnexpress.net/tin-tuc/thoi-su/con-hon-nua-trieu-liet-si-chua-xac-minh
-duoc-thong-tin-3253460.html. The statistics included soldiers of the first Indochina War (or the French War as the Vietnamese call it) from 1945 to 1954, the
Vietnam War (or the American War) from the 1950s to 1975, and the conflicts
with the Khmer Rouge and China in the late 1970s.

95 Trở Về Từ Ký Ức, "Home," Trở Về Từ Ký Ức, https://web.archive.org/web
/20150405023800/http://trovetukyuc.vn/.

96 Người Đưa Đò, "Home," Người Đưa Đò, accessed Septembr 27, 2020, http://
www.nguoiduado.vn.

Conclusion

1 "Returning for Redemption," *Tuoi Tre News*, April 1, 2013, http://tuoitrenews.vn
/features/8365/returning-for-redemption.

2 "Returning for Redemption."

3 Akira Iriye, *Global and Transnational History: The Past, Present, and Future*
(Basingstoke, UK: Palgrave Macmillan, 2013)

4 Donna Seaman, "A Conversation with John Balaban," *Triquarterly*, no. 114.

5 John Balaban, "The Invisible Powers," David L. Jannetta Distinguished Lectureship in War, Literature and the Arts, United States Air Force Academy, CO, October 13, 2009.

6 Balaban, "The Invisible Powers"; John Balaban, *Remembering Heaven's Face: A
Story of Rescue in Wartime Vietnam* (Athens: University of Georgia, 2002).

7 Balaban, "The Invisible Powers"; for more information, see http://www.john
balaban.com. In Vietnam, folk poems have rhythmic formats and are sung in
particular ways, depending on their patterns of rhythm.

8 Elizabeth Farnsworth, "Voices from Vietnam," PBS Newshour, June 27, 2001,
http://www.pbs.org/newshour/bb/entertainment-jan-june01-vietnam_06-27.

9 Vietnamese Nôm Preservation Foundation, "About," Vietnamese Nôm Preservation Foundation, accessed September 27, 2020, http://www.nomfoundation.org.

10 Farnsworth, "Voices from Vietnam."

11 Excerpted from the poem "Fuku," in Yevgeny Yevtushenko, *The Collected Poems, 1952–1990*, edited by Albert C. Todd with the author and James Ragan
(New York: Henry Holt, 1991), 586–587.

Sources in English

Allen, Kevin Minh. "Identity at War's End: The Amerasian Legacy."*International Examiner*, May 4, 2011.

"Americans Begin 'Peace Walk' through Vietnam." *United Press International*, August 29, 1991.

Anderson, Benedict. *Imagined Communities: Reflections on the Origin and Spread of Nationalism*. London: Verso, 1991.

Anzaldúa, Gloria. *Borderlands*. 2nd ed. San Francisco: Aunt Lute Books, 1999.

Arnett, Peter. "Refugees from 'Boat with No Smiles' Find New Life in U.S." *Los Angeles Times*, June 23, 1978.

_____. "'Worse Off Than I Ever Expected': Monsoons Halt Aid for 'Boat People.'" *Los Angeles Times*, November 16, 1978.

"Art that Reaches into Our Guts." Opinion, *Battle Creek Enquirer*, September 11, 1991.

Ashkenazy, Elinor. "Is Sending Plows to Vietnam 'Trading with the Enemy?'" *Los Angeles Times*, November 7, 1975.

Bacon, William, III, dir. *Friendship Village: A Place of Healing*. 2003; produced by Reed Bovee.

Bahadur, Gaiutra. "Citizenship Bill Holds Promise for Disenfranchised Amerasians." *Philadelphia Inquirer*, October 27, 2003.

Balaban, John. "The Invisible Powers." David L. Jannetta Distinguished Lectureship in War, Literature and the Arts, Air Force Academy, CO, October 13, 2009.

_____. *Remembering Heaven's Face: A Story of Rescue in Wartime Vietnam*. Athens: University of Georgia, 2002.

Bass, Thomas A. *Vietnamerica: The War Comes Home*. New York: Soho Press, 1996.

Beech, Keyes. "'Boat People' Easy Prey for Asia's Pirates." *Los Angeles Times*, August 7, 1979.

Belkin, Lisa. "Children of 2 Lands in Search of Home." *New York Times*, May 19, 1988.

Bennetts, Leslie. "The Vietnam War as Theater and an Act of Exorcism." *New York Times*, January 27, 1985.

Bernstein, Fred. "Vet-Turned-Vip Tom Bird Is Stuck on New York's 'Mayflower Madam'" *People*, June 17, 1985.

Biddle, Wayne. "The Ragtag and Regimental Legacies of Vietnam." *New York Times*, May 30, 1984.

Black, George. "The Lethal Legacy of the Vietnam War." The Nation, February 25, 2015. https://www.thenation.com/article/archive/lethal-legacy-vietnam-war/.

Bleakney, Julia. *Revisiting Vietnam: Memoirs, Memorials, Museums*. New York: Routledge, 2006.

Bly, Laura. "Vietnam Tour Ban Comes under Fire." *Orlando Sentinel*, June 18, 1989.

"The Boat People." *Los Angeles Times*, December 14, 1976.

Bowen, Kevin. Interview. Voices Compassionate Education, 2001, http://www.voic-eseducation.org/node/372.

———. "Notes from When the War Was Over: Remembering the Embargo." *Massachusetts Review* 36, no. 4 (Winter 1995): 527–538.

Briggs, Kenneth A. "Church Group Reports on Vietnam." *New York Times*, June 2, 1978.

Broder, David "To Bind up Wounds of Vietnam, Lewis B. Puller, Jr." *Orlando Sentinel*, May 19, 1994.

Brody, Jeffrey. "Amerasians Exploited as Ticket to United States." *Orange County Register*, April 7, 1991.

Brooke, Pankaja, dir. *You're the Enemy—Welcome Back!* 2014; Holland, OH: Dreamscape Media, 2015.

Brown Z., Frederick. "Vietnam since the War (1975–1995)." *Wilson Quarterly* 19, no. 1 (Winter 1995): 64–87.

Brusseau, Jerilyn. "Greetings from family of Dan Cheney." Northwest Vets, January 6, 2013. http://www.northwestvets.com/spurblog/2013/01/06/greetings-from -family-of-dan-cheney.

Callo, Kathleen. "Americans Begin 'Peace Walk' in Vietnam Against U.S. Embargo." Reuters News Agency, August 29, 1991.

Campbell, Colin. "Outcast Vietnam Children Still Hope." *New York Times*, June 5, 1982.

Carlson, Elof Axel. "Commentary: International Symposium on Herbicides in the Vietnam War: An Appraisal." *BioScience* 33, no. 8 (September 1983): 507–512.

Champagne, Fredy. "The Founding of the VVRP." Veterans Vietnam Restoration Project. https://web.archive.org/web/20150225032712/http://www.vvrp.org/?page _id=133.

Chanola, Harish. "New Pacific Doctrine." *Economic and Political Weekly*, January 10, 1976.

Cherry, Daniel, and Fran Erickson. *My Enemy, My Friend: A Story of Reconciliation from the Vietnam War*. 2nd ed. Bowling Green, KY: Aviation Heritage Park, 2009.

"Churches Ship Wheat to Vietnam." *New York Times*, April 4, 1978.

Church World Service. "History." Church World Service, accessed September 19, 2020. http://www.cwsglobal.org/who-we-are/history.html.

"Church World Service to Ship $2 Million in Wheat to Vietnam." *Washington Post*, November 23, 1977.

Clavin, Patricia. "Defining Transnationalism." *Contemporary European History* 14, no. 4. (2005): 438.

Constable, Pamela "For Area's Amerasians, More Struggle: Many Children of GI's Find It Hard to Adjust." *Washington Post*, April 13, 1998.

Cooper, Gay-Wynn. "Peace Trees, Vietnam." *Yes! Magazine*, June 30, 1999. http:// www.yesmagazine.org/issues/cities-of-exuberance/peace-trees-vietnam.

Crossette, Barbara. "Hanoi Asks to End Amerasians' Issue." *New York Times*, October 20, 1985.

———. "Veterans to Help Mine-Field Victims." *New York Times*, April 19, 1992.

_____. "Vietnam Is Giving American Tourism a Trial Run." *New York Times*, November 3, 1985.

Dao, James. "Vietnam Legacy: Finding G.I. Fathers, and Children Left Behind." *New York Times*, September 15, 2013.

Dean, Paul. "Coming to the Aid of the Boat People." *Los Angeles Times*, July 23, 1979.

DeBonis, Steven. *Children of the Enemy: Oral Histories of Vietnamese Amerasians and Their Mothers*. Jefferson, NC: McFarland, 1995.

Desbarats, Jacqueline. "Population Redistribution in the Socialist Republic of Vietnam." *Population and Development Review* 13, no. 1 (March 1987): 43–76.

"Dismissal Sought in Cooperman Case after Hung Trial." *Morning Call*, February 22, 1985.

Downie, Sue. "Wisconsin Teacher Aids Vietnamese." *Sun-Sentinel*, April 16, 1989.

Duarte, Carmen. "Cousin Finds Closure after 36 Years." *Arizona Daily Star*, April 5, 2003.

Dumbrell, John. *Clinton's Foreign Policy: Between the Bushes, 1992–2000*. London and New York: Routledge, 2009.

Earthstewards. "Home." Earthstewards, accessed September 27, 2020. http://www.earthstewards.org.

Edelman, Marian Wright "Vietnam's Hungry Children." *New York Times*, August 14, 1977.

"11 Amerasian Kids Leave Vietnam and Happily Embrace Their U.S. Families." *People*, October 18, 1982.

"11 American-Vietnamese Fly to New Home." *Boston Globe*, October 1, 1982.

Elinson, Elaine "Fellow Traveler's Notebook." *Veteran* 43, no. 2 (Fall 2013). http://www.vvaw.org/veteran/article/?id=2481

Elkins, David J. "Globalization, Telecommunication, and Virtual Ethnic Communities." *International Political Science Review* 18, no. 2 (April 1997): 139–152.

Escobedo, M. Geneva. "Remembering Raymond." TOP Vietnam Veterans, February 25, 2003.

Esper, George. "Amerasians: Vietnam's Misbegotten Legacy." *Los Angeles Times*, April 30, 1989.

Farnsworth, Clyde. "Vietnam: To Aid or Not to Aid?" *New York Times*, June 26, 1977. http://search.proquest.com.www2.1ib.ku.edu:2048/docview/123444285.

Farnsworth, Elizabeth. "Voices from Vietnam." PBS Newshour, June 27, 2001. http://www.pbs.org/newshour/bb/entertainment-jan-june01-vietnam_06–27.

Fforde, Adam. "Economics, History, and the Origins of Vietnam's Post-War Economic Success." *Asian Survey* 49, no. 3 (May/June 2009): 484–504.

FitzGerald, Frances. "Punch In! Punch Out! Eat Quick!" *New York Times*, December 28, 1975.

Ford, Gerald R. "Address at a Tulane University Convocation." April 23, 1975. The American Presidency Project, accessed November 9, 2020. http://www.presidency.ucsb.edu/ws/index.php?pid=4859.

"Four Veterans Defend Visit to Vietnam." *New York Times*, December 29, 1981.

Gage, Sue-Je Lee. "The Amerasian Problem: Blood, Duty, and Race." *International Relations* 21, no. 1 (2007): 86–102.

Genova, Jessica. "A Case of Academic Good Will: How a UW-Madison Professor Kept a Scientific Link Open to Vietnam." *Wisconsin State Journal*, December 3, 1995.

Goldberg, Trista. "The 35th Anniversary." Vietnamese Adoptees, April 28, 2010, http://www.vietnameseadoptees.com.

Gowen, Annie. "Legacies of War." *Washington Post*, April 17, 2015.

Green, Larry. "Refugee Gets Transplant of Bone Marrow." *Los Angeles Times*, May 14, 1985.

Greene, A. Richard. "Decades after War, U.S. and Vietnam Swap Slain Troops' Papers." CNN, June 5, 2012. http://www.cnn.com/2012/06/04/us/us-vietnam-war-letters.

Growald, Richard H. "Odyssey of a 'Boat People' Family: Safety at Last." *Los Angeles Times*, August 15, 1979.

Hagopian, Joachim "The Life and Death of Vietnam War Veteran Jack Wheeler: A Good Man in an Evil World." Global Research, April 7, 2015. http://www.globalresearch.ca/the-life-and-death-of-vietnam-war-veteran-jack-wheeler-a-good-man-in-an-evil-world/5441165.

Hayslip, Le Ly. "A Vietnam Memoir." *People*, December 18, 1989. https://people.com/archive/a-vietnam-memoir-vol-32-no-25/.

Hedges, Chris. "The Last U.S. Hostage." *New York Times*, December 5, 1991.

Heinemann, Larry. *Black Virgin Mountain: A Return to Vietnam.* New York: Doubleday, 2005.

———. Personal conversation with the author. College Station, Texas, March 23, 2013.

"He Looks Like Me: Two Amerasians Seek Their Dads -and Their Missing Heritage." *Los Angeles Times*, July 7, 1991.

Hershberger, Mary. *Traveling to Vietnam: American Peace Activists and the War.* Syracuse, NY: Syracuse University Press, 1998.

Hess, Bill. "Sierra Vista Man's Trips Help Make Peace." *Sierra Vista Herald*, September 16, 2005. http://www.topvietnamveterans.org/SVHearald/index.html.

Hess, Gary R. *Vietnam and the United States: Origins and Legacy of War.* New York: Prentice Hall International, 1998.

Hicks, Jerry. "Inmate Says Lam Told of Political Plot behind Killing of Cooperman." *Los Angeles Times*, January 8, 1985.

———. "Lam Attorney Asks Court to Bar Handwriting Expert." *Los Angeles Times*, January 15, 1985.

———. "Professor's Killer Freed from Prison." *Los Angeles Times*, July 1, 1986.

———. "2nd Inmate Says Lam Called Killing Deliberate." *Los Angeles Times*, March 26, 1985.

Horvath, Alex. "Veterans Heal through Laughter." *Press Democrat*, March 17, 2015.

Huntington, Samuel P. "The Bases of Accommodation." *Foreign Affairs* 46, no. 4 (July 1968): 642–656.

Hupy, Joseph P. "The Environmental Footprint of War." *Environment and History* 14, no. 3 (August 2008): 405–421.

Hurst, Steven. *The Carter Administration and Vietnam*. London and New York: Macmillan, 1996.

Hyer, Marjorie. "Quakers Get Approval for Vietnam Aid." *Washington Post*, November 17, 1975.

_____. "Quakers to Flout Law on Viet Aid." *Washington Post*, November 11, 1975.

Indochina Arts Partnership. "As Seen by Both Sides." Indochina Arts Partnership, accessed September 25, 2020. https://web.archive.org/web/20160701043214 /http://indochinaartspartnership.org/as-seen-by-both-sides/.

Iriye, Akira. *Cultural Internationalism and World Order*. Baltimore and London: Johns Hopkins University Press: 1997.

_____. *Global and Transnational History: The Past, Present, and Future*. Basingstoke, UK: Palgrave Macmillan, 2013.

Istvan, Zoltan. "Vietnam Villagers Find Profit, Risk in Bomb Hunting." *National Geographic News*, January 7, 2004.

Ives, Mike. "Dr. Sam Axelrad, Former U.S. Military Physician, Returns to Vietnam to Give Back Arm to Soldier." Huffington Post, July 1, 2013.

Jacobsen, Kurt. "Larry Heinemann in Conversation with Kurt Jacobsen." *Logos Online* 2, no. 1 (Winter 2003).

Jennings, Robin. "Michigan Man Reunites with His Half-Vietnamese Children." Michigan Live, May 16, 2009. https://www.mlive.com/news/2009/05/michigan _man_reunites_with_his.html.

Jenny Do for City Council. "Home." Jenny Do for City Council, accessed November 21, 2020. https://web.archive.org/web/20160223033352/http://www.jennydo forcouncil.com/.

Johnson, Janis. "U.S. Urged to End Vietnam Ban." *Washington Post*, May 7, 1976.

Kamm, Henry. "Geneva Meeting Yields Few Pledges of Aid for Indochinese Refugees: Thai Delegation Supports Plan." *New York Times*, December 17, 1978.

_____. "Vietnam's Premier Says He Wants U.S. Friendship: Vietnam's 'Duty' to Help." *New York Times*, August 8, 1978.

Karnow, Stanley. "Amerasians—Tragic Legacy of the U.S. Era in Vietnam." *Los Angeles Times*, March 16, 1981.

Keohane, Robert O., and Joseph S. Nye. *Transnational Relations and World Politics*. Cambridge, MA: Harvard University Press, 1981

Klein, Dianne. "Child of War Still Searching for Father." *Los Angeles Times*, September 29, 1992.

_____. "He Looks Like Me: Two Amerasians Seek Their Dads—and Their Missing Heritage." *Los Angeles Times*, July 7, 1991.

_____. "Search for Father Is a Search for Self." *Los Angeles Times*, July 4, 1991.

_____. "Vietnam's Lingering Casualties." *Los Angeles Times*, June 30, 1991.

Kneeland, Douglas E. "Wide Hostility Found as First Exiles Arrive." *New York Times*, May 2, 1975.

Kurtis, Bill. "The Plight of the Children Abandoned in Vietnam." New York Times, March 2, 1980.

Lakshmanan, Indira A. R. "The Children They Left Behind." *Boston Globe*, October 26, 2003.

Lamb, David. "Children of the Vietnam War." *Smithsonian Magazine*, June 2009.

Landmine and Cluster Munition Monitor. "Explosive Remnants of War." Landmine and Cluster Munition Monitor, accessed September 27, 2020. http://www.the -monitor.org/en-gb/the-issues/erw.aspx

Lang, Michael H. "Locational Components of Urban and Regional Public Policy in Postwar Vietnam: The Case of Ho Chi Minh City (Saigon)." *GeoJournal, South East Asia* 4, no. 1 (1980): 13–18.

Latham, Michael E. "Redirecting the Revolution? The USA and the Failure of Nation-Building in South Vietnam." *Third World Quarterly* 27, no. 1 (2006): 29–30.

LeBoutillier, John. *Vietnam Now: A Case for Normalizing Relations with Hanoi.* New York: Praeger, 1989.

Lederer, Edith M. "Singer Adapts to U.S.-Vietnam Roots." Associated Press, April 29, 2000.

Le-Tormala, Hang. Interview by the author, August 22, 2015, Ho Chi Minh City, Vietnam.

Levy, Marc. "An Interview with Bao Ninh: Part Two." *Veteran* 30, no. 1 (Spring/Summer 2000): 16.

Lewis, Flora. "North Vietnam Demands U.S. Fulfill Its Promise of Postwar Aid." *New York Times*, March 30, 1976.

Lloyd Roberts, Sue. "A US Soldier Searches for His Vietnamese Son." BBC News, April 27, 2014. https://www.bbc.com/news/magazine-27159697#:~:text=Thous ands%20of%20children%20were%20fathered,daughters%20they%20 have%20never%20known.&text=His%20latest%20client%2C%20the%20 American,Vietnam%20to%20find%20his%20son.

Locke, Colleen. "William Joiner Center Director Receives Award in Vietnam." University of Massachusetts, Boston, April 17, 2011. https://www.umb.edu/news /detail/william_joiner_center_director_receives_award_in_vietnam#:~:text =For%20more%20than%2025%20years,of%20the%20effects%20of%20expo sure.

MacLeod, Andrew. "Amerasian Daughter Adapts to U.S. after Rough Start." United Press International, January 23, 1983.

"'Madame Viet Nam' Finds Her Final Resting Place in Ha Noi." *Vietnam News*, July 22, 2013.

Madden, Richard L. "Ford Still Seeks More Saigon Aid: Wants Military Assistance Despite Declaration on End of Involvement." *New York Times*, April 25, 1975.

Makhijani, Arjun. *Manifesto for Global Democracy: Two Essays on Imperialism and the Struggle for Freedom.* New York: Apex Press, 2004.

Manegold, C. S. "Born in Vietnam: An American Veteran Returns to Asia to Claim His Son." *Ottawa Citizen*, July 23, 1988.

Mann, Jim. "U.S. May Let Groups Travel, Do Business in Vietnam " *Los Angeles Times*, April 11, 1991.

Manuel, Susan. "Vietnam Top Capitalist Predicts U.S. Ties." *Star Bulletin*, October 29, 1988.

Marcus, Erin. "A Search for Family, Amerasian Odyssey: Few Find the Fathers Who Left Them Behind in Vietnam." *Washington Post*, March 8, 1992.

Martini, Edwin A. "Invisible Enemies: The American War on Vietnam, 1975–2000." In *Culture, Politics, and the Cold War*, edited by Christian G. Appy. Amherst: University of Massachusetts Press, 2007.

Mason, Michelle, dir. "The Friendship Village." 2003; Cypress Park Productions.

McArthur, George. "Viet Refugees Victimized at Sea: Helpless 'Boat People' Known as Easy Pickings." *Los Angeles Times*, June 11, 1978.

McDonald, R. Robin. "Vietnamese Gangs: War's Bitter Fruit Prosecutors Are Tageting Amerasians in Atlanta Who Prey on Asian Merchants." *Atlanta Journal Constitution*, July 14, 1996.

McGraw, Carol. "Vietnamese Teen Reunited with American Father, Family." *Los Angeles Times*, June 11, 1988.

McKelvey, Robert S. *The Dust of Life: America's Children Abandoned in Vietnam*. Seattle: University of Washington Press, 1999.

McMichael, H. William. "Work Starts on Puller School." *Daily Press (Newport News, Virginia)*, October 1, 1994.

Miller, Alan C. "Veterans Find Peace in Vietnam." *Los Angeles Times*, July 5, 1990
_____. "Veterans Testify on Bill Allowing Trips to Vietnam." *Los Angeles Times*, March 14, 1990.

Mishrin, Ahrin. "Vietnamese Gangs: Identity and Discourse in 'Little Saigon.'" Grad thesis, University of Southern California, August 1993. Quoted in Yarborough, Trin, *Surviving Twice: Amerasian Children of the Vietnam War*. Washington, DC: Potomac Books, 2005.

Morrison, Keith. "Coming Home: One Veteran Heals through a Battlefield Keepsake." Dateline NBC, May 25, 2008. http://www.nbcnews.com/id/24818399/ns /dateline_nbc-international/t/coming-home.

Muller, Robert O. "The Land Mine Scourge—How Much Longer?" *Christian Science Monitor*, February 8, 1996.

Mydans, Seth. "Diary of North Vietnam Doctor Killed in U.S. Attack Makes War Real." *New York Times*, June 6, 2006.

Needham, John, and Thuan Le. "Slaying Mars Youth's Dreams of a New Life." *Los Angeles Times*, April 5, 1992.

Negron, Edna. "Le Van Minh's Americanization." *Newsday*, November 16, 1987.

Northrop, Sandy, pro. "Pete Peterson: Assignment Hanoi." PBS, documentary, 1999.

O'Neill, Anne-Marie. "Seeds of Hope: American Jerilyn Brusseau Turns Minefields into Peace Arbors." *People*, May 1, 2000.

Orians, Gordon H., and E. W. Pfeiffer. "Ecological Effects of the War in Vietnam." *Science, New Series* 168, no. 3931 (May 1970): 551

"Orphan Singer Returns in Search of Peace." Việt Nam News, December 6, 2010. http://vietnamnews.vn/Sunday/Features/206427/Orphan-singer-returns-in -search-of-peace.html.

Osborne, Milton. "The Indochinese Refugees: Cause and Effects." *International Affairs* 56, no. 1 (January 1980): 37–53.

Ottaway, David B. "Covert Military Aid for Cambodia Is Debated." *Washington Post*, June 13, 1989.

"PBS History Detectives Returns Soldier's Diary to Vietnam through U.S. Department of Defense." PBS Press Release, June 3, 2012. http://www.pbs.org/about /blogs/news/pbs-history-detectives-returns-soldiers-diary-to-vietnam-through -us-department-of-defense.

"Peace Profile: Bobby Muller." *Peace Review* 13, no. 1 (2001): 129–133.

PeaceTrees Vietnam. "Home." PeaceTrees Vietnam, accessed September 27, 2020. http://www.peacetreesvietnam.org.

Peang-Meth, Abdulgaffar. "A Study of the Khmer People's National Liberation Front and the Coalition Government of Democratic Kampuchea." *Contemporary Southeast Asia* 12, no. 3 (1990): 172–185. http://www.jstor.org/stable/42707623.

Pfeiffer, E. W. "Final Word on Defoliation Effects." *Science, New Series* 171, no. 3972 (February 1971): 625–626.

———, and Gordon H. Orians. "Ecological Effects of the War in Vietnam." *Science, New Series* 168, no. 3931 (May 1970): 544–554.

Plummer, William, and Richard Woodley. "A Vietnamese Novelist Makes Peace with Some Wartime Foes." *People*, November 14, 1988.

Porter, Cynthya. "A Long, Hard Trip to Visit the Past and See the Future." TOP Vietnam Veterans, April 16, 2003. https://web.archive.org/web/20160418123919 /http://topvietnamveterans.org/WinonaPost/April-16-2003.html.

Porter, Gareth. "The U.S. And Vietnam: Between War and Friendship." *Southeast Asian Affairs* (1977): 325–338.

Pressler, Larry. "We Can't Isolate Vietnam Forever." *New York Times*, May 23, 1988

Price, Jay "Having Changed America, the League of POW/MIA Families Fades." National Public Radio, October 19, 2017. https://www.npr.org/2017/10/19/5581 37698/having-changed-america-the-league-of-pow-mia-families-fades.

Project RENEW. "A Study of Explosive Remnants of War Accidents and the Knowledge — Attitudes — Practices–Beliefs of People in Quang Tri Province, Vietnam." Project RENEW, 2011. http://landmines.org.vn/publications/a-study-of-erw-ac cidents-in-quang-tri-province.

Project RENEW. "What We Do." Project RENEW, accessed September 27, 2020. http://www.landmines.org.vn/what-we-do

"Quakers, Friends, Set to Hold Prayer Vigil at Home of Jimmy Carter." *Philadelphia Tribune*, December 18, 1976.

"Quakers to Flout Law on Viet Aid." *Washington Post*, November 11, 1975.

"Quakers Will Defy Curb on Vietnam Aid." *New York Times*, July 29, 1975.

"Randy Tran: An Amerasian Singer." Amerasian Voice, November 22, 2012.

Rawls, Walton. *Offerings at the Wall: Artifacts from the Vietnam Veterans Memorial Collection*. Atlanta, GA: Turner Publishing, 1995.

"Religious Leaders Plan Vietnam Tour." *Washington Post*, March 5, 1976.

"Replies by the President (Carter) to Questions Asked at a News Conference, Washington, D.C., March 24, 1977." *American Foreign Policy Basic Documents 1977–1980*. Washington, DC: US Department of State, 1983.

"Returning for Redemption." *Tuoi Tre News*, January 4, 2013. http://tuoitrenews.vn /features/8365/returning-for-redemption

Reuther, David. Interview with Ambassador David Lamberston. Association for Diplomatic Studies and Training, Foreign Affairs Oral History Project, August 31, 2004, 90–92. https://tile.loc.gov/storage-services/service/mss/mfdip/2007/2007lam03 /2007lam03.pdf.

"Rice on Way to Vietnam from 4 Relief Agencies." *New York Times*, December 22, 1976.

Roberts, Sue Lloyd. "A U.S. Soldier Searches for His Vietnamese Son." BBC News, April 27, 2014.

Rogers, David. "Senate Panel Votes to End Covert Aid to Non-Communist Forces in Cambodia." *Wall Street Journal*, June 29, 1990.

Rummel, Rudolph J. *Statistics of Democide: Genocide and Mass Murder since 1900*. Munster: LIT Verlag, 1998.

Safire, William. "The Chinese Key." *New York Times*, January 12, 1976.

Saunier, Pierre-Yves. *Transnational History*. Basingstoke, UK: Palgrave Macmillan, 2013.

Schulzinger, Robert D. *A Time for Peace: The Legacy of the Vietnam War*. New York: Oxford University Press, 2006.

Schwenkel, Christina. *The American War in Contemporary Vietnam: Transnational Remembrance and Representation*. Bloomington: Indiana University Press, 2009.

Seadia, Wendy. "Artist Profile—C. David Thomas." *Wellesley Weston*, February 18, 2010.

Seaman, Donna. "A Conversation with John Balaban." *Triquarterly*, no. 114 (Fall 2002).

"Search for Father Is a Search for Self." *Los Angeles Times*, July 4, 1991.

Searcy, Chuck. "A Personal Note from Chuck Searcy about Project RENEW." *"Lemon Juice" Bruce* (blog), January 18, 2013. http://lemonjuicebruce.blogspot .com/2013/01/a-personal-note-from-chuck-searcy-about.html.

Secter, Bob. "Amerasians Will Join Fathers: 11 Vietnam Children Fly to a New World—The U.S." *Los Angeles Times*, October 1, 1982.

Shanahan, Eileen. "Aid Group Says U.S. Curbs Export of Items to Vietnam." *New York Times*, July 26, 1975.

Shawcross, William. "Refugees and Rhetoric." *Foreign Policy* 36 (Autumn 1979): 3–11.

Siegelaub, Marc. "A Man Reborn," *Long Island Newsday*, October 16, 2001. https:// www.newsday.com/lifestyle/a-man-reborn-bobby-muller-went-to-vietnam -gung-ho-and-naive-he-came-home-paralyzed-from-the-waist-down-and-altered -forever-from-the-neck-up-1.783471.

Stein, Barry. "The Geneva Conferences and the Indochinese Refugee Crisis." *International Migration Review* 13, no. 4 (Winter 1979): 716–723.

Stone, Jeremy J. *Every Man Should Try: Adventures of a Public Interest Activist.* New York: Public Affairs, 1999.

"A Study of Explosive Remnants of War Accidents and the Knowledge—Attitudes—Practices–Beliefs of People in Quang Tri Province, Vietnam." Project RENEW, 2011. http://landmines.org.vn/publications/a-study-of-erw-accidents-in-quang-tri-province.

Sullivan, Michael. "A Wartime Diary Touches Vietnamese." National Public Radio, November 15, 2006.

Susan Schindehette, "Against the Odds." *People*, May 1, 2000

Tara Leaman, "A Memoir of an Amerasian Orphan," Amerasian Voice, newsletter 2, no. 3, November 2009. http://www.vvaohio.com.

Tarlow, Lois. "The Indochina Arts Partnership Turns Twenty-Five." Art New England, accessed September 25, 2020. http://artnewengland.com/ed_picks/the-indochina-arts-partnership-turns-twenty-five.

Taylor, Clyde. "A Black Teacher's Agonized Message to the Vietnamese Refugees." *Los Angeles Times*, May 26, 1975.

TedxSeattle. "Jerilyn Brusseau." TedxRainier, December 2, 2010. http://www.tedxrainier.com/speakers/jerilyn-brusseau

Teltsch, Kathleen. "Many Agencies Joined in Retrieving Vietnam Children." *New York Times*, October 1, 1982.

_____. "3 Faiths' Leaders in Refugee Plea: Catholic Groups Involved." *New York Times*, June 29, 1979.

_____. "U.N. Panel Votes Priority Economic Aid for Vietnam." *New York Times*, October 7, 1977.

Temin, Christine. "An Artist Returns to Faces of Vietnam's Children." *Boston Globe*, February 28, 1988.

_____. "A Time for War, a Time for Art." *Boston Globe*, January 13, 1991.

"Thirty-Three Americans to Start 'Peace Walk' in Vietnam." *Agence France-Presse*, August 28, 1991.

Thow, George D. "Reconstruction Aid for Vietnam." *Los Angeles Times*, March 31, 1977.

Thuy Tram, Dang. *Last Night I Dreamed of Peace: The Diary of Dang Thuy Tram.* Translated by Andrew X. Pham. New York: Random House, 2007.

TOP Vietnam Veterans. "Home." TOP Vietnam Veterans, accessed November 9, 2020. https://web.archive.org/web/20160316152218/http://topvietnamveterans.org/index.html.

TOP Vietnam Veterans. "Personal Effects Program." TOP Vietnam Veterans, accessed November 9, 2020. https://web.archive.org/web/20160315031201/http://topvietnamveterans.org/p-pe.html.

TOP Vietnam Veterans. "TOP Vietnam Veterans Finds Captain Marshall's Family, Reunites Personal Effect." TOP Vietnam Veterans, accessed November 9, 2020. https://web.archive.org/web/20160315031201/http://topvietnamveterans.org/p-pe.html.

Tran, My-Thuan. "Children of Vietnam War Servicemen Seek U.S. Citizenship." *Los Angeles Times*, October 10, 2008.

"Travel Advisory: U.S. Lifts Ban on Travel to Vietnam." *New York Times*, February 5, 1992.

Treaster, Joseph B. "Black Market Down, Saigon Hopes Rise." *New York Times*, January 29, 1972.

Triplett, William. "On a Mission to Win 21st Century Hearts and Minds." *VVA Veteran*, March/April 2012. https://vvaveteran.org/32-2/32-2_vwam.html.

Turley, William S. "Urban Transformation in South Vietnam." *Pacific Affairs* 49, no. 4 (1976–1977): 607–624.

Unger, David C. "Editorial Notebook: How to Look for M.I.A.'S; Travel Barriers Invite Scams." *New York Times*, August 4, 1991.

United Nations. "Universal Declaration of Human Rights." United Nations, accessed September 25, 2020. https://www.un.org/en/universal-declaration-human-rights/.

University of Wisconsin-Madison. "Ladinsky Memorial Fund Receives Gift, Launches Lecture." International Division, University of Wisconsin-Madison, August 22, 2015. https://international.wisc.edu/ladinsky-fund-lecture/.

"U.S. Commits to 3,000,000 in Humanitarian Aid to Vietnam." Veterans Vietnam Restoration Project newsletter, no 14, June 1992.

Usdansky, Margaret L. "Amerasians: Caught between Cultures." *USA Today*, May 18, 1993.

US Embassy. "Chronology of U.S.-Vietnam Relations." U.S. Embassy & Consulate in Vietnam. https://vn.usembassy.gov/our-relationship/policy-history/chronology-of-us-vietnam-relations/.

"U.S. Groups Seeking Help for Vietnam." *New York Times*, October 3, 1975.

"U.S. Spent $141-Billion in Vietnam in 14 Years." *New York Times*, May 1, 1975.

Vesey, Tom. "A Project of Love: Driven by Memories of Son in Vietnam, Veteran Seeks Help for Amerasian Youth." *Washington Post*, September 1, 1982.

Vets With A Mission. *Medical Team Overcomes Major Obstacles to Complete Mission*. Vets With A Mission, accessed September 24, 2020. https://web.archive.org/web/20150426173943/http://www.vetswithamission.org/2014_March-April_Medical_Team_Report.pdf/.

"Vietnam Asks U.S. to Take More Refugees." *Los Angeles Times*, June 25, 1984.

Vietnam Children's Fund, "About Us," Vietnam Children's Fund, accessed November 21, 2020. http://www.vietnamchildren.org/about.html.

"Vietnamese Sell $40,000 Worth Daily: Refugee Camps Become Gold Mines." *Los Angeles Times*, July 27, 1975.

"Vietnam Gets $150,000 for Mylai Hospital." *Washington Post*, March 17, 1977.

"Vietnam Inaugurates Puller School." *Associate Press / Daily Press (Newport News, Virginia)*, April 25, 1995.

"Vietnam Offers Amity to the U.S.: Hanoi Leader Conciliatory at Third-World Meeting." *New York Times*, August 18, 1976.

"Vietnam Official Wants Talks on Amerasians." *New York Times*, July 31, 1984.

"Vietnam Peace Walk." Associated Press, August 29, 1991.

"Vietnam's Lingering Casualties." *Los Angeles Times*, June 30, 1991.

Virag, Irene. "In the Land of Their Fathers." *Newsday*, June 15, 1986.

———. "Lawmakers Ask Shultz to Help Amerasian." *Newsday*, March 7, 1987.

———. "Long Island Diary: Orphan Becomes a Symbol of Diplomacy." *Newsday*, March 23, 1987.

The Virtual Wall. "Daniel Bernard Cheney." The Virtual Wall, accessed September 27, 2020. http://www.virtualwall.org/dc/CheneyDB01a.htm.

Ward, Chuck. "Reconciliation, Forgiveness and Charity." Vets With A Mission, April 27, 2015. http://www.vetswithamission.org.

Watts, Jonathan. "GIs Return to End 30 Years of Pain for Vietnam's Children of the Dust." *Guardian*, May 1, 2005.

Wedel, Paul. "Viets Allow U.S. Charity to Aid Amerasians." United Press International, March 22, 1989.

Weinraub, Bernard. "Four Veterans End Vietnam Trip Nervous about Return to U.S." *New York Times*, December 25, 1981.

———. "Vietnam Veterans Take an Emotional Journey to Hanoi: 'Nothing Has Changed.'" *New York Times*, December 19, 1981.

Weiss, Cora. "Vietnam: To Heal Wounds." Letter to the editor, *New York Times*, December 17, 1976.

Winnacker, Martha "By Aiding the Future, U.S. Could Ease the Burden of the Past: My Lai—Where the Rice Will Grow Again." *Los Angeles Times*, July 25, 1977.

Woodward, Robert. "Ex-GI Dedicates Life to Help Amerasians." *Los Angeles Times*, October 15, 1989.

Woollacott, Martin. "The Boat People." *Guardian*, December 3, 1977. https://www.theguardian.com/century/1970-1979/Story/0,,106868,00.html.

Yarborough, Trin. *Surviving Twice: Amerasian Children of the Vietnam War*. Washington, DC: Potomac Books, 2005.

Yevtushenko, Yevgeny. *The Collected Poems, 1952–1990*. Edited by Albert C. Todd, with the author and James Ragan. New York: Henry Holt, 1991.

Sources in Vietnamese

Cẩm Giang. "Phi Nhung: Con lai bị chối bỏ và nỗi đau đớn khó quên về mẹ ruột" (Phi Nhung: An unwanted biracial child and an unforgettable, painful memory of her mother). *Soha News*, March 3, 2015. http://soha.vn/giai-tri/phi-nhung-con-lai-bi-choi-bo-va-noi-dau-don-kho-quen-ve-me-ruot-20151002084131798.htm.

"Chuyện kinh hoàng chưa biết về tội ác diệt chủng của Pol Pot ở Tây Ninh" (Unknown horror of Pol Pot's genocidal crime in Tay Ninh). VTC News. September 10, 2015. https://vtc.vn/chuyen-kinh-hoang-chua-biet-ve-toi-ac-diet-chung-cua-pol-pot-o-tay-ninh-ar222068.html.

"David Thomas: Họa sĩ Mỹ đầu tiên vẽ chân dung Bác Hồ" (David Thomas: The first American artist to portray Uncle Ho). *Thời báo Ngân hàng*, August 30, 2013.

Giao Chỉ. "Giới Thiệu 'Đường Khuynh Diệp'" (introduction to "The roads of eucalyptus"). Việt Báo, October 15, 1915. http://www.Vietbao.com.

"Hành trình 28 năm tìm cha của ca si 'Xe đạp ơi' Phương Thảo" ("Phuong Thao, Singer of the song "Xe Đạp Ơi" found her father after 28 years). Zing News, May 20, 2011. http://trithucsong.com/van-hoa/hanh-trinh-28-nam-tim-cha-cua-ca-si -xe-dap-oi-phuong-thao-c31979.html.

Hoàng Phương. "Còn hơn nửa triệu liệt sĩ chưa xác minh được thông tin" (More than a half million of fallen soldiers unidentified). VnExpress. July 25, 2015. http://vn express.net/tin-tuc/thoi-su/con-hon-nua-trieu-liet-si-chua-xac-minh-duoc-thong -tin-3253460.html.

Hồng Quân. "BTV Thu Uyên với chương trình truyền hình 'Như Chưa Hề Có Cuộc Chia Ly': Lại một cuộc dấn thân" (TV show host Thu Uyen and "as if they had never been separated": Another adventure). Thanh Niên, November 14, 2007.

Huy Thông. "Nhà văn Lê Lựu: Kể chuyện 'đi sứ' Văn học đến Mỹ" (Writer Le Luu remembers his literary "ambassadorial" trip to the United States). Thể thao Văn Hóa, May 31, 2010.

Lâm Nguyễn. "Phi Nhung và chuyện đời đầy nước mắt trước khi nổi tiếng" (Phi Nhung and her ordeals before becoming famous). Đời sống & Pháp luật, August 10, 2015. http://www.doisongphapluat.com/giai-tri/nguoi-trong-cuoc/phi-nhung -va-chuyen-doi-day-nuoc-mat-truoc-khi-noi-tieng-a105335.html.

Lan Dung. "Thời Xa vắng Đoạt Giải Thưởng tại LHP Quốc Tế Thượng Hải" (A Time Far Past winning award at Shanghai International Film Festival). Thanh Niên, June 20, 2005. http://www.thanhnien.com.vn/news/pages/200525/113254.aspx.

"Luật sư Jenny Đỗ tâm sự về Cuộc đời bên bờ sinh tử" (Attorney Jenny Do discussing life on the edge). Interview, Cali Today, October 22, 2015. http://baocalitoday .com/vn/tin-tuc/cong-dong/luat-su-jenny-do-tam-su-ve-cuoc-doi-ben-bo-sinh -tu.html.

Minh Quynh. "Giao lưu hội ngộ Babylift tại Báo Tuổi Trẻ" (Babylift Reunion at Tuoi Tre's newspaper headquarters). Announcement, Tuoi Tre, April 29, 2011.

Minh Thu. "Mothers Share Sorrow of War." Viet Nam News, September 16, 2010. https://vietnamnews.vn/society/203707/mothers-share-sorrow-of-war.html.

Ngày Phát Sóng. "Truyền Hình." Hãy Lên Tiếng, July 6, 2020. http://www.haylen tieng.vn.

Ngọc Nga. "Món nợ cuộc đời" (A debt to life). Tuổi Trẻ, May 20, 2012.

Người Đưa Đò. "Home." Người Đưa Đò, accessed September 27, 2020. http://www .nguoiduado.vn.

"Người Mẹ Việt và Đứa Con Lai Ca Sĩ Nổi Tiếng" (A Vietnamese mother and a famous Amerasian singer). VnExpress, August 2, 2012.

Nguyễn Mỹ. "Cuộc chia ly màu đỏ" (A red separation). Cuộc chia ly màu đỏ. Hanoi: Hanoi Publisher, 1979.

Nguyễn Phạm Thu Uyên. "NCHCCCL Gala 2014: Phút giây này, có ai ngờ, chợt đến" (NCHCCCL gala 2014: The unexpected moment arrived, video), February 4, 2014. Hãy Lên Tiếng. http://www.haylentieng.vn.

————. "NCHCCCL số 16" (NCHCCCL no. 16, video), March 14, 2009. Hãy Lên Tiếng. http://www.haylentieng.vn.

————. "NCHCCCL số 18: Những người con nuôi từ đường 7" (NCHCCCL no 18: Adopted children from Route 7, video), May 16, 2009. Hãy Lên Tiếng. http://www.haylentieng.vn.

————. "NCHCCCL số 31: Những chiếc mũ rơm" (NCHCCCL no 31: The straw hats, video), June 6, 2010. Hãy Lên Tiếng. http://www.haylentieng.vn.

————. "NCHCCCL số 70: Lá rụng về cội" (NCHCCCL no 70: Returning to the roots, video), January 4, 2014. Hãy Lên Tiếng. http://www.haylentieng.vn.

————. "NCHCCCL số 79: Như dòng đời xô dạt" (NCHCCCL no 79: In the drift of life, video), October 4, 2014. Hãy Lên Tiếng. http://www.haylentieng.vn.

————. "NCHCCCL số 81: Luôn hướng về nhau" (NCHCCCL no 81: Always in each other's thoughts, video), January 3, 2015. Hãy Lên Tiếng. http://www.haylentieng.vn.

————. "NCHCCCL số 84: Sự đối nghịch của chiến tranh" (NCHCCCL no 84: Paradoxes of war, video), April 4, 2015. Hãy Lên Tiếng. http://www.haylentieng.vn.

Nguyễn Quốc Chính. "Một dự án nghệ thuật—Một dự án hòa bình" (An art project—a peace project). *Hà Nội Mới*, April 20, 1991.

Nguyễn Trinh. "'Đại sứ' hàn gắn vết thương chiến tranh" (The "ambassador" who heals the wounds of war). *Sức khỏe & Đời sống*, April 29, 2013.

Nguyễn Trường. "Rung động cựu binh Mỹ trả lại xương cánh tay cho người lính Bắc Việt" (A touching story of an American veteran wishing to return arm bones to a north Vietnamese soldier). *Tiền Phong*, November 11, 2012.

Như Chưa Hề Có Cuộc Chia Ly. http://www.haylentieng.vn.

Phạm Xuân Hướng. Interview with film director Phạm Quang Minh. *Nhân Dân*, August 14, 2004. http://www.nhandan.com.vn/vanhoa/dien-dan/item/10336102-.html.

"Phi Nhung: 'Kiếp này tôi chọn sống độc thân'" (Phi Nhung: "I chose to stay single for the rest of this life"). *Cali Today*, February 23, 2015. http://baocalitoday.com/vn/nguoi-noi-tieng/phi-nhung-kiep-nay-toi-chon-song-doc-than.html.

"Randy Tran: An Amerasian and a Singer." Amerasian Voice, November 22, 2012. https://amerasianvoice.wordpress.com/2012/11/22/randy-tran-an-amerasian-and-a-singer/.

"Randy và hành trình tìm mẹ" (Randy and the journey to look for his mother; documentary). *Người Việt Bốn Phương*, channel VTV4, July 30, 2012. https://www.youtube.com/watch?v=_6B4XwqD87M.

Trane, Randy. "Mẹ" (Mother). *Mẹ*, 2000.

Trần Quỳnh Hoa. "Kỷ vật lạ lùng của một cựu bác sĩ quân y Mỹ" (A strange keepsake of an American military physician). *Thanh Niên*, November 11, 2012.

Tran Thuy Duong. "Talk Vietnam: American Mothers Plant Peace Trees in Vietnam." Television interview.

Trinh Nguyễn. "'Đại sứ' hàn gắn vết thương chiến tranh" (The "ambassador" who heals the wounds of war). *Sức khỏe & Đời sống*, April 29, 2013.

Trở Về Từ Ký Ức. "Home." Trở Về Từ Ký Ức, accessed November 9, 2020. https://
web.archive.org/web/20150405023800/http://trovetukyuc.vn/.

Trường Kỳ. "Randy—Người ca sĩ mồ côi" (Randy—the orphaned singer). Radio
interview, Chương trình Nghệ sĩ và Đời sống, 2005. https://www.voatiengviet
.com/a/a-19-2005-09-06-voa14-81660467/505850.html.

Tử Văn. "Phi Nhung và mối lương duyên với trẻ em" (Phi Nhung and her predetermined bonds with children). Người Đưa Tin, September 28, 2015. http://www
.nguoiduatin.vn/phi-nhung-va-moi-luong-duyen-voi-tre-em-a208349.html.

"Vượt Biên Sau 30/4/1975—Nhân Chứng Sống Nguyễn Ngọc Ngạn Kể Lại" (Ocean
crossing after April 30, 1975: Told by living witness Nguyen Ngoc Ngan).
YouTube, 5:40, April 25, 2013. https://web.archive.org/web/20140407123342
/https://www.youtube.com/watch?v=7KmZnnp6YwM.

Xuân Anh. "Lê Lựu—Nhà Văn Cộng Sản Việt Nam đầu tiên đến Mỹ" (Le Luu—The
first Vietnamese communist writer to visit the United States). Phong Điệp.Net,
May 1, 2008. http://phongdiep.net/default.asp.

Archival Documents

American Public Welfare Association. Indochinese Refugee Reports, vol. 1, no. 1,
May 1, 1979. Folder 03, Box 03, Douglas Pike Collection: Other Manuscripts—
Jackson-Desbarats Study. The Vietnam Center and Archive, Texas Tech Univer-
sity, Lubbock, Texas [hereafter VCA, TTU, LT].

Bird, Thomas. Letter to Ngo Quynh Giao, August 15, 1986. Folder 36, Box 39, Vietnam Veterans of America–Vietnam Project Collection. VCA, TTU, LT.

———. Letter to Nguyen Dang Quang, May 15, 1986. Folder 36, Box 39, Vietnam
Veterans of America–Vietnam Project Collection. VCA, TTU, LT.

Brzezinski, Zbigniew, to President Jimmy Carter. Memorandum, July 1, 1977. Office
of Staff Secretary, Presidential Files, Folder 7/15/77[3], Container 31. Jimmy
Carter Presidential Library and Museum, Atlanta, Georgia.

Brzezinski, Zbigniew, to President Jimmy Carter. Memorandum, July 15, 1977. Office of Staff Secretary, Presidential Files, Folder 7/15/77[3], Container 31. Jimmy
Carter Presidential Library and Museum, Atlanta, Georgia.

Brzezinski, Zbigniew, to President Jimmy Carter. Memorandum, December 19, 1977.
Office of Staff Secretary, Presidential Files, Folder 12/20/77[1], Container 55.
Jimmy Carter Presidential Library and Museum, Atlanta, Georgia.

Bulletin of the US Committee for Scientific Cooperation with Vietnam 6, no. 1 (Summer 1987). Folder 8, Box 44, Vietnam Veterans of America–Vietnam Project Collection. VCA, TTU, LT.

California Legislature. Senate Joint Resolution No. 24, Amended Version of Relative
to the Arrival of Indochinese Refugees in the United States, July 16, 1979. Folder
15, Box 01, Douglas Pike Collection: Other Manuscripts—Jackson-Desbarats
Study. VCA, TTU, LT.

Church World Service, Mennonite Central Committee, and American Friends Service Committee. Letter to American Council of Voluntary Agencies and other NGOs, September 2, 1982. Folder 2, Box 44, Vietnam Veterans of America–Vietnam Project Collection. VCA, TTU, LT.

————. Letter to Senator Carl M. Levin, August 11, 1982. Folder 2, Box 44, Vietnam Veterans of America–Vietnam Project Collection. VCA, TTU, LT.

Collection #329 (Vietnam Veterans of America—Vietnam Project), 1979–1990. Boxes 37–50, 52, and 53. VCA, TTU, LT.

Condon, Tom. "Statement before the Subcommittee on International Economic Policy and Trade Committee on Foreign Affairs," US House of Representatives, Washington, DC, March 13, 1990. Folder 4, Box 50, Vietnam Veterans of America–Vietnam Project Collection. VCA, TTU, LT.

Cranston, Alan. "Opening statement before the Subcommittee on East Asian and Pacific Affairs, Committee on Foreign Relations," September 19, 1990. Folder 28, Box 42, Vietnam Veterans of America–Vietnam Project Collection. VCA, TTU, LT.

"Current Situation in Indochina." Report. June 1, 1979, Folder 06, Box 22, Douglas Pike Collection: Unit 06—Democratic Republic of Vietnam, VCA, TTU, LT.

East Meets West flyer. Folder 14, Box 40, Vietnam Veterans of America–Vietnam Project Collection. VCA, TTU, LT.

Facts about Refugees from Indochina. July 31, 1979. Folder 13, Box 32, Douglas Pike Collection: Unit 03—Refugees and Civilian Casualties. VCA, TTU, LT.

Families of Vietnamese Political Prisoners Association. *Special Issue 1988*—re: Report of Activities, Poems, Personal Narratives, and Correspondence between Khuc Minh Tho and Freedom Committee for Imprisoned Pastors, 1988. Folder 16, Box 01, Vietnam Archive Collection. VCA, TTU, LT.

Ford, Gerald R. Address at a Tulane University Convocation, April 23, 1975. The American Presidency Project, accessed September 29, 2020. http://www.presidency.ucsb.edu/ws/index.php?pid=4859.

————. Address at the University of Hawaii. December 7, 1975. Gerald R. Ford Presidential Library and Museum, Ann Arbor, Michigan.

Gardner, Paul F. Letter to Robert O. Muller, March 1984. Folder 2, Box 50, Vietnam Veterans of America–Vietnam Project Collection. VCA, TTU, LT.

Hatfield, Mark O. "Statement before the Senate Subcommittee on East Asian and Pacific Affairs," August 2, 1988. Folder 22, Box 42, Vietnam Veterans of America–Vietnam Project Collection. VCA, TTU, LT.

Hearing Before the Subcommittee on Immigration, Nationality and International Law (1982) Statement of Fr. Alfred Keane, n.d. Folder 1, Box 44, Vietnam Veterans of America–Vietnam Project Collection. VCA, TTU, LT.

Holt International Children's Services. "Amerasian Project: Vietnam. A Proposal for Participation by Holt International Children's Services, Inc.," July 1982. Folder 2, Box 44, Vietnam Veterans of America–Vietnam Project Collection. VCA, TTU, LT.

Holt International Children's Services. Letter to Congressman Peter W. Rodino, September 1982. Folder 2, Box 44, Vietnam Veterans of America–Vietnam Project Collection. VCA, TTU, LT.

House of Representatives. *Hearings Before the Subcommittee on Asian and Pacific Affairs of the Committee on Foreign Affairs*, 96th Cong., 1st Sess. on 1979: Tragedy in Indochina: War, Refugees, and Famine, 1980. Folder 21, Box 10, Douglas Pike Collection: Unit 11—Monographs. VCA, TTU, LT.

House of Representatives. *Hearings Before the Subcommittee on Immigration, Citizenship, and International Law of the Committee on the Judiciary*, May 7, 1975. Folder 05, Box 32, Douglas Pike Collection: Unit 03—Refugees and Civilian Casualties. VCA, TTU, LT.

House of Representatives. *Refugee Crisis in Indochina, 1978: Hearings Before the Subcommittee on Asian and Pacific Affairs*, 1978. Folder 09, Box 09, Douglas Pike Collection: Unit 11—Monographs. VCA, TTU, LT.

House of Representatives. "Statement by David Lamberston Before the Subcommittee on East Asian and Pacific Affairs," June 30, 1988. Senate. Folder 21, Box 42, Vietnam Veterans of America–Vietnam Project Collection. VCA, TTU, LT.

Indochina Refugee Action Center. *Special Report: Physical and Emotional Health Care Needs of Indochinese Refugees*, March 20, 1980. Folder 17, Box 01, Douglas Pike Collection: Other Manuscripts—Jackson-Desbarats Study. VCA, TTU, LT.

International Rescue Committee Inc. *Annual Report 1981*, 1981. Folder 33, Box 03, Douglas Pike Collection: Other Manuscripts—Jackson-Desbarats Study. VCA, TTU, LT.

Kane, Gregory. Letter to Nguyen Can, October 26, 1984. Folder 2, Box 50, Vietnam Veterans of America–Vietnam Project Collection. VCA, TTU, LT.

_____. Letter to Nguyen Dang Quang, January 23, 1985. Folder 11, Box 40, Vietnam Veterans of America–Vietnam Project Collection. VCA, TTU, LT.

Kleven, Greg. Letter to Congressman Miller, April 22, 1989. Folder 4, Box 50, Vietnam Veterans of America–Vietnam Project Collection. VCA, TTU, LT.

_____. Letter to John Myers, n.d. Folder 3, Box 53, Vietnam Veterans of America–Vietnam Project Collection. VCA, TTU, LT.

Lafatch, Joseph M. Letter to the Return Trip Committee, February 28, 1990. Folder 3, Box 53, Vietnam Veterans of America–Vietnam Project Collection. VCA, TTU, LT.

_____. "Statement of Joe Lafatch, Vietnam veteran, before the Subcommittee on International Economic Policy and Trade Committee on Foreign Affairs," US House of Representatives, Washington, DC, March 13, 1990. Folder 31, Box 42, Vietnam Veterans of America–Vietnam Project Collection, VCA, TTU, LT.

Letter of intent between the Social Science Research Council and the Vietnam Committee for the Social Sciences, May 1988. Folder 3, Box 38, Vietnam Veterans of America–Vietnam Project Collection. VCA, TTU, LT.

Martin, Kate. Letter to Abraham D. Sofaer, May 4, 1988. Folder 18, Box 52, Vietnam Veterans of America–Vietnam Project Collection. VCA, TTU, LT.

McAuliff, John. "Testimony to the Committee on the Judiciary. Subcommittee on

Courts, Intellectual Property, and the Administration of Justice." 1988–1989. Folder 21, Box 38, Vietnam Veterans of America–Vietnam Project Collection. VCA, TTU, LT.

McCausland, Mark J. Letter to John Myers/Don Mills, March 3, 1990. Folder 3, Box 53, Vietnam Veterans of America–Vietnam Project Collection. VCA, TTU, LT.

McDonnell, Mary Byrne. "Indochina Activity by Nongovernmental Organizations." May 1988. Folder 3, Box 38, Vietnam Veterans of America–Vietnam Project Collection. VCA, TTU, LT.

Memorandum, July 15, 1977. Office of Staff Secretary, Presidential Files, Folder 7/15/77[3], Container 31. Jimmy Carter Presidential Library and Museum, Atlanta, Georgia.

Memorandum, December 19, 1977. Office of Staff Secretary, Presidential Files, Folder 12/20/77[1], Container 55. Jimmy Carter Presidential Library and Museum, Atlanta, Georgia.

Muller, Robert O. Letter to George P. Shultz, February 8, 1984. Folder 2, Box 50, Vietnam Veterans of America–Vietnam Project Collection. VCA, TTU, LT.

Muskie, Edmund S. Testimony of the Honorable Edmund S. Muskie to the U.S. Senate Committee on Foreign Relations, Subcommittee on East Asian and Pacific Affairs, February 28, 1990. Folder 29, Box 40, Vietnam Veterans of America–Vietnam Project Collection. VCA, TTU, LT.

Notes from Solarz's press briefing on his trip to China, Cambodia, Vietnam, Thailand, Singapore, and the Philippines, April 7, 1989. Folder 21, Box 42, Vietnam Veterans of America–Vietnam Project Collection. VCA, TTU, LT.

Olson, Clifford G., Jr. Letter to U.S. House of Representatives, May 3, 1984. Folder 2, Box 50, Vietnam Veterans of America–Vietnam Project Collection. VCA, TTU, LT.

Parker, Gary. Letter to Don Mills and John Myers, March 4, 1990. Folder 3, Box 53, Vietnam Veterans of America–Vietnam Project Collection. VCA, TTU, LT.

Pinter, Stephen. Letter from Department of Treasury to Don Mills and John Myers, February 10, 1989. Folder 31, Box 42, Vietnam Veterans of America–Vietnam Project Collection. VCA, TTU, LT.

Report on the Possibilities for an International Organizational Role in the Postwar Recovery and Development of North and South Vietnam. March 1972, Folder 10, Box 16, Douglas Pike Collection: Unit 06—Democratic Republic of Vietnam, VCA, TTU, LT.

Roberts, Alden, and Paul Starr. *Attitudes Toward Indochinese Refugees: An Empirical Study*, n.d. Folder 01, Box 01, Alden Roberts Collection. VCA, TTU, LT.

Rubin, Saul. "Both Sides Now: Artists Depict Vietnam War from 2 Perspectives," n.d. Folder 7, Box 44, Vietnam Veterans of America–Vietnam Project Collection. VCA, TTU, LT.

Special Study on Indochina Refugee Situation, July 1979. Folder 09, Box 33, Douglas Pike Collection: Unit 01—Assessment and Strategy VCA, TTU, LT.

Stadtmiller, Jerry. Open letter, n.d. Folder 14, Box 40, Vietnam Veterans of America–Vietnam Project Collection. VCA, TTU, LT.

Statistical Update on Indochina Refugee Situation from the Indochina Refugee Action Center, September 24, 1980. Folder 13, Box 32, Douglas Pike Collection: Unit 03—Refugees and Civilian Casualties. VCA, TTU, LT.

Stone, Jeremy J. "Preventing the Return of Pol Pot: Conventional Wisdom versus New Appraisal." Washington, DC: Federation of American Scientists, 1989. Folder 1, Box 40, Vietnam Veterans of America–Vietnam Project Collection. VCA, TTU, LT.

Sutter, Robert G. "Vietnam-U.S. Relations: The Missing-In-Action (MIA) and the Impasse over Cambodia." *Congressional Research Service*, May 20, 1988. Folder 21, Box 42, Vietnam Veterans of America–Vietnam Project Collection. VCA, TTU, LT.

Terzano, John F. *Restrictions on International Travel: Hearing.* "Statement of John F. Terzano, President, Vietnam Veterans of America Foundation, before the Subcommittee on International Economic Policy and Trade Committee on Foreign Affairs," US House of Representatives, Washington, DC, March 13, 1990. Folder 31, Box 42, Vietnam Veterans of America–Vietnam Project Collection. VCA, TTU, LT.

Theisen, Maribeth. Letter to John Myers, March 6, 1990. Folder 3, Box 53, Vietnam Veterans of America–Vietnam Project Collection. VCA, TTU, LT.

US Committee for Refugees. *Vietnamese Boat People-Pirates' Vulnerable Prey*, February 1984. Folder 03, Box 01, James Banerian Collection. VCA, TTU, LT.

US Department of Health, Education, and Welfare. *Report to the Congress, Indochinese Refugee Assistance Program*, December 31, 1979. Folder 18, Box 01, Douglas Pike Collection: Other Manuscripts—Jackson-Desbarats Study. VCA, TTU, LT.

US Department of State. General office files—Correspondence, Incoming—Department of Health & Human Services, Family Support Administration, Office of Refugee Resettlement, April 26, 1989. Folder 016, Box 119, Families of Vietnamese Political Prisoners Association (FVPPA) Collection. VCA, TTU, LT.

US Department of State. General office files—Office Correspondence—Incoming, n.d. Folder 047, Box 164, Families of Vietnamese Political Prisoners Association Collection. VCA, TTU, LT.

US Senate. *Hearing Before the Subcommittee on Immigration and Refugee Policy of the Committee on the Judiciary*, 97th Cong., 2nd Sess. on S. 1698, a Bill to Amend the Immigration and Nationality Act to Provide Preferential Treatment in the Admission of Certain Children of the United States Armed Forces Personnel, June 21, 1982, 60–63. Opening Statement of Hon. Senator Edward M. Kennedy, US senator from the state of Massachusetts, Library of Congress, Washington, DC. http://www.loc.gov/law/find/hearings/pdf/00139298329.pdf.

US Senate. *Hearing Before the Subcommittee on Immigration and Refugee Policy of the Committee on the Judiciary*, 97th Cong., 2nd Sess. on S. 1698, a Bill to Amend the Immigration and Nationality Act to Provide Preferential Treatment in the Admission of Certain Children of the United States Armed Forces Personnel, June 21, 1982, 60–631982. Statement of Hon. Senator Carl Levin, US senator from the state of Michigan, Library of Congress, Washington, DC.

US Senate. *Report to the Committee on Foreign Relations*, 94th Cong., 1st Sess. on Indochina Migration and Refugee Assistance Act of 1975, May 12, 1975. Folder 21, Box 10, Douglas Pike Collection: Unit 11—Monographs. VCA, TTU, LT.

"U.S. Veterans Build Surgical Ward for Children's Hospital in Northern Vietnam." Press release, Veterans Vietnam Restoration Project, October 31, 1989. Folder 13, Box 40, Vietnam Veterans of America–Vietnam Project Collection. VCA, TTU, LT.

Vance, Cyrus, to President Jimmy Carter. Memorandum, June 23, 1977. Office of Staff Secretary, Presidential Files, Folder 7/15/77[3], Container 31. Jimmy Carter Presidential Library and Museum, Atlanta, Georgia.

Vance, Cyrus, to President Jimmy Carter. Memorandum, December 6, 1977. Office of Staff Secretary, Presidential Files, Folder 12/20/77[1], Container 55. Jimmy Carter Presidential Library and Museum, Atlanta, Georgia.

"VFW Tells VVA to Step Aside." VFW news release, March 20, 1984. Folder 8, Box 44, Vietnam Veterans of America–Vietnam Project Collection. VCA, TTU, LT.

The Vietnam-Cambodia Emergency, 1975, Part I: The Vietnam Evacuation and Humanitarian Assistance, H.R. 5960 and H.R. 5961 (1976). Folder 14, Box 01, John Haseman Collection. VCA, TTU, LT.

Vietnam Veterans of America Trip to Vietnam, March 28–April 12, 1984, report to VVA board of directors, July 1984. Folder 2, Box 50, Vietnam Veterans of America–Vietnam Project Collection. VCA, TTU, LT.

Organizations' Websites

Adopted Vietnamese International: http://www.adoptedvietnamese.org/avi-community/other-vn-adoptee-orphan-groups/operation-reunite.

Agent Orange Record Project: http://www.agentorangerecord.com.

Ao Dai Festival: www.aodaifestival.com.

Cambodia Tribunal Monitor: http://www.cambodiatribunal.org.

Church World Service: https://cwsglobal.org/about/history/.

Church World Service Vietnam. http://cws.org.vn.

The Earth Stewards Network: www.earthstewards.org.

Embassy of the United States, Hanoi, Vietnam: www.vietnam.usembassy.gov.

Father Founded: http://www.fatherfounded.org.

The Fund for Reconciliation and Development: www.ffrd.org.

Global Security: http://www.globalsecurity.org.

The International Campaign to Ban Landmines: http://www.icbl.org/en-gb/the-treaty/treaty-status.aspx.

The International Center: http://www.theintlcenter.org.

Jenny Do for City Council: ww.jennydoforcouncli.com.

John Balaban: http://www.johnbalaban.com.

Landmine and Cluster Munition Monitor: http://www.the-monitor.org/en-gb/the-issues/erw.aspx.

Người Đưa Đò: www.nguoiduado.vn.

Như Chưa Hề Có Cuộc Chia Ly: http://haylentieng.vn.

PeaceTrees Vietnam: www.peacetreesvietnam.org.

The Peoples of the World Foundation: http://www.peoplesoftheworld.org/individuals /amerasians/Adopted.

Project RENEW: http://landmines.org.vn.

TOP Vietnam Veterans: http://www.topvietnamveterans.org/vietnam.

Trở Về Từ Ký Ức: www.trovetukyuc.vn.

Veterans Vietnam Restoration Project: http://www.vietvet.org/vetviet.htm.

Vets With A Mission: http://www.vetswithamission.org/past_projects.html.

Vietnam Children's Fund: www.vietnamchildren.org/about.

Vietnamese Nôm Preservation Foundation: http://www.nomfoundation.org.

Vietnam Friendship Village Project USA: http://www.vietnamfriendship.org/word press/project-history.

Vietnam Veterans of America: www.vva.org.

The Virtual Wall: www.virtualwall.org/dc/CheneyDB01a.htm.

VUFO-NGO Resource Centre Vietnam: http://www.ngocentre.org.vn.

William Joiner Institute for the Study of War and Social Consequences: https://www .umb.edu/joinerinstitute.